UNJUST ENRICHMENT AND COUNTERVAILING OBLIGATIONS

This book examines the relationship between the English law of unjust enrichment and countervailing legal obligations arising from other branches of the law.

The book examines this relationship primarily by considering cases in which the enrichment was received by the defendant in discharge of a valid legal obligation. Is an unjust enrichment claim available in these cases? If so, in what circumstances? If not, why not?

In the foreword, Lord Burrows observes that these issues are 'of fundamental importance to our understanding of the law of unjust enrichment.' They have also been the subject of a large body of recent case law, including at the highest appellate levels in the United Kingdom and Australia.

By applying insights from the theory of unjust enrichment to cases from England, Australia, New Zealand, Canada, South Africa and the United States of America, the book offers a clear, simple and cogent explanation of a complex and topical question in the law of unjust enrichment.

Volume 51 in the series Hart Studies in Private Law

Hart Studies in Private Law

This monograph series brings together in one place two types of book: works which examine in-depth the fundamental doctrines and principles of private law, and works which engage with the theoretical underpinnings of private law. The series thus aims to contribute to ever-evolving debates about the nature of private law such as problems of classification and taxonomy, remedies, the relationship with public law and the boundaries of private law generally.

The series includes, but is not confined to, works on contract, tort, unjust enrichment, equity, property and the conflict of laws, welcoming work which intersects with other fields of study to enable a deeper understanding of private law theory and practice.

Unjust Enrichment and Countervailing Obligations

KV Krishnaprasad

•HART•
OXFORD • LONDON • NEW YORK • NEW DELHI • SYDNEY

HART PUBLISHING

Bloomsbury Publishing Plc

Kemp House, Chawley Park, Cumnor Hill, Oxford, OX2 9PH, UK

1385 Broadway, New York, NY 10018, USA

29 Earlsfort Terrace, Dublin 2, Ireland

HART PUBLISHING, the Hart/Stag logo, BLOOMSBURY and the Diana logo are trademarks of Bloomsbury Publishing Plc

First published in Great Britain 2025

A catalogue record for this book is available from the British Library.

A catalogue record for this book is available from the Library of Congress.

Library of Congress Control Number: 2024944193

ISBN: HB: 978-1-50996-639-4
ePDF: 978-1-50996-641-7
ePub: 978-1-50996-640-0

Typeset by Compuscript Ltd, Shannon

Foreword

IN RECENT YEARS, much of the scholarship on unjust enrichment has reverted to discussing whether the subject exists at all. It is therefore refreshing to read this book where the author takes as his starting point the traditional approach of there being a law of unjust enrichment, organised around unjust factors, and then sets himself the task of analysing how we are to understand two closely connected rules that appear to deny restitution. Those rules are labelled the "good consideration rule" and the "obligation rule".

It is argued that both rules do exist in English law, that they are treated as two separate rules rather than one, and that each has a sound justification. Moreover, although there is an overlap between them and, in the final analysis, the latter largely swallows up the former, each can be regarded as having a distinct role to play.

The first rule is justified, so the author argues, because, by reason of the good consideration, the defendant's enrichment is offset by an equivalent "disenrichment". Overall, therefore, there is no net enrichment of the defendant. Drawing on German law, it is argued that a net enrichment theory is preferable to one resting on there being a claim and counterclaim. Various alternative explanations (eg based on change of position or "at the expense of" or bona fide purchase) are considered and rejected.

The second rule is presented as drawing a bright line rather than resting on a flexible weighing up of the unjust factor against the defendant's legal entitlement (which includes an extensive and interesting criticism of some of my own views). Ultimately, having rejected other explanations, the author finds a justification for this rule by applying an equality thesis based on the need for equal protection of the claimant's and defendant's interests. That is, the claimant's protection of its pre-existing entitlement (not to have its entitlements transferred away without consent) is matched by the need to respect the pre-existing entitlement of the defendant.

The author writes in a clear, succinct and engaging way and makes illuminating and extensive use of hypothetical examples to work out, and help the reader to understand, what is the best interpretation of the law.

Throughout, the rigour and depth of the analysis are an example to all of us. The author is not only a master of the details of the decided English case law but draws on comparative law and philosophical writings to develop and explain his views. The issues he discusses are of fundamental importance to our understanding of the law of unjust enrichment.

All academics and students with an interest in the common law, and especially in the law of unjust enrichment, will benefit from reading this book. It will also be of considerable assistance, in providing an invaluable guide, to solicitors, barristers and judges alike who may have to grapple with these issues in practice.

Like all great law books, this one goes a long way to reducing complexity to relative simplicity. Dr Krishnaprasad is to be warmly congratulated on his achievement.

Andrew Burrows
Lord Burrows, Justice of the UK Supreme Court
20 August 2024

Acknowledgements

I am indebted to a large number of people in connection with this book.

Robert Stevens supervised my doctoral research upon which the book is based. The reader will see his influence throughout the book, on matters of substance (e.g. Chapters 4 and 5) as well as style (e.g. the use of hypothetical examples).

Andrew Burrows examined my doctoral thesis at three different stages, each time with characteristic care, diligence and insight. He was also kind enough (to agree to be appointed a Justice of the UK Supreme Court in good time) to write a foreword for this book. It will be obvious to any reader of the book that he was the most fitting person to do so.

William Swadling, Ben McFarlane and Robert Chambers examined my doctoral thesis at various stages. Their comments have saved me from many errors.

Andrew Burrows, William Swadling, Robert Stevens, Michael Watkins and Frederick Wilmot-Smith introduced me to the law of restitution through their BCL seminars and tutorials. I am especially grateful to Michael Watkins for his tutorial question: "*Can there ever be restitution of an unjust enrichment where money is paid by the claimant to the defendant in order to discharge a legal duty arising under statute or contract?*"

My research at Exeter College was funded by Harish Salve through the Dr Mrs Ambriti Salve Scholarship. Without his support, this book would not have been written.

On various aspects of the book, I have benefited from helpful conversations with Ajay Ratan, Dimitrios Kyriazis, Eli Ball, Frederick Wilmot-Smith, Maximilian Hocke, Mihir Naniwadekar, Mohammud Jaamae Hafeez-Baig, Niranjan Venkatesan, Samuel Williams, Sonja Meier, Steven Elliott and Timothy Liau.

I presented draft chapters of the book at the Obligations IX Conference at the Melbourne Law School (2018) and the Society of Legal Scholars Conference at the University of Nottingham (2014). On both occasions, questions and comments from the conference participants prompted me to rethink and refine my analysis.

Most of all, I am fortunate to have had the love and support of G, N and M during the many times when the completion of a doctoral thesis – let alone a book based upon it – seemed nearly impossible.

KV Krishnaprasad
London
10 November 2024

Contents

PART II
THE OBLIGATION RULE

Table of Cases

Table of Legislation

United Kingdom

Australia

Canada

France

Germany

Italy

Netherlands

Portugal

Introduction

A CLAIM BASED on unjust enrichment will fail if the enrichment was received by the defendant in discharge of a valid legal obligation. As Lord Sumption observed, this proposition is 'supported by more than a century and a half of authority'.[1] Yet its justification remains unclear. Why is an unjust enrichment claim not available if the defendant has a valid legal right to the enrichment? This book attempts to answer that question.

In a landmark decision of the House of Lords on unjust enrichment, Lord Scott emphasised the importance of answering this question. He said:[2]

> If a contract has been entered into that would not have been entered into but for a mistake, but the contract is then completed by a payment of the price for the goods or services that the payee has supplied, the payment cannot be recovered unless the contract can be set aside. The proposition seems such an obviously correct one that it may seem pointless to ask why it is that it is correct. But I think the question does need to be asked for the answer casts, in my opinion, valuable light on the nature of the restitutionary remedy for the recovery of money paid under a mistake.

The relationship between unjust enrichment claims and countervailing legal obligations owed to the defendant has received much judicial and academic attention since then. Burrows identifies this as a 'hotly debated issue'[3] in the law of unjust enrichment. That observation is borne out by the volume of caselaw on this topic over the last decade, including at the highest appellate levels in the United Kingdom and in Australia.[4]

The decision of the UK Supreme Court in *International Energy Group v Zurich Insurance*[5] is a notable example. In that case, this issue narrowly divided seven Justices of the Supreme Court. Unassisted by a convincing account of the relationship between unjust enrichment and other areas of the law, the judges in

[1] *DD Growth Premium 2X Fund v RMF Market Neutral Strategies* [2017] UKPC 36, [2018] Bus LR 1595 [62] (Lord Sumption).

[2] *Deutsche Morgan Grenfell Group Plc v Inland Revenue Commissioners* [2006] UKHL 49, [2007] 1 AC 558 [84] (Lord Scott).

[3] Andrew Burrows, 'Restitution of Mistaken Enrichments' (2012) 92 Boston University Law Review 767, 774.

[4] See *Fairfield Sentry Ltd (In Liquidation) v Migani* [2014] UKPC 9, [2014] 1 CLC 611; *International Energy Group Ltd v Zurich Insurance plc* [2015] UKSC 33, [2015] 2 WLR 1471; *DD Growth Premium 2X Fund* (n 1); *ICICI Bank UK Plc v Assam Oil Co Ltd* [2019] EWHC 750 (Comm); *Skatteforvaltningen v Solo Capital Partners LLP* [2020] EWHC 1624 (Comm), [2020] 4 WLR 98; *Dargamo Holdings Ltd v Avonwick Holdings Ltd* [2021] EWCA Civ 1149, [2022] 1 All ER (Comm) 1244; *Redland City Council v Kozik* [2024] HCA 7.

[5] *International Energy Group Ltd v Zurich Insurance plc* [2015] UKSC 33, [2015] 2 WLR 1471.

that case fundamentally disagreed about how conflicts between unjust enrichment claims and countervailing legal obligations should be resolved.

The confusion caused by *Zurich Insurance* was then compounded by the decision of the Court of Appeal in *Equitas Insurance Ltd v Municipal Mutual Insurance Ltd*.[6] In that case, Leggatt LJ (as he then was) expressed 'concern' about the reasoning of the Supreme Court in *Zurich Insurance*.[7] Relying, among other sources, on material that forms part of Chapter 4 of this book, Leggatt LJ concluded that the approach in *Zurich Insurance* should be 'regarded as an absolutely last resort, if not a counsel of despair'.[8]

For many years now, restitution lawyers have debated many foundational aspects of the law of unjust enrichment. Is there a unified law of unjust enrichment? If so, is this area of the law best conceptualised as consisting of claims based on different unjust factors? Or is the 'absence of basis' for a performance or enrichment the common thread that unites it? The central issue considered in this book has proved to be a key battleground for many of these debates. For example, proponents of the absence of basis model rely upon the inability of the 'unjust factors' framework to account for cases where restitution is denied on the basis that the enrichment was owed to the defendant as a reason for rejecting the unjust factors framework.

This book does not attempt to resolve these foundational issues.[9] Instead, it proceeds on the basis that there is a unified English law of unjust enrichment and that, in order to bring a claim based on unjust enrichment, that law requires the claimant to prove the existence of an 'unjust factor' such as mistake, duress or failure of basis. This book attempts to account for the relationship between restitution claims and countervailing legal obligations owed to the defendant within the orthodox 'unjust factors' scheme of the law of unjust enrichment.

The book is structured in the following way. **Chapter 1** argues that, from a doctrinal standpoint, there are two distinct rules that deny restitution claims on the basis of the defendant's entitlement to the enrichment: 'the good consideration rule' and 'the obligation rule'.

Part I of the book examines the good consideration rule. **Chapters 2 and 3** argue that the good consideration rule is an enrichment-based principle. In cases where the good consideration rule applies, the defendant's enrichment is offset by its equivalent dis-enrichment. Overall, this leaves the defendant in an enrichment-neutral position. This is why a restitution claim is not available.

Part II considers the obligation rule. **Chapter 4** argues that this principle ought to be conceptualised as a bright-line rule rather than as a flexible principle. **Chapter 5** rejects the commonly offered academic explanations for the

[6] *Equitas Insurance Ltd v Municipal Mutual Insurance Ltd* [2019] EWCA Civ 718.
[7] ibid [143].
[8] ibid [145].
[9] Although Section B of the Conclusion demonstrates that the questions considered in this book are not as straightforward for the 'absence of basis' framework as its proponents suggest.

obligation rule. **Chapters 6 and 7** set out the positive case. They use, as their framework, two prominent accounts of the normative basis for unjust enrichment claims: the entitlement thesis and the corrective justice theory. On both accounts, it is suggested that the justification for the obligation rule is based on the need to maintain equality between the claimant and the defendant. This explanation is referred to in this book as the 'equality thesis'.

Chapter 8 sets out the doctrinal consequences of the equality thesis. It demonstrates that these consequences are consistent with the prevalent judicial and academic approach regarding the operation of the obligation rule.

In the light of the equality thesis advanced in **Chapters 6 and 7**, the **Conclusion** revisits the relationship between the good consideration rule and the obligation rule. It is suggested that, although there is a large degree of overlap between these principles, neither renders the other redundant. As to when each of these rules should apply, the preferable analysis is as follows. If the defendant received the enrichment in discharge of a valid legal obligation, whether owed by the claimant or by a third party, restitution is precluded by the obligation rule. The good consideration rule has no useful role to play in these cases. However, there are cases in which the defendant may have provided 'good consideration' without discharging any legal obligation owed to it. For example, the claimant and the defendant may have exchanged benefits pursuant to a common basis, only to discover later that they did so pursuant to a void contract. In such cases, restitution is denied by the good consideration rule whereas the obligation rule is inapplicable.

The law is stated as at February 2024.

1

The Good Consideration Rule and the Obligation Rule

AN UNJUST ENRICHMENT claim may fail because the defendant gave 'good consideration' for the enrichment or because the defendant received the enrichment in discharge of a valid legal obligation. I will call the former principle the 'good consideration rule' and the latter the 'obligation rule'.[1] It is necessary to separate out these distinct principles before asking whether they should exist and why. This chapter will explain the distinction between the good consideration rule and the obligation rule, while the remainder of this book will examine their scope and justification.

> *Example 1*: X owed debts to C and D. X conveyed Blackacre to C to discharge the debt owed by X to C. Blackacre was subject to a mortgage securing X's debt to D. X and C agreed that C would pay off the debt owed by X to D. After doing so, C realised that X was in fact not entitled to Blackacre. C's claim for restitution from D failed.[2]
>
> *Example 2*: C owed £100 each to D and X. C intended to pay X but mistakenly paid D, thereby discharging the debt owed to D. C's claim for restitution from D failed.[3]

It has often been assumed that, in both cases, C's restitution claim is precluded by the same principle.[4] However, the better view is that there are two distinct principles at play, namely the good consideration rule and the obligation rule.

[1] The term 'obligation rule' is based on *Dargamo Holdings Ltd v Avonwick Holdings Ltd* [2021] EWCA Civ 1149, [2022] 1 All ER (Comm) 1244 [70] (Carr LJ).

[2] *Aiken v Short* [1856] 1 Hurl & N 210, 156 ER 1180.

[3] Based on dicta in *Platt v Bromage* [1854] 24 LJ Ex 63, 65. See also, Andrew Burrows, *A Restatement of the English Law of Unjust Enrichment* (Oxford, Oxford University Press, 2012) 32–33.

[4] See eg Graham Virgo, 'Demolishing the Pyramid – the Presence of Basis and Risk-Taking in the Law of Unjust Enrichment' in Andrew Robertson and Tang Wu (eds), *The Goals of Private Law* (Oxford, Hart, 2009) 493–495; Charles Mitchell, Paul Mitchell and Stephen Watterson (eds), *Goff & Jones: The Law of Unjust Enrichment* (10th edn, London, Sweet & Maxwell, 2016) [29-02]; Graham Virgo, *The Principles of the Law of Restitution* (3rd edn, Oxford, Oxford University Press, 2015) 172; Keith Mason, John Carter and Gregory Tolhurst, *Mason & Carter's Restitution Law in Australia* (2nd edn, Melbourne, LexisNexis Butterworths, 2008) 440; George Palmer, *The Law of Restitution*, vol 3 (Boston, Little, Brown and Company, 1978) 496ff.

I. TWO DISTINCT RULES: THE AUTHORITIES

The authorities support the distinction between the good consideration rule and the obligation rule. A comparison of Lord Sterndale's judgment in *Steam Saw Mills*[5] and Goff J's decision in *Barclays Bank*[6] is a useful starting point to explore this distinction.

In *Steam Saw Mills*, the claimant held a licence from the Russian Government to import timber. As a condition of the licence, the claimant was required to deposit the purchase price with the defendant. The dispute concerned certain payments made by the claimant on 9 November 1917. By then, the Russian government had been overthrown by revolution. The claimant sought restitution on the basis that, had it been aware of this fact, it would not have made the payments. Lord Sterndale dismissed the claim, explaining that 'if a man pays money under a mistake of fact, there being a liability to pay it, if the fact of which he was ignorant does not discharge him from that liability, he cannot recover it back'.[7]

In *Barclays Bank*, the claimant bank had mistakenly overlooked a countermand order by its customer in making a payment to the defendant. The bank was granted restitution of the payment because it was unauthorised and therefore incapable of discharging a debt owed by the bank's customer to the defendant. Had the bank's payment discharged that debt, Goff J would have dismissed the claim. That is because, he said, a restitution claim will fail if:[8]

> the payment is made for good consideration, in particular if the money is paid to discharge, and does discharge, a debt owed to the payee (or a principal on whose behalf he is authorised to receive the payment) by the payer or by a third party by whom he is authorised to discharge the debt.

In some respects, the principle articulated by Goff J in *Barclays Bank* is more restrictive than the one applied by Lord Sterndale in *Steam Saw Mills*. Goff J's formulation suggests that the payment must have been made 'to discharge' the debt. An unintentional payment is unlikely to meet this requirement.[9] In Example 2, for instance, C's payment was intended to discharge the debt owed by C to X, but the debt it discharged was owed by C to D; C's payment was not made 'to discharge' the debt owed to D. Goff J also qualified the good consideration rule by reference to the payee's state of mind. He said that the defence may fail 'if the payer's mistake was induced by the payee, or possibly even where the payee, being aware of the payer's mistake, did not receive the money in good faith'.[10]

[5] *Steam Saw Mills Company Ltd v Baring Brothers* [1922] 1 Ch 244 (CA).

[6] *Barclays Bank Ltd v WJ Simms Son & Cooke (Southern) Ltd* [1980] QB 677 (Goff J).

[7] *Steam Saw Mills* (n 5) 250. See also, *Deutsche Morgan Grenfell Group Plc v Inland Revenue Commissioners* [2006] UKHL 49, [2007] 1 AC 558 [85] (Lord Scott); *Re Magarey Farlam Lawyers Trust Accounts (No 3)* [2007] SASC 9, 96 SASR 337 [177].

[8] *Barclays Bank* (n 6) 695 (Goff J).

[9] This is considered in more detail in Section II(B) below.

[10] *Barclays Bank* (n 6) 695 (Goff J). See further, Section II(C) below.

By contrast, Lord Sterndale did not consider the payor's or the payee's state of mind relevant in *Steam Saw Mills*. They also do not feature in subsequent judicial formulations of the obligation rule. For example, in *Portman Building Society v Hamlyn Taylor Neck*,[11] Lord Millett said that 'where money is paid under a legally effective transaction, neither misrepresentation nor mistake vitiates consent or gives rise by itself to an obligation to make restitution'. In *Kleinwort Benson Ltd v Lincoln City Council*,[12] Lord Hope explained that 'the payee cannot be said to have been unjustly enriched if he was entitled to receive the sum paid to him.' In *Dargamo Holdings Ltd v Avonwick Holdings Ltd*,[13] Carr LJ said, 'an unjust factor will not override a valid and subsisting legal obligation of the claimant to confer the benefit on the defendant'. There was no suggestion in any of these cases that the operation of the obligation rule was contingent on the state of mind of the payor or the payee.

In one respect, however, Goff J's formulation is broader than Lord Sterndale's dictum in *Steam Saw Mills*. Lord Sterndale's formulation requires a legal liability owed to the defendant whereas Goff J's language does not. The words 'in particular' in Goff J's analysis suggest that the discharge of a debt is only one way in which the payee may give 'good consideration'. Goff J left open the possibility that the defendant may give 'good consideration' by other means that do not involve the discharge of a legal obligation owed to the defendant.

The doctrinal distinction between the obligation rule and the good consideration rule is reflected in cases decided after *Steam Saw Mills* and *Barclays Bank*. For instance, in *DD Growth Premium v RMF Strategies*,[14] Lord Sumption said,

> It is fundamental that a payment cannot amount to enrichment if it was made for full consideration [***the good consideration rule***]; and that it cannot be unjust to receive or retain it if it was made in satisfaction of a legal right [***the obligation rule***].

Similarly, in *ICICI Bank UK Plc v Assam Oil Co Ltd*,[15] Andrew Burrows QC (sitting as a Judge of the High Court) distinguished between the two rules. He said:

> It is a well-established proposition of law that a mistaken payer is not entitled to restitution of payments that were owed by the payer under a valid contract between the payer and the payee [***the obligation rule***] … it is also the law that a mistaken payer is not entitled to restitution 'if the money is paid to discharge, and does discharge, a debt owed to the payee … by a third party by whom [the payer] is authorised to discharge the debt' (per Robert Goff J in *Barclays Bank Ltd v WJ Simms, Son and Cooke (Southern) Ltd* [1980] QB 677, 695) [***the good consideration rule***].

[11] [1998] 4 All ER 202, 207 (Lord Millett).
[12] [1999] 2 AC 349, 408 (Lord Hope).
[13] [2021] EWCA Civ 1149, [2022] 1 All ER (Comm) 1244 [70] (Carr LJ).
[14] *DD Growth Premium 2X Fund v RMF Market Neutral Strategies* [2017] UKPC 36, [2018] Bus LR 1595 [62] (Lord Sumption).
[15] [2019] EWHC 750 (Comm) [38(ii)].

There is support for this distinction in Australian cases too. Consider, for example, the decision of the Supreme Court of Queensland in *Queensland University of Technology v Project Constructions*.[16] The claimant university sought restitution of its payments to the defendant builder, arguing that the defendant had committed a breach of contract by failing to maintain its building licence. The defendant relied on two defences: (a) the payments were made for good consideration (the good consideration rule); and (b) the defendant's breach 'did not affect existing obligations to pay for past work' (the obligation rule).[17]

The Court held that the contract only provided for a temporary suspension of payments.[18] The payment received by the defendant was, therefore, owed to it under the contract and thus the restitution claim was barred by the obligation rule. The Court analysed the good consideration rule as a separate restriction, albeit that in the light of the Court's conclusion on the obligation rule it was unnecessary to decide whether it applied.[19] The recognition of this distinction in Australia is confirmed by the decision of the High Court of Australia in *Redland City Council v Kozik*.[20] In that case, Godson, Edelman and Steward JJ analysed the good consideration rule and the obligation rule as two distinct restrictions on the availability of an unjust enrichment claim.[21]

The American *Third Restatement on Restitution and Unjust Enrichment* also reflects the distinction between the two principles. The obligation rule is reflected in §62, which provides that a prima facie right to restitution may be defeated if 'the benefit conferred did not unjustly enrich the recipient when the challenged transaction is viewed in the context of the parties' further obligations to each other'.[22] Although this provision is opaquely worded, its operation is made clear by the illustrations to §62. Illustration 2 is identical to Example 2 above. §67 of the Restatement reflects the good consideration rule. It states that the payee has a valid defence if it 'accepts the funds in satisfaction or reduction of the payee's valid claim as creditor of the payor or of another person'.[23] Illustrations to §67 resemble the leading English cases on the good consideration rule.[24]

Thus, the current state of the authorities suggests that the good consideration rule and the obligation rule are two distinct restrictions on the availability of an unjust enrichment claim. This vindicates Burrows's observation that the

[16] *Queensland University of Technology v Project Constructions* [2002] QCA 224, [2003] ALMD 2309.

[17] ibid [6].

[18] ibid [26].

[19] ibid [28].

[20] *Redland City Council v Kozik* [2024] HCA 7.

[21] Good consideration rule: ibid [181], [189], [199], [205]–[207]. Obligation rule: ibid [221].

[22] American Law Institute, *Restatement Third: Restitution and Unjust Enrichment* (Philadelphia, American Law Institute, 2011) §62.

[23] ibid §67.

[24] See eg §67, illustration 1.

'factual distinction [between Examples 1 and 2] appears to mark an important conceptual divide'.[25]

II. DISTINGUISHING FEATURES

The remainder of this chapter will demonstrate that there are three main features that distinguish the good consideration rule and the obligation rule: (1) the obligation rule requires a legal obligation owed to the defendant whereas the good consideration rule may apply even if there was no such obligation; (2) it is relevant to the good consideration rule whether the claimant intended to confer the enrichment on the defendant whereas this is irrelevant to the obligation rule; (3) the operation of the good consideration rule is contingent on the state of mind of the payee. The application of the obligation rule is not qualified in this way.

A. Good Consideration Rule does not Require Discharge of a Legal Liability

As explained above, in order for the obligation rule to apply, a legal obligation owed to the defendant must have been discharged by the defendant's receipt of the enrichment. However, the good consideration rule does not require this. The 'consideration' given by the defendant does not have to involve the discharge of a legal liability; it suffices that the defendant gave up a benefit on the basis of its receipt of the enrichment. This may be illustrated by three examples.

In the decision of the Victoria Court of Appeal in *Ovidio Carrideo*,[26] a landlord had failed to provide the tenant with a disclosure statement. Under the relevant statute, this meant that the tenant was not obliged to pay rent. In ignorance of this rule, the tenant paid rent. Although the rent was not owed to the landlord,[27] the tenant's claim for restitution failed because the landlord had given 'good consideration' by permitting the tenant to use the premises. Chernov JA explained that:[28]

> the tenant here has received good consideration for the money it paid, namely, exclusive possession of the premises that were obviously of use and benefit to it … on the evidence, it is apparent that the tenant received such a benefit and, thus, from its point of view, it received good consideration for its payments.

[25] Andrew Burrows, 'Is There a Defence of Good Consideration?' in Charles Mitchell and William Swadling (eds), *The Restatement Third, Restitution and Unjust Enrichment: Critical and Comparative Essays* (Oxford, Hart, 2013) 168. See also, Robert Stevens, *The Laws of Restitution* (Oxford, Oxford University Press, 2023) 84–89 (the obligation rule) and 385 (the good consideration rule).

[26] *Ovidio Carrideo Nominees Pty Ltd v The Dog Depot Pty Ltd* [2006] VSCA 6, 1 BFRA 612.

[27] ibid [33] (Nettle JA).

[28] ibid [21]. See also, [56] (Ashley JA).

In *Adrenaline Pty Ltd*,[29] the claimant had entered into an agreement with the defendant Council to hire a motor racing circuit. For five years, the claimant used the circuit and paid the sums purportedly due under the agreement. The claimant then sought restitution of these payments on the basis that the Council had not complied with its statutory obligations in setting the fee under the agreement. The New South Wales Court of Appeal held that the restitution claim should be dismissed because the Council gave 'good consideration' for the payments it received. Leeming JA said:[30]

> [The claimant] must be taken to have received precisely what it bargained for … It obtained good consideration for the fees it paid each year … there can be no injustice in Council retaining the monies paid by [the claimant] for services bargained for and received by [the claimant].

The third example is the decision of the High Court of Australia in *Redland City Council*.[31] In that case, the Council had levied special charges on certain persons who owned land with water frontage. It was subsequently found that the Council resolutions levying these charges were invalid. The Council refunded the portion of the charges that it had not spent, but refused to refund the remainder on the basis that these amounts had been spent on services that benefited the claimants. Before the High Court, the Council did not contend that its resolutions to impose the charges were valid. Nor did the Council argue that the charges were owed to it under any legal obligation. Rather, the Council's submission was that the payers were not entitled to restitution because they had received 'good consideration'.[32] The majority judgment by Gordon, Edelman and Steward JJ makes it clear that the good consideration rule may apply even if the defendant's enrichment was not owed to it under a legal obligation.[33] The majority held that the good consideration rule was inapplicable on the facts of *Redland City Council* for a different reason: the receipt of the charges was not the basis upon which Council had provided its services. The Council was under a statutory obligation to perform the services anyway.[34]

B. Intention to Discharge the Debt

This section addresses a second feature that separates the good consideration rule from the obligation rule: the good consideration rule operates only if the claimant's payment was intended to discharge the debt. Goff J's insistence in

[29] *Adrenaline Pty Ltd v Bathurst Regional Council* [2015] NSWCA 123.
[30] ibid [86].
[31] *Redland City Council* (n 20).
[32] ibid [150], [181].
[33] See eg ibid [200]–[203].
[34] ibid [206].

Barclays Bank that the payment must have been made 'to discharge'[35] the debt supports this view.

> *Example 3*: C, D1 and D2 were victims of X's fraud. X misrepresented to C that C was paying D1 and D2 for the supply of goods. Meanwhile, X induced D1 and D2 to believe that the payment from C was made in discharge of debts owed by X's companies. D1 and D2 accepted the payment in discharge of those debts. Upon discovering the fraud, C sought restitution from D1 and D2.

C's payment was not intended to discharge the debts owed to D1 and D2. Does the good consideration rule nevertheless apply? This led to a division of views in the New South Wales Court of Appeal in *Hills Industries*,[36] with Allsop P and Meagher JA reaching opposite conclusions. Allsop P accepted that 'the expression of the matter in proposition (2)(b) in *Barclays Bank* appears to require the intention of the payer to pay off a debt'.[37] Ultimately, however, he preferred the analysis in some American cases that adopted the contrary view. Meagher JA, on the other hand, declined to apply the good consideration rule outside of the confines of its formulation in *Barclays Bank*. On that basis, he found that the good consideration rule was inapplicable to the facts.[38] On appeal, the High Court of Australia preferred Meagher JA's view, concluding that the good consideration rule had no application since '[C's] payments were not made to discharge [X's companies'] debts to [D1] and [D2]'.[39]

In 1926, the House of Lords had considered a similar issue in *RE Jones*.[40] A fraudster owed the defendant company £5000. He induced the claimant to make that payment based on the misrepresentation that the claimant was paying a deposit for the purchase of motorcars. The defendant accepted the payment in discharge of the fraudster's debt. When the fraud was discovered the claimant sought restitution of the deposit. The House of Lords held that the claimant was entitled to restitution. Why did the good consideration rule not preclude restitution? The best explanation is that the good consideration rule was inapplicable because the claimant's payment was not intended to discharge the defendant's debt.[41]

[35] *Barclays Bank* (n 6) 695.
[36] *Hills Industries Ltd v Australian Financial Services & Leasing Pty Ltd* [2012] NSWCA 380, [2012] 295 ALR 147.
[37] ibid [113].
[38] ibid [200]. See also, Andrew Burrows, 'Good Consideration in the Law of Unjust Enrichment' (2013) 129 Law Quarterly Review 329, 332.
[39] *Australian Financial Services & Leasing Pty Ltd v Hills Industries Ltd* [2014] HCA 14, (2014) 88 ALJR 552 [101] (Hayne, Crennan, Kiefel, Bell and Keane JJ) (emphasis added).
[40] *RE Jones Ltd v Waring & Gillow Ltd* [1926] AC 670 (HL).
[41] Daniel Friedmann, 'Payment of Another's Debt' (1983) 99 Law Quarterly Review 534, 551; Daniel Friedmann and Nili Cohen, 'Payment of Another's Debt' in *International Encyclopedia of Comparative Law* X (1991) 63; Sonja Meier, 'Mistaken Payments in Three-Party Situations: A German View of English Law' (1999) 58 Cambridge Law Journal 567, 579.

In *Hills Industries* and *RE Jones*, the payor did not intend to discharge the debt because the payor did not know there was a debt. The payor may also not have intended to discharge the debt because the payor was mistaken as to the debtor's identity.[42] This is illustrated by *Durrant*.[43] The question in that case was whether the claimant could recover tithe charges it paid the defendant under the mistaken impression that they were due from the claimant whereas, in fact, the liability was owed by a third party. Restitution was denied. Again, the preferable analysis is that the good consideration rule did not apply because the claimant did not intend to discharge the third party's liability to the defendant.[44]

It may be said that the decision of the Court of Appeal in *Lloyds Bank Plc v Independent Insurance Co Ltd*[45] is inexplicable on this view. In that case, the claimant bank paid £162,388 to the defendant as instructed by the bank's customer which discharged a debt owed by the customer to the defendant. The bank made the payment believing that certain cheques deposited by its customer had been cleared. However, one of these cheques was in fact dishonoured. Consequently, the customer's account was substantially overdrawn. The bank sought restitution from the defendant. The Court of Appeal held that the claim should be dismissed. It was held that by discharging the debt owed by the customer, the defendant had provided 'good consideration' for the bank's payment. But it is unlikely that the bank intended to discharge that debt. As Burrows says, 'the claimant bank had no knowledge of the underlying purpose of the payment and did not know that it was to discharge a debt'.[46]

However, on analysis, the decision in *Lloyds Bank* is consistent with the requirement that the payor must have intended to discharge the debt owed to

[42] Scottish Law Commission, *Recovery of Benefits Conferred Under Error of Law* (Discussion Paper Number 95, Vol 2, 1993) [2.163].

[43] *Durrant v Ecclesiastical Commissioners for England & Wales* [1880] 6 QBD 234. See also, *Bank of New York v North British Steel Group* [1992] SLT 613 (OH) 614 (Lord Caplan) (where the payee did not intend to discharge the debt because of a mistake as to the identity of the payee). Many civilian jurisdictions insist that the payment must have been intended to discharge the debt: see Schlechtriem P, Coen C and Hornung R, 'Restitution and Unjust Enrichment in Europe' (2001) 9 European Review of Private Law 377, 412.

[44] Friedmann, 'Payment of Another's Debt' (n 41) 550; Robin Evans-Jones, 'Identifying the Enriched: Some Complex Relationships Involving the Condictio Indebiti' (1992) 4 Scots Law Times 25, 29. The payor's intention to discharge the debt is an element of the 'suum recepit' rule, which is the Roman law equivalent of the good consideration rule: see Helen Scott, 'Unjustified Enrichment' [2012] Annual Survey of South African Law 1046, 1048; Patrick Elchies, *Annotations on Lord Stair's Institutions of the Law of Scotland* (Edinburgh, Bell & Bradfute, 1824) 39–40; Andrew Bankton, *An Institute of the Laws of Scotland in Civil Rights* (Edinburgh, Stair Society, 1993–1995) 217–218; David Hume, *Baron David Hume's Lectures, 1786–1822*, vol 3 (George Paton ed, Edinburgh, Stair Society, 1939) 34; Scottish Law Commission (n 42) [2.175]; Alexander Schall, 'Three-party Situations in Unjust Enrichment Epitomised by Mistaken Bank Transfers' [2004] Restitution Law Review 110, 128.

[45] *Lloyds Bank Plc v Independent Insurance Co Ltd* [2000] QB 110 (CA).

[46] Burrows, 'Is There a Defence of Good Consideration?' (n 25) 171.

the defendant. This is apparent when one considers the nature of the banker-customer relationship. As Zyl explains:[47]

> A bank which effects payment of a cheque in accordance with its mandate and within its authority has no interest in the underlying agreement or in the reason for the payment by cheque. It is for all practical purposes, no more than a conduit or 'neutral functionary' whose payment of the cheque facilitates performance by the customer, as debtor in terms of the underlying agreement, to the third party payee, as creditor in terms thereof. By paying the cheque the bank does not effect performance of the customer's obligation to the third party. It is the customer who performs with the assistance or through the mediation of the bank.

Therefore, the relevant intention in *Lloyds Bank* is that of the customer, not the bank. As long as the customer's payment was intended to discharge the debt, the interposition of the bank is immaterial. Waller LJ recognised this in *Lloyds Bank*, where he explained that:[48]

> It must be remembered that the formulation in the *Simms* case [1980] Q.B. 677 itself contemplates that 'the money is paid to discharge and does discharge a debt owed …' The case further recognises that where the bank meet[s] a cheque payable to A which in fact pays a debt that C owes to A, the bank are paying money <u>to discharge</u> that debt.

C. State of Mind of the Payee

The third feature that distinguishes the good consideration rule from the obligation rule is the relevance of the payee's state of mind. As Goff J said in *Barclays Bank*, the good consideration rule may not be available 'if the payer's mistake was induced by the payee, or possibly even where the payee, being aware of the payer's mistake, did not receive the money in good faith'.[49] The genesis of this qualification appears to be *Ward v Wallis*[50] which Goff J expressly referred to in *Barclays Bank*.

In *Ward v Wallis*, the defendant contractor had sub-contracted the claimant to supply pavements at the cost of £125.5. Having done the work, the claimant demanded this sum from the defendant. A dispute ensued between the defendant and the architect of the project regarding which, among the two, was liable to the claimant. The claimant issued a writ seeking the value of its work from the defendant. The writ ought to have been issued for the sum of £125.5. However, mistakenly, the writ only sought to recover £50.5s from the defendant. Upon being served with the writ, the defendant paid £50.5 to the claimant and

[47] DH Zyl, 'Unauthorised Payment and Unjust Enrichment in Banking Law' in Francis Rose (ed), *Restitution and Banking Law* (Oxford, Mansfield, 1998) 3.
[48] *Lloyds Bank* (n 45) 127 (Waller LJ) (emphasis added).
[49] [1980] QB 677 (QB) 695 (Goff J).
[50] [1900] 1 QB 675.

obtained a receipt that the entire sum due to the claimant had been satisfied. Subsequently, the claimant discovered the mistake and sought to recover £75 from the defendant. In response, the defendant argued that the claim must fail in view of the earlier settlement between the parties.

Kennedy J rejected the defendant's contention. He recognised that, as a general rule, the claimant was not entitled to bring a claim in this scenario. However, he said, the defendant must have known that credit of £75 was given as a result of a mistake on the plaintiff's part.[51] This, according to Kennedy J, was a 'special circumstance'[52] that allowed the claimant to seek recovery from the defendant. As he put it, in order to rely on the defence that the payment was received in discharge of a debt created pursuant to a valid settlement, '[t]here must be bona fides on the part of the party who has got the benefit of his opponent's payment'.[53]

The relevance of the payee's state of mind was confirmed by the Court of Appeal in *Lloyds Bank*.[54] In that case, Peter Gibson LJ pointed out that, in formulating the good consideration rule in *Barclays Bank*,[55] Goff J had said that the claim 'may' fail if certain conditions were satisfied. According to Peter Gibson LJ,[56]

> The use of the word "may" in "His claim may however fail" is explicable by [Goff J's] qualification of his proposition (b), viz. where the payer's mistake is induced by the payee or possibly where the payee, being aware of the payer's mistake, did not receive the money in good faith: in such cases there will be no defence to the payer's claim even though the payee has given consideration for the payment by accepting the payment in discharge of a debt owed to him by a third party on whose behalf the payer is authorised to discharge it.

III. OVERLAP BETWEEN THE OBLIGATION RULE AND THE GOOD CONSIDERATION RULE

In *Barclays Bank*, Goff J said that the defendant may give good consideration by discharging a debt owed 'by the payer or by a third party'.[57] Thus, the good consideration rule may apply whether discharged debt was owed by the claimant to the defendant (a two-party case) or by a third-party to the defendant (a three-party case).

[51] ibid 679.
[52] ibid 678.
[53] ibid.
[54] See also, *Skatteforvaltningen v Solo Capital Partners LLP* [2020] EWHC 1624 (Comm), [2020] 4 WLR 98 [141] (Andrew Baker J) (summary judgment was denied, inter alia, on the basis that the payor may be able to establish at trial that the payee did not receive the money in good faith).
[55] [2000] QB 110.
[56] ibid 130.
[57] *Barclays Bank* (n 6) 695 (Goff J) (emphasis added).

The application of the good consideration rule to two-party cases is exemplified by the decision of the New Zealand Supreme Court in *Stiassny*.[58] The dispute in that case concerned the liability of the claimant partnership to pay GST. The claimant paid GST because its receivers believed that a failure to pay would lead to their personal liability. This was in fact a misapprehension. The claimant therefore sought restitution of mistakenly paid GST. The claim failed. The New Zealand Court of Appeal applied the good consideration rule as formulated in *Barclays Bank*. In particular, the Court considered it relevant that the payment was made 'to discharge' the debt[59] and that the defendant received the payment in good faith.[60] On appeal, this approach was confirmed by the New Zealand Supreme Court.[61]

The applicability of the good consideration rule to two-party cases means that there may be cases in which both the good consideration rule and the obligation rule apply.

> *Example 4*: C owed £100 to D. Intending to discharge the debt, C paid £100 to D which D accepted in discharge of the debt. C later realised that he had misread his bank balance. Had he known the true position, he would not have paid D. D was at all material times unaware of C's mistake. C seeks restitution from D. C's claim will fail.

On these facts, D may rely on either the good consideration rule or the obligation rule. Both principles produce the same result, that C is not entitled to restitution. But this overlap leads to important normative questions: does the law of unjust enrichment need both the good consideration rule and the obligation rule? Does one render the other redundant?

In order to answer these questions, it is necessary to understand the justification(s) for each of these principles first. That task is undertaken in Chapters 2 to 8 of this book. Based on the analysis in those chapters, Section A of the Conclusion revisits the relationship between the good consideration rule and the obligation rule. As explained in more detail there, the analysis in this book suggests that there is a large degree of overlap between the good consideration rule and the obligation rule. In particular, many 'good consideration' cases are capable of being analysed or decided based on the obligation rule. However, there is one category of case in which the good consideration rule applies and the obligation rule does not. Accordingly, neither principle is otiose.

This chapter sought to demonstrate that the good consideration rule and the obligation rule are two distinct restrictions on the availability of claims in unjust enrichment. There are three features that distinguish these rules: (a) the obligation rule requires a legal obligation owed to the defendant, while the good

[58] *Stiassny v Commissioner of Inland Revenue* [2012] NZSC 106. See also, *National Mutual Life Association v Walsh* [1987] 8 NSWLR 585 (NSWSC) (Clarke J); *Orix Australia Corporation Ltd v Moody Kiddell & Partners* [2005] NSWSC 1209.

[59] *Commissioner of Inland Revenue v Stiassny* [2012] NZCA 93, [2012] 10 NZBLC 99-704 [85].

[60] ibid [105].

[61] *Stiassny* (NZSC) (n 58).

consideration rule does not. The defendant may give 'good consideration' even though there was no legal obligation owed to the defendant; (b) in order for the good consideration rule to apply the claimant must have intended to confer the enrichment on the defendant. The obligation rule is not subject to such a restriction; and (c) the good consideration rule does not apply if the defendant was not acting in good faith, for example, because the defendant was aware of the claimant's mistake. The application of the obligation rule is not qualified in this way.

Part I

The Good Consideration Rule

2

The Enrichment Explanation

THIS CHAPTER ARGUES that the best explanation for the good consideration rule is based on the absence of the defendant's enrichment. That claim is advanced in two parts. Section I suggests that, in evaluating the defendant's enrichment, any conditionally-related disenrichments of the defendant must be taken into account. I call this the 'net benefit approach'. Section II uses the net benefit approach to explain the good consideration rule as an enrichment-related principle.

I. THE NET BENEFIT APPROACH

> *Example 1*: C pays £10,000 to D for a car worth £8,000. Realising that D had misrepresented the value of the car, C rescinds the contract and seeks restitution of £10,000.

There are two ways of characterising D's enrichment. On one view ('the independent claims theory') D is enriched by £10,000. On that view, C's claim against D is subject to a counter-claim for £8,000.[1] On another view, D is only enriched by the 'net benefit' (£2,000).[2] The second idea, the net benefit approach, is based on the notion that in certain circumstances enrichments and disenrichments of the defendant are to be netted off against each other.

English law's choice between these methodologies is seemingly equivocal.[3] By contrast, German law adopts the net benefit approach. The German *Saldotheorie* ('the doctrine of balance') states that, when parties' performances are mutually conditional, the defendant is only enriched by the difference between the values of those performances.[4] The remainder of this section will argue that the net benefit thesis is the preferable approach under English law.

[1] Elise Bant, *The Change of Position Defence* (Oxford, Hart, 2009) 96–101; Andrew Lodder, *Enrichment in the Law of Unjust Enrichment and Restitution* (Oxford, Hart, 2012) 21–22.

[2] Peter Birks, *Unjust Enrichment* (2nd edn, Oxford, Oxford University Press, 2005) 225–226; Robert Stevens and Ben McFarlane, 'In Defence of Sumpter v. Hedges' (2002) 118 Law Quarterly Review 569, 583–584; Ben McFarlane, 'Unjust Enrichment, Rights and Value' in Donal Nolan and Andrew Robertson (eds), *Rights and Private Law* (Oxford, Hart, 2012) 584.

[3] See *School Facility Management Ltd v Governing Body of Christ the King College* [2021] EWCA Civ 1053, [2021] 1 WLR 6129 [34], [78], [83] (Popplewell LJ, with whom Dingemans and Nicola Davies LJJ agreed).

[4] Basil Markesinis, Werner Lorenz and Gerhard Dannemann, *The German Law of Obligations – The Law of Contracts and Restitution: A Comparative Introduction*, vol 1 (Oxford, Clarendon,

A. The Positive Case for the Net Benefit Approach

> *Example 2*: C swaps her horse for D's cow. After the transaction, the cow dies while it is in C's possession. C discovers a ground for rescission, avoids the contract and demands the return of the horse.[5]

Under the independent claims theory, C's claim to the horse and D's claim to the cow are autonomous. Each party bears the risk that the other may raise a defence. Thus, C can rely on change of position in response to D's claim for the cow. In effect, therefore, C can recover the horse and pay nothing for the value of the cow.

Consider two variations of Example 2:

> *Example 2A*: C swaps her horse for D's cow. After the transfer, the cow dies due to C's negligence. C rescinds the contract and demands the return of the horse.
>
> *Example 2B*: C swaps her horse for D's cow. After the transfer, C intentionally kills the cow believing in good faith that the loss is her own. C rescinds the contract and demands the return of the horse.[6]

C is entitled to the return of the horse (or its value) in both cases while D has no claim in either case. That is because C's negligence does not prevent it from relying on the defence of change of position.[7] Consequently, in Example 2A, C can plead change of position on the basis of the death of the cow. Similarly, in Example 2B, as long as C was unaware of the ground for rescission, even C's intentional act of killing the cow does not disentitle it from relying on change of position.[8] These results seem unjust. They are also unprincipled, as explained below.

i. The Net Benefit Approach: Principle

The independent claims thesis leads to an allocation of risks that is very difficult to justify. As a general rule, the party in control of an asset must bear the risk of its loss.[9] Ensuring the identity of control and risk in this way protects

1997) 764–765; John Dawson, 'Erasable Enrichment in German Law' (1981) 61 Boston University Law Review 271, 295.

[5] Birke Häcker, *Consequences of Impaired Consent Transfers: A Structural Comparison of English and German Law* (Oxford, Hart, 2013) 73.

[6] ibid.

[7] *Dextra Bank & Trust Co Ltd v Bank of Jamaica* [2001] UKPC 50, [2002] 1 All ER (Comm) 193.

[8] Thomas Krebs, *Restitution at the Crossroads: A Comparative Study* (London, Cavendish, 2001) 102.

[9] Konrad Zweigert and Hein Kötz, *Introduction to Comparative Law* (Tony Weir tr, 3rd rev edn, Oxford, Clarendon, 1998) 593; Phillip Hellwege, 'Unwinding Mutual Contracts: *Restitutio in Integrum* v. the Defence of Change of Position' in David Johnston and Reinhard Zimmermann (eds), *Unjustified Enrichment: Key Issues in Comparative Perspective* (Cambridge, Cambridge University Press, 2002) 274; Daniel Visser, 'Unjustified Enrichment in Comparative Perspective' in Mathias Reimann and Reinhard Zimmermann (eds), *The Oxford Handbook of Comparative Law* (Oxford, Oxford University Press, 2006) 982.

parties from losses they cannot prevent. It also respects the autonomy of parties to decide whether they wish to incur expenses for the protection of their assets.[10] The consequence of the independent claims theory is that the claimant recipient of an asset no longer assumes the risk that its own actions may destroy the asset.[11] Instead, that risk is passed on to the defendant even though the defendant was incapable of exercising any control over that asset.[12] As a result, each party acts as 'the insurer of the other; each bears the risk for the mistakes that the other might make'.[13]

It may be said that this reasoning proves too much. If it is correct, it seemingly suggests that change of position defence should not apply even to unilateral transfers. After all, 'the accidental destruction … of a benefit … forms the paradigm example of disenrichment that attracts the application of the … change of position defence'.[14]

The answer to this suggestion leads me to a second objection to the independent claims thesis. That is based on the notion of 'conditionality'. When mutual exchanges are conditional on each other, their 'factual reciprocity' must also influence their unwinding.[15] In the case of mutually conditional performances, each party confers a benefit on the other on the basis that the other party will reciprocate. Splitting the transaction up into two individual transfers ignores this aspect. Since the parties conferred enrichments on each other acting in furtherance of a common basis, reversing the transaction without regard to that basis also violates their autonomy.[16]

This explains why the change of position defence does not apply in the same way to unilateral transfers and mutual exchanges of benefits.

> *Example 3*: C pays £10,000 to D for a car worth £8,000. C sells the car and invests the price in shares. The shares are rendered worthless due to a market fall. Later, realising that D misrepresented the value of the car, C rescinds the contract and seeks restitution of £10,000 from D.

Under the independent claims thesis, C has a change of position defence against D's claim. On one view, this defence protects C's autonomy.[17] In Example 3, however, that defence must be weighed against D's autonomy, as D's decision to

[10] Daniel Visser, *Unjustified Enrichment* (Cape Town, Juta, 2008) 499.

[11] Reinhard Zimmermann, 'Restitution after Termination for Breach of Contract in German Law' [1997] Acta Juridica 121, 129; Visser, *Unjustified Enrichment* (n 10) 498.

[12] Reinhard Zimmermann and Jacques Du Plessis, 'Basic Features of the German Law of Unjustified Enrichment' [1994] Restitution Law Review 14.

[13] Visser, *Unjustified Enrichment* (n 10) 104.

[14] Bant, *The Change of Position Defence* (n 1) 99.

[15] Gerhard Dannemann, *The German Law of Unjustified Enrichment and Restitution: A Comparative Introduction* (Oxford, Oxford University Press, 2009) 142–143; Häcker (n 5) 73; Hellwege (n 9) 271.

[16] Hellwege (n 9) 274. See also, James Edelman, 'Change of Position: A Defence of Unjust Disenrichment' (2012) 92 Boston University Law Review 1009, 1024–1025.

[17] Edelman (n 16).

transfer the car was based on the expectation of C's payment. Therefore, reversing that payment without restoring the value of the car infringes D's autonomy.

Excluding the application of the change of position defence to conditional transfers is well-recognised in English law. This is illustrated by *Goss v Chilcott*.[18] The defendants, Mr and Mrs Goss, had obtained a loan from the claimant. The loan agreement was found to be void. The claimant brought a claim for restitution of the loan. The defendants argued that they had passed on the loan to Mr Haddon, a third party, and were hence entitled to rely on change of position. Lord Goff rejected this submission:[19]

> [The defendants] had … allowed the money to be paid over to Mr. Haddon in circumstances in which, as they well knew, the money would nevertheless have to be repaid to the company. They had, therefore, in allowing the money to be paid to Mr. Haddon, deliberately taken the risk that he would be unable to repay the money.

A similar approach was adopted in *Haugesund Kommune*[20] where the defendant municipality argued that it had changed its position by investing, unsuccessfully, the sums it received under a swap agreement. In a passage that closely mirrors the risk-allocation reasoning, Tomlinson J rejected this contention:[21]

> The case is far removed from that where the recipient of what he reasonably believes is an out and out payment to him pays that amount away to charity. Here the municipalities always knew that they had to repay the money … I can see no basis upon which it can begin to be suggested that in these circumstances it would be inequitable to require the municipalities to make restitution. That would be to impose upon Depfa the risk of investments over which they were not consulted and over which they had no control.

The decisions in *Goss* and *Haugesund Kommune* are best rationalised on the basis that change of position is ruled out by the conditionality of the transfer.[22]

Yet another difficulty with the independent claims theory is that it treats like cases differently.

> *Example 4A*: C buys a pen from D for £4. C pays £5 and D returns the £1 balance. Later, C rescinds the transaction for misrepresentation.
>
> *Example 4B*: The facts are identical to Example 4A, except that C pays £4 for the pen. C rescinds the transaction for misrepresentation.

[18] *Goss v Chilcott* [1996] AC 788 (PC).

[19] ibid 799 (Lord Goff).

[20] *Haugesund Kommune v Depfa ACS Bank* [2010] EWCA Civ 579, [2012] QB 549.

[21] *Haugesund Kommune v Depfa ACS Bank* [2009] EWHC 2227 (Comm), [2010] Lloyd's Rep PN 21 [163] (Tomlinson J) (emphasis added). Affirmed on appeal: *Haugesund Kommune* (CA) (n 20). This reasoning was not applied in *Banca Intesa Sanpaolo Spa v Comune Di Venezia* [2023] EWCA Civ 1482 because, unlike in *Goss* and *Haugesund*, the defendants in that case did not know that the receipt of the enrichment was conditional: see [195] (Sir Julian Flaux C, with whom Males and Falk LJJ agreed).

[22] Edelman (n 16) 1025; Robert Stevens, 'Is There a Law of Unjust Enrichment?', in Simone Degeling and James Edelman (eds), *Unjust Enrichment in Commercial Law* (Sydney, Thomson Reuters, 2008) 32; Robert Stevens, *The Laws of Restitution* (Oxford, Oxford University Press, 2023) 359–360.

Adopting the independent claims theory leads to D's enrichment being calculated differently in Examples 4A and 4B. According to the independent claims theory, D's enrichment is £5 in Example 4A whereas it is £4 in Example 4B even though the factual difference between these examples is entirely fortuitous. Faced with this difficulty, proponents of the independent claims theory may contend that D's enrichment is £4 in both cases as that was the 'value' transferred to D. However, my objection to the independent claims thesis is that it does not permit one to reach that result. The result that D's enrichment is £4 can only be reached by defining enrichment in terms of the net value transferred to D. The proposition that the value transferred to D is £4 is an implied acceptance of the net benefit theory. It is therefore difficult to disagree with Birks's conclusion that:[23]

> [T]he two-claim approach can produce bizarre results. One claimant may fortuitously encounter an obstacle or bar which the other escapes, with the consequence that for very slight reasons the parties to the one exchange may end up in very different situations.

ii. The Net Benefit Approach: Authorities

The net benefit approach has also been accepted by the courts. A commonly cited example is Hobhouse J's decision in *Westdeutsche*.[24] One of the claims in that case sought to reverse payments made under a void interest rate swap between Kleinwort Benson and Sandwell Borough Council. Kleinwort Benson had made a net payment of £196,322 to the Council. However, the Council argued that the six-year limitation period had to be calculated from the date of each payment, which would have meant that the recovery of the first three payments was time-barred. Rejecting this argument, Hobhouse J held that the claim could only be for the defendant's net enrichment:[25]

> Where there have been a whole succession of payments one way and the other in respect of a single underlying transaction, both equity and justice require that one should have regard to the totality of those payments and the resultant overall benefit and detriment … At no time during the history of this transaction has there been a cause of action for more than the net balance existing at any given time.

The net benefit approach also derives support from Lord Templeman's speech in *Lipkin Gorman*.[26] Lord Templeman considered that the defendant club was

[23] Birks, *Unjust Enrichment* (n 2) 226.

[24] *Westdeutsche Landesbank Girozentrale v Islington London Borough Council* [1994] 4 All ER 890 (QB) (Hobhouse J). See also *Foskett v McKeown* [2000] UKHL 29, [2001] 1 AC 102, 129; Charles Mitchell, Paul Mitchell and Stephen Watterson (eds), *Goff & Jones: The Law of Unjust Enrichment* (10th edn, London, Sweet & Maxwell, 2022) [4-59]–[4-66].

[25] *Westdeutsche* (n 24). See also, *South Tyneside Metropolitan Borough Council v Svenska International Plc* [1995] 1 All ER 545 (QB) 548 (Clarke J).

[26] *Lipkin Gorman v Karpnale Ltd* [1991] 2 AC 548 (HL).

only enriched by the difference between the sums staked with it (£561,014.06) and the winnings it paid out (£378,294.06). He explained:[27]

> [I]f Cass had paid £20,000 derived from the solicitors to a car dealer for a motor car priced at £20,000, the car dealer would not have been enriched. The car dealer would have received £20,000 for a car worth £20,000. But an innocent recipient of stolen money will be enriched if the recipient has not given full consideration.

Lord Goff analysed the club's disenrichment in terms of change of position. However, that was because Lord Goff found that independent bets could not be aggregated as though they constituted a single transaction.[28] In other words, enrichments and disenrichments across different bets were not conditional on each other. This was also Hobhouse J's view in *Kleinwort Benson*.[29] The facts were identical to *Westdeutsche*. However, the claimant attempted to circumvent the limitation period by aggregating payments across five different interest rate swaps. This was rejected on the basis that 'each interest rate swap contract was an independent transaction'.[30]

Henderson J's decision in *Littlewoods*[31] also impliedly accepts the net benefit approach. The question was whether corporation tax that would have been paid had it not been for the disputed VAT payments should be taken into account in computing the Revenue's enrichment. The Court held that it should not. However, this was because it could not be said that these two liabilities 'arose out of the same underlying transaction'.[32] Consequently, 'the position is not analogous with that considered … in [*Westdeutsche*]'.[33]

The net benefit approach has been approved in other commonwealth jurisdictions. Consider the New Zealand High Court's decision in *Nimmo*.[34] A fraudster embezzled money from the claimant and converted it into cheques at the defendant bank. Rejecting a 'knowing receipt' claim against the bank, Blanchard J held:[35]

> [The bank] undoubtedly received the moneys … [It] immediately put Mr. Eaton in possession of bank cheques and travellers cheques and debited its books accordingly. The net result … was that [the bank] was in no better position as a result of the transaction. It had not been enriched.

On similar facts, in *Cigna Insurance*,[36] the Court refused to hold a bank liable as a constructive trustee for 'knowing receipt' because it had paid out an amount

[27] ibid 560 (Lord Templeman).
[28] ibid 582 (Lord Goff).
[29] *Kleinwort Benson Ltd v South Tyneside Metropolitan Borough Council* [1994] 4 All ER 972 (QB).
[30] ibid 979 (Hobhouse J).
[31] *Littlewoods Retail Ltd v Revenue & Customs Commissioners* [2014] EWHC 868 (Ch), [2014] BVC 23 (Henderson J).
[32] ibid [434].
[33] ibid. Although the issue came up before the Court of Appeal in *School Facility Management Ltd v Governing Body of Christ the King College* [2021] EWCA Civ 1053, [2021] 1 WLR 6129, the Court did not express a conclusive view: see [34], [78], [83] (Popplewell LJ, with whom Dingemans and Nicola Davies LJJ agreed).
[34] *Nimmo v Westpac Banking Corporation* [1993] 3 NZLR 218 (NZHC).
[35] ibid 224–225 (Blanchard J).
[36] *Cigna Life Insurance New Zealand v Westpac Securities* [1996] 1 NZLR 80 (NZHC).

equal to an initial deposit. The bank, the Court held, was 'merely a depository or channel through which the moneys are transferred'.[37]

iii. The Net Benefit Approach: Operation

It was explained above that the net benefit thesis is supported by principle as well as authority. This section makes two brief points about its operation.

First, it must be apparent from the justification for the net benefit approach that it can apply only when the defendant's enrichment and disnenrichment are conditional on each other. In other words, the exchange between the claimant and the defendant must have taken place in furtherance of a common basis shared by the parties.

Second, the requirement of 'conditionality' precludes the application of the net benefit approach to cases where the defendant was aware of the claimant's mistake. A leading German decision illustrates this.[38] The plaintiff bought a used car from the defendant. The defendant had knowingly misrepresented to the plaintiff that the car was accident-free. The plaintiff later learnt that this was false. A claim for restitution was brought. The question was whether *Saldotheorie* – the German equivalent of the net benefit approach – applied here. The Bundesgerichtshof held that *Saldotheorie* did not apply:[39]

> The basic principle of the Saldotheorie … also illustrates the limits of its application … The defendant caused the purchaser to conclude the sale contract by fraud, which the plaintiff, as the defendant knew, had he known that the car purchased had been involved in an accident, would certainly not have concluded … The defendant company must therefore allow itself to be treated as if … <u>it had already known when it received the purchase price and transferred the car to the plaintiff of the defect in the legal basis for the exchange of performances rendered by both parties</u> … Thereby however, the internal justification for an application of the Saldotheorie in the present case lapses.

Notably, the Court emphasised the fact that the defendant was aware of the claimant's mistake. This is relevant because it is the defendant's knowledge of the claimant's mistake that vitiates the common basis underlying the transaction. This is fatal to the application of the net benefit approach.[40]

B. Objections to the Net Benefit Approach

This section considers three common objections to the net benefit thesis. These objections raise three questions: (i) Are there material differences between the

[37] ibid 87.
[38] BGH 14 October 1971, BGHZ 57, 137.
[39] ibid cited in Dannemann (n 15) 237 (emphasis added).
[40] Hellwege (n 9) 279.

English and German legal systems that preclude the adoption of *Saldotheorie* in England? (ii) Is the net benefit thesis based on a misapprehension as to what 'transfer of value' means? (iii) How does the net benefit thesis operate when the enrichment consists of 'rights' rather than 'value'?

i. Differences between English and German Legal Systems

Two differences between the English and German legal systems have been relied upon as precluding the adoption of the net benefit approach in England. The first among them is the dichotomy between immediate enrichment and extant enrichment. English law adopts the former[41] and German law the latter. The second difference is that German law adopts the 'absence of basis' approach whereas English law requires positive reasons for the restitution of an unjust enrichment.[42]

a. Immediate Enrichment and Extant Enrichment

The distinction between the immediate and extant enrichment approaches has been relied upon to support two distinct arguments. First, it has been argued that the net benefit thesis is derived from the extant enrichment approach adopted by German law.[43] Second, it has been suggested that *Saldotheorie* is inconsistent with English law's commitment to the immediate enrichment approach.[44] I will examine each of these points in turn.

The extant enrichment approach is embodied in §818(3) of the German Bürgerliches Gesetzbuch ('BGB'). It provides that the obligation to surrender or replace value is excluded if the recipient is no longer enriched. However, the net benefit approach does not follow from this rule. The rule in §818(3) is entirely compatible with the independent claims theory.

> *Example* 5: C pays £10,000 to D for a car worth £8,000. The car is destroyed while it is in C's possession. Later, realising that D misrepresented the value of the car, C seeks restitution of £10,000.

One could apply §818(3) in conjunction with the independent claims thesis to this example. On that approach, C's claim against D and D's claim against C are both restricted to the value surviving. This has the consequence that C is entitled to restitution of £10,000 whereas C is not liable to return the car or its value. German law had adopted this approach (Zweikondiktionenlehre) in the past.[45] Some pockets of German law (e.g. claims by the mentally incapable

[41] Mitchell, Mitchell and Watterson (eds), *Goff & Jones* (10th edn) (n 24) [4-67].
[42] *Woolwich Equitable Building Society v Inland Revenue Commissioners* [1993] AC 70, 172 (HL) (Lord Goff).
[43] Bant, *The Change of Position Defence* (n 1) 98.
[44] Lodder (n 1) 22.
[45] Zimmermann and Du Plessis (n 12) 41.

and minors) still follow that view.[46] Such claims are not exceptions to §818(3). This shows that *Saldotheorie* is not contingent on §818(3). Indeed, some German commentators view the net benefit approach as an *exception* to §818(3).[47] Consider, for instance, this passage from Dawson's influential article:[48]

> The effort so far has been to show that 'innocent' receivers of unjustified enrichment have been protected by every available means against every loss that can cause enrichment to diminish or disappear … the addition of only one other feature will be enough to throw into reverse the usual exemption from all forms of risk that is granted to 'innocent' receivers of gain. If the receiver gave something of value in exchange for his gain that has since diminished or vanished, then to the extent of the value given the risk of loss shifts and any loss that occurs is his. This is the result of the 'net balance' (Saldo) theory.

Similarly, Zimmermann and Du Plessis have argued that the net benefit theory is 'an exception to the protection normally granted to the enrichment debtor by … §818(3)'.[49] In short, the net benefit thesis does not follow from the extant enrichment rule in German law. Nor is its validity conditional on the acceptance of that approach.

Lodder argues that the net enrichment theory is inconsistent with the immediate enrichment approach adopted by English law. This argument is flawed as it conflates two distinct issues: first, at what point in time should the defendant's enrichment be evaluated?; and second, are conditionally related disenrichments of the defendant relevant in computing the defendant's enrichment? A test of timing – which is what immediate enrichment is – cannot resolve the second question. This is clear from the fact that the defendant's disenrichment may be antecedent to or simultaneous with the enrichment. Lodder seems to admit that 'antecedent or simultaneous events and conduct' are not relevant if they are 'extraneous to the receipt of value in a defective transaction factually enriching the defendant'.[50] Disenrichments on which the conferral of a benefit are conditional are almost never 'extraneous to the receipt of value'. Therefore, in effect, Lodder's approach draws a sharp distinction between disenrichments that are antecedent to or simultaneous with the enrichment on the one hand and disenrichments that are subsequent to the enrichment on the other. This is difficult to justify because, within a transaction, whether the defendant's disenrichment is antecedent or subsequent to the enrichment is often fortuitous.

Furthermore, the authorities that Lodder relies upon for the immediate enrichment argument[51] are cases in which the courts did not have occasion to

[46] Häcker (n 5) 73.

[47] Reinhard Zimmermann, 'Unjustified Enrichment: The Modern Civilian Approach' (1995) 15 Oxford Journal of Legal Studies 403, 413; Michael Jewell, 'The Boundaries of Change of Position – A Comparative Study' [2000] Restitution Law Review 1, 31.

[48] Dawson (n 4) 294 (emphasis added).

[49] Zimmermann and Du Plessis (n 12) 40. See also, Jewell (n 47) 31.

[50] Lodder (n 1) 198.

[51] *Baker v Courage & Co* [1910] 1 KB 56 (KB); *Craven-Ellis v Canons Ltd* [1936] 2 KB 403 (CA); *William Lacey (Hounslow) Ltd v Davis* [1957] 1 WLR 932 (QB); *Pavey & Mathews Pty Ltd v Paul*

consider the implications of a conditionally-related disenrichment of the defendant. In many of these cases, the reason the claim was restricted to original receipt was because subsequent benefits were not 'at the expense of' the claimant.[52] In *Greenwood*,[53] for example, the defendant was simultaneously enriched by two different benefits: the value of services rendered (£226) and appreciation in the car's value (£325). The claimant was only awarded restitution of the value of his services. It is difficult to see how this result can be said to have been dictated by the immediate enrichment rule. Lodder admits that the 'at the expense of' requirement may provide 'a second reason in support of the immediate enrichment approach'.[54] The better view is that this was the only reason for the results in the cases that Lodder relies upon.

Therefore, English law's commitment to the immediate enrichment approach does not rule out the net benefit approach.

b. Absence of Basis and Unjust Factors

English and German legal systems adopt different approaches to the 'unjust' enquiry. This has also been relied upon as precluding the adoption of the net benefit approach in English law.[55]

The net benefit analysis does not follow from the commitment of a legal system to the absence of basis approach. Indeed, some civilian jurisdictions which follow the 'absence of basis' approach do not adopt the net benefit analysis. In Spanish law, for example, the general rule is that disadvantages sustained in exchange for or after the enrichment are not relevant in determining the defendant's enrichment.[56] Similarly, Romanian law distinguishes between claims arising out of payment of an undue debt and other claims in unjust enrichment. The net enrichment approach only applies to the latter category.[57] Under the Portuguese Civil Code enrichment is understood broadly as 'the thing acquired'. It is unclear whether this precludes the net benefit approach. Both the net benefit approach as well as the independent claims theory have therefore attracted adherents in Portugal.[58] The same is the case in Dutch law.[59]

[1987] HCA 5, (1987) 162 CLR 221; *Kleinwort Benson Ltd v Lincoln City Council* [1998] UKHL 38, [1999] 2 AC 349; *Sempra Metals Ltd (formerly Metallgesellschaft Ltd) v Inland Revenue Commissioners* [2007] UKHL 34, [2008] 1 AC 561; *Yeoman's Row Management Limited v Cobbe* [2008] UKHL 55, [2008] 1 WLR 1752.

[52] Robert Stevens, 'Three Enrichment Issues' in Andrew Burrows and Alan Rodger (eds), *Mapping the Law: Essays in Memory of Peter Birks* (Oxford, Oxford University Press, 2006) 54.

[53] *Greenwood v Bennett* [1973] QB 195 (CA). See also, *Yeoman's Row Management* (n 51).

[54] Lodder (n 1) 204.

[55] Bant, *The Change of Position Defence* (n 1) 98.

[56] Christian Bar and Stephen Swann, *Principles of European Law: Unjustified Enrichment* (Stephen Swann, Padraic McCannon and Susan Singleton trs, Oxford, Oxford University Press, 2010) 359.

[57] ibid 362.

[58] ibid 362.

[59] ibid 363.

Thus, the net benefit thesis does not follow from the absence of basis approach. Nor does English law's commitment to unjust factors necessarily commit it to the independent claims theory.

c. The 'Transfer of Value' Objection

Lodder builds a case against the net benefit approach based on the notion of 'transfer of value'. According to him, the net benefit approach rests on the assumption that a transaction at market value involves no transfer of value. He argues that this is incorrect and that, even in such cases, there are two equal and opposite transfers of value.[60]

There are two responses to this argument. First, let us assume that Lodder is correct. On that supposition, a transaction at market value involves two opposing transfers of value. But that still leaves open the question of whether these transfers of value must be treated independently or netted off against each other. Second, his argument ascribes insufficient weight to the fact that 'value' is an inherently relational concept,[61] a proposition Lodder accepts.

The label 'relational' represents two distinct ideas here. The first of them is that value is a quantitative notion that facilitates comparison of distinct assets by reducing them to a single comparable dimension.[62] Thus, 10 apples and 20 oranges are comparable when reduced to monetary terms. Lodder accepts this. 'Relationality' has a second meaning too. This is what Klimchuck calls relationality in a 'deeper sense':[63]

> Value … is not a kind of asset, first in the transferor's and then in the transferee's possession. Instead it is an intrinsically relational concept, because <u>the value of a thing is ascertained only in the process of exchange</u>… Saying that there has been a transfer of value in a transaction expresses the fact that <u>the transferee has got something for nothing</u>… the substance of the transfer at issue conforms, in a deep way, to the correlativity essential to the structure of corrective justice, because <u>we cannot identify a transfer of value outside of a particular transaction</u>.

The inherently relational nature of value means that the question of whether there has been a transfer of value cannot be answered outside of a transaction. Weinrib is therefore right to say that '[e]xchange features a movement of things of value … from each party to the other. It does not, however, feature

[60] Lodder (n 1) 22.

[61] Ernest Weinrib, 'The Normative Structure of Unjust Enrichment' in Charles Rickett and Ross Grantham (eds), *Structure and Justification in Private Law: Essays for Peter Birks* (Oxford, Hart, 2008) 21; Ernest Weinrib, 'Correctively Unjust Enrichment' in Robert Chambers, Charles Mitchell and James Penner (eds), *Philosophical Foundations of the Law of Unjust Enrichment* (Oxford, Oxford University Press, 2009) 36.

[62] Lodder (n 1) 20.

[63] Dennis Klimchuk, 'The Normative Foundations of Unjust Enrichment' in Robert Chambers, Charles Mitchell and James Penner (eds), *Philosophical Foundations of the Law of Unjust Enrichment* (Oxford, Oxford University Press, 2009) 88–89 (emphasis added).

any movement of value'.[64] For this reason, the notion of a 'transfer of value' supports rather than detracts from the net benefit approach.

ii. Enrichment as Value and Enrichment as Rights

Some commentators have argued that enrichment may consist in either value or rights.[65] Assuming the correctness of that argument, this section considers whether the 'value and rights' theory is consistent with the net benefit approach. It will be argued that it is.

> *Example 6*: C buys a car worth £10,000 from D for £10,000. D had represented to C that the manufacturer of the car follows ethical labour practices. This is found to be untrue. C seeks rescission and restitution of the £10,000.

Assuming that C's payment is traceable in D's hands, C may frame D's enrichment as consisting of either rights or value.[66] On the net benefit analysis, D is not enriched in the form of value. Can C overcome this result by arguing that D is enriched by the receipt of the right to £10,000? If so, can C recover £10,000 from D? The answer is that C cannot.

In Example 6, D's enrichment consists only of rights, not value. D's enrichment in the form of value was netted off by a corresponding disenrichment. When a defendant's enrichment consists only in rights, restitution must also consist of rights alone. This process cannot involve an incidental reversal of value, which is what permitting C to recover £10,000 from D would amount to. As Lodder explains, when combining claims for restitution of rights and value, it must be ensured that 'restitution of one would not incidentally achieve restitution of the other'.[67]

Thus, the net benefit thesis does not apply if the defendant's enrichment consists of rights alone. However, this does not preclude the application of that approach to cases where enrichment takes the form of value.

II. THE GOOD CONSIDERATION RULE AS AN ENRICHMENT QUALIFICATION

The previous section demonstrated that the net benefit approach to evaluating conditional enrichments is well founded in English law. When the defendant's enrichments and disenrichments are conditional on each other, they must be netted off. This section uses the net benefit thesis to explain the good consideration rule as an enrichment-related principle.

[64] Weinrib, 'Correctively Unjust Enrichment' (n 61) 36–37.

[65] Robert Chambers, 'Two Kinds of Enrichment' in Robert Chambers, Charles Mitchell and James Penner (eds), *Philosophical Foundations of the Law of Unjust Enrichment* (Oxford, Oxford University Press, 2009) 242; Lodder (n 1) chs 3, 4 and 5.

[66] Lodder (n 1) 219.

[67] ibid.

A. Applying the Net Benefit Thesis to the Good Consideration Rule

> *Example 7*: X owed debts to C and D. X conveyed Blackacre to C in discharge of X's debt to C. However, Blackacre was subject to a mortgage securing X's debt to D. X and C agreed that C should pay off D's debt. After doing so, C realised that X was not entitled to Blackacre. C's claim against D for restitution failed.[68]

Is D enriched here? On the net benefit methodology, D is not. D is seemingly enriched by the payment from C. However, that payment was intended to clear X's debt to D and was 'conditional' on it. The common basis between C and D was that D would accept that payment in discharge of X's debt. The net benefit approach suggests that D's enrichment (the payment from C) and disenrichment (discharge of X's debt) must be netted off against each other. This leaves D in an enrichment-neutral position.

The fact that D's disenrichment does not result in C's enrichment does not preclude the application of the net benefit thesis. No part of the justification for the net benefit thesis relies on the mutual enrichment of both parties.

> *Example 8*: Under a contract between C and D, C gives a horse to D on the basis that D will give a cow to X. The cow dies while it is in X's possession. C later discovers that D had misrepresented the value of the cow. C rescinds the transaction and seeks restitution from D.

The reasons that justify the net benefit methodology apply with equal force to this example. Consider the risk-allocation reasoning. In Example 8, the cow is in X's possession, but the independent claims theory places the risk of its death on D. Characterising C's claim against D and D's claim against X as independent claims also fails to take into account the conditionality underlying the transaction, which is another aspect of the justification for the net benefit thesis. D's transfer of the cow to X was premised on the common basis between C and D that C would transfer a horse to D. If the transaction is to be unwound, it must be unwound as a whole.

There is some judicial support for the application of the net benefit approach to Example 8. In *Lumbers*,[69] a building sub-contractor claimed the value of its work from the owner of the land. In computing the owner's enrichment, the Court took account of his disenrichment in the form of his obligation to pay the main contractor, a third party to the claim:[70]

> [I]t was said that the [owners] would receive a "benefit", a "gain" or a "windfall" if they were not found to be liable to [the sub-contractors] … The accuracy and the relevance of any such characterisation depends upon whether the [owners] had

[68] *Aiken v Short* (1856) 1 Hurl & N 210, 156 ER 1180.

[69] *Lumbers v W Cook Builders Pty Ltd (In Liquidation)* [2008] HCA 27, (2008) 232 CLR 635. See also, *NIML Ltd v MAN Financial Australia Ltd* [2004] VSC 449, 1 BFRA 204 [79] (Harper J).

[70] *Lumbers* (n 69) [119]–[120].

> performed their obligations under their contract with [the main-contractor]. If the [owners] have not fully performed their obligations under their contract with [the main-contractor], by not paying all that is due to [it], it is evident that the [owners] have not received any benefit, gain or windfall. They would remain liable to [the main contractor]. Questions of benefit, gain or windfall could arise only if [the main contractor] has no further claim against the [owner].

In other words, the owner is enriched only if the benefit consisting of the building work is not offset by an obligation owed by him to the main contractors.[71] Thus, the owner's disenrichment (consisting of the obligation owed to the main contractor) is relevant in evaluating his enrichment. The fact that the disenrichment moved from the defendant to a third party and not the claimant does not preclude the application of the net benefit approach.

The same view was adopted by the New Zealand High Court in *Cigna Insurance*.[72] In that case, the Court declined to hold a bank liable as a constructive trustee for 'knowing receipt' on the basis that it had paid out to a third party (not the claimant) an amount equal to the initial deposit.

In *Barclays Bank*, Goff J imposed two qualifications on the application of the good consideration rule, one concerning the state of mind of the payor and the other relating to the state of mind of the payee. The enrichment thesis explains both these restrictions. It was explained earlier in this chapter that the net benefit approach applies only when the enrichment and disenrichment are conditional on each other or, in other words, linked by a common basis shared by the parties.[73] This requirement explains both qualifications.

Consider the requirement that the good consideration rule only applies if the payment was intended to discharge the debt.[74] When analysed through the lens of the net benefit approach, this requirement confines the good consideration rule to cases where the claimant's payment is made on the basis, shared by both parties, that the debt will be discharged.

> *Example 9*: C owes £100 each to D and X. C intends to pay X but mistakenly pays D. C seeks restitution from D. C's claim will fail.[75]

The condition underlying C's payment here was not the discharge of the debt owed to D. However, that was the basis on which D accepted the payment. There was no shared basis between the parties and, therefore, the good consideration rule is inapplicable.[76]

[71] Angus O'Brien, 'The Relationship Between the Laws of Unjust Enrichment and Contract: Unpacking *Lumbers v Cook*' (2011) 32 Adelaide Law Review 83, 99.

[72] *Cigna Life Insurance* (n 36). See also, *Compagnie Commerciale Andre SA v Artibell Shipping Company Ltd (No 2)* [2001] SC 653 (OH) [16].

[73] See Section (I)(A)(iii) above.

[74] See Chapter I, Section II(B) above.

[75] Based on dicta in *Platt v Bromage* (1854) 24 LJ Ex 63, 65.

[76] Note, however, that restitution in this case is precluded by the obligation rule.

The second qualification concerns the state of mind of the payee, which Goff J formulated in the following terms:[77]

> [E]ven if the payee has given consideration for the payment … that transaction may itself be set aside (and so provide no defence to the claim) if the payer's mistake was induced by the payee, or possibly even where the payee, being aware of the payer's mistake, did not receive the money in good faith.

The net benefit thesis explains this qualification too. As the previous section demonstrated, the net benefit approach has no application in cases where the defendant is aware of the claimant's mistake.[78] The fact that the payor's mistake was induced by the payee, or the payee's knowledge of the mistake, defeats the common basis between the parties. This is fatal to the application of the net benefit approach and, therefore, the good consideration rule.[79] As explained earlier, courts in Germany have treated the defendant's awareness of the claimant's mistake as precluding the application of *Saldotheorie*. German courts have also applied this qualification to the good consideration rule. Thus, in claims for restitution of mistaken payments by banks that discharged a debt owed to the payee by a third party, German courts have awarded restitution if the payee was aware of the bank's mistake.[80]

B. The Enrichment Explanation: Authorities

There is considerable support in academic writing for the view that the good consideration rule is best explained on the basis of the absence of the defendant's enrichment.[81]

[77] *Barclays Bank Ltd v WJ Simms Son & Cooke (Southern) Ltd* [1980] QB 677 (QB) 695 (Goff J). See also, *Lloyds Bank Plc v Independent Insurance Co Ltd* [2000] QB 110 (CA) 130.

[78] See Section (I)(A)(iii) above.

[79] Hellwege (n 9) 279.

[80] BGH 16 June 1983, BGHZ 87, 393; BGH 19 January 1984, BGHZ 89, 376, cited in Markesinis, Lorenz and Dannemann (n 4) 734, 796, 798.

[81] Graham Virgo, 'Recent Developments in Restitution of Mistaken Payments' (1999) 58 Cambridge Law Journal 478, 481; William Swadling, 'Restitution and *Bona Fide* Purchase' in William Swadling (ed), *The Limits of Restitutionary Claims: A Comparative Analysis* (United Kingdom National Committee of Comparative Law 1997) 79; Daniel Friedmann, 'Valid, Voidable, Qualified, and Non-Existing Obligations: An Alternative Perspective on the Law of Restitution' in Andrew Burrows (ed), *Essays on the Law of Restitution* (Oxford, Clarendon Press, 1991) 247; DH Zyl, 'Unauthorised Payment and Unjust Enrichment in Banking Law' in Francis Rose (ed), *Restitution and Banking Law* (Oxford, Mansfield, 1998) 25; Ross Grantham, 'Security of Contract: The Challenge from Restitution' (2000) 16 Journal of Contract Law 102, 112–113; Visser, *Unjustified Enrichment* (n 10) 200, 203; Daniel Visser, 'Searches for Silver Bullets: Enrichment in Three-Party Situations' in David Johnston and Reinhard Zimmermann (eds), *Unjustified Enrichment: Key Issues in Comparative Perspective* (Cambridge, Cambridge University Press, 2002) 534–542; Niall Whitty, 'Indirect Enrichment in Scots Law: Part 1' (1994) 2 Juridical Review 200, 203; Hector MacQueen, 'Payment of Another's Debt' in David Johnston and Reinhard Zimmermann (eds), *Unjustified Enrichment: Key Issues in Comparative Perspective* (Cambridge, Cambridge University Press, 2002) 482; Andrew Kull, 'Rationalizing Restitution' (1995) 83 California Law Review 1191, 1236–1239; Jacques Du Plessis,

The enrichment explanation has also attracted judicial support. For example, in his speech in *Kleinwort Benson*,[82] Lord Hope analysed the defendant's receipt of a payment he was entitled to in the following way:[83]

> As for the concept of enrichment, a person is enriched when he receives a payment which the payer was not bound by any obligation to make to him … The common law accepts that the payee is enriched where the sum was not due to be paid to him, but it requires the payer to show that this was unjust.

In *DD Growth Premium 2X Fund*,[84] Lord Sumption adopted the enrichment explanation. He said, '[i]t is fundamental that a payment cannot amount to enrichment if it was made for full consideration'.[85] A similar analysis was adopted by the High Court of Australia in *Redland City Council*,[86] where Gordon, Edelman and Steward JJ explained: '[a]lthough this defence of good consideration in the sense of counter-restitution has been described as a "counterclaim", the better view is that it is not a separate claim but is instead a defence that recognises that respective benefits must be "netted off"'.[87]

South African courts have also adopted the enrichment explanation for the good consideration rule. The leading decision is *Govender*,[88] where a customer ('S') of the claimant bank entered into a contract with the defendant for hiring a bus. S later decided not to use the bus. Although the agreement with the defendant was not terminated S instructed the claimant bank to stop payment on a cheque he had issued to the defendant. The bank paid overlooking the countermand order. Upon discovering the mistake, the bank sought restitution from the defendant. The bank's claim failed.[89] The Court held:

> The question which must be posed is whether plaintiff has shown that defendant was unjustifiably enriched by the payment of the cheque. The fact of the payment of money is itself prima facie proof of enrichment, but not conclusive proof. In assessing whether defendant has been enriched by the payment account must be taken of any performance rendered by defendant which was juridically connected with his receipt of the money.[90]

'Fraud, Duress & Unjustified Enrichment: A Civil Law Perspective' in David Johnston and Reinhard Zimmermann (eds), *Unjustified Enrichment: Key Issues in Comparative Perspective* (Cambridge, Cambridge University Press, 2002) 213; Lionel Smith, 'Property, Subsidiarity and Unjust Enrichment, Key Issues in Comparative Perspective' in D Johnston and R Zimmermann (eds), *Unjustified Enrichment: Key Issues in Comparative Perspective* (Cambridge, Cambridge University Press, 2010) 605; John Dawson, 'The Self-Serving Intermeddler' (1974) 87 Harvard Law Review 1446–467; D Laycock, 'Restoring Restitution to the Canon' (2012) 110 Michigan Law Review 929, 940.

[82] *Kleinwort Benson Ltd v Lincoln City Council* [1998] UKHL 38, [1999] 2 AC 349.

[83] ibid 408–409 (Lord Hope).

[84] *DD Growth Premium 2X Fund v RMF Market Neutral Strategies* [2017] UKPC 36, [2018] Bus LR 1595.

[85] ibid [62] (Lord Sumption).

[86] *Redland City Council v Kozik* [2024] HCA 7.

[87] ibid [199].

[88] *Govender v Standard Bank of South Africa* [1984] 2 All SA 497 (C).

[89] The result is different from *Barclays Bank* (n 77) because, in South African law, even an unauthorised payment is capable of discharging a debt: ibid 513.

[90] ibid 511.

> [T]he defendant who has performed, or held himself ready and willing to perform a contractual obligation, here the hiring out of the bus, is prima facie not unjustifiably enriched by the receipt of a payment in consideration for the hire of the bus.[91]

A little over a decade later, a similar issue arose in *B & H Engineering*.[92] In that case, the Supreme Court of South Africa reiterated that:[93]

> If this payment served to discharge [the defendant's] debt, [the defendant] would have lost its claim for that amount against [a third party]. [The defendant's] net position would accordingly have remained the same. There would have been no enrichment.

C. Explaining the Case Law on the Good Consideration Rule

This section demonstrates that the enrichment thesis can explain the results in the leading cases on the good consideration rule. Three categories of case are considered below: (i) three-party cases; (ii) two-party cases; and (iii) cases in which the defendant's disenrichment took place other than through the discharge of a debt.

i. Three Party Cases

The facts of *Aiken v Short*[94] are identical to Example 7 above. In that case, Bramwell B dismissed the claim on the basis of the now-discredited 'supposed liability' test.[95] Platt B dismissed the claim because the payment was owed to the defendant.[96] Although Pollock CB agreed with this reasoning, his speech offers some guidance on what 'consideration' means in this context. He said:[97]

> The [claimant] had paid the money in one sense without any consideration, but the defendant had a perfect right to receive the money from [the third party], and the [claimant] paid for him.

In other words, it is immaterial that the 'consideration' did not benefit the claimant. 'Good consideration' is a defendant-oriented enquiry. This is entirely consistent with the enrichment explanation. The application of the defence turns on the enrichment of the defendant. Whether the relevant disenrichment moved to the claimant or to a third party is immaterial.[98]

[91] ibid 513.
[92] *B & H Engineering v First National Bank of South Africa Ltd* [1995] 1 All SA 545 (A).
[93] ibid 546. See also, *ABSA Bank Ltd v Lombard Insurance Company Ltd* [2012] 4 All SA 485 (SCA) [14], [19].
[94] *Aiken* (n 68).
[95] ibid Hurl & N 215, ER 1182.
[96] ibid Hurl & N 214–215, ER 1182.
[97] ibid Hurl & N 214, ER 1181 (Pollock CB).
[98] Graham Virgo, *The Principles of the Law of Restitution* (3rd edn, Oxford, Oxford University Press, 2015) 175–176.

For the purposes of the good consideration rule, what matters is that the payment discharged a debt owed to the defendant.[99]

The two leading English cases on the good consideration rule, namely *Barclays Bank* and *Lloyds Bank*, are explicable on this basis. The results in these cases turned on whether the claimant bank's payment discharged a debt owed to the defendant.[100] In *Barclays Bank*, the customer had countermanded the cheque. The bank's payment was, therefore, unauthorised and did not discharge the defendant's debt.[101] Consequently, the defendant was enriched by the receipt of the payment and the claim succeeded. In *Lloyds Bank*, by contrast, the claim failed. In that case, the mistake arose from the bank's unawareness that the customer's account was overdrawn. This did not affect the bank's authority to pay and, therefore, the payment did discharge the defendant's debt. As a result, the defendant was not enriched.

ii. Two Party Cases

The enrichment explanation also accounts for the application of the good consideration rule to two-party cases. The only difference here is that the defendant's debt is owed by the claimant and not a third party. From the perspective of the enrichment explanation, this is not a material distinction. The decision of the New Zealand Supreme Court in *Stiassny* illustrates this.[102] In that case, the claimant sought restitution of GST it paid by mistake. However, the GST paid was owed to the Revenue. Applying Goff J's reasoning in *Barclays Bank*, the Court dismissed the claim. It held that 'the [claimant] did owe the amount of GST which it paid … Therefore [the defendant] gave good consideration in accepting its payment in discharge of the debt'.[103]

iii. Disenrichment Other than Through the Discharge of a Debt

A logical corollary of the enrichment explanation is that the 'consideration' provided by the defendant may not necessarily take the form of the discharge of a debt. This is apparent from Goff J's formulation in *Barclays Bank*, where he

[99] See also, *Australian Financial Services & Leasing Pty Ltd v Hills Industries Ltd* [2014] HCA 14, (2014) 88 ALJR 552.

[100] Carmel McLure, 'Failure of Consideration and the Boundaries of Restitution and Contract' in Simone Degeling and James Edelman (eds), *Unjust Enrichment in Commercial Law* (Sydney, Thomson Reuters, 2008) 214.

[101] For a contrary view see, Roy Goode, 'The Bank's Right to Recover Money Paid on a Stopped Cheque' (1981) 97 Law Quarterly Review 254.

[102] *Stiassny v Commissioner of Inland Revenue* [2012] NZSC 106. For other examples of application of the good consideration rule to two-party cases, see *National Mutual Life Association v Walsh* [1987] 8 NSWLR 585 (NSWSC) (Clarke J); *Orix Australia Corporation Ltd v Moody Kiddell & Partners* [2005] NSWSC 1209.

[103] *Stiassny* (NZSC) (n 102) [65].

said that the good consideration rule applies '*in particular* if the money is paid to discharge, and does discharge, a debt'.[104] The disenrichment of the defendant may therefore consist of the discharge of any other obligation or even the provision of other benefits. This is why, as explained in Chapter 1, the good consideration rule is capable of application even if no legal obligation was owed to the defendant.[105] The 'consideration' provided by the defendant may consist of the provision of services[106] or security,[107] or even the release of an obligation to pay tortious damages.[108]

In summary, this chapter explained that the good consideration rule is explicable on the basis of the defendant's lack of enrichment. Despite the receipt of a benefit, the corresponding discharge of an obligation negates the defendant's net enrichment. Judicial reasoning and academic commentary support this view. The results in the cases applying the good consideration rule are also explicable on this basis.

[104] *Barclays Bank* (n 77) 695 (Goff J) (emphasis added).
[105] See Chapter 1, Section II(A).
[106] *National Mutual Life Association* (n 102).
[107] *Spaulding v Kendrick* 51 NE 453 (Mass 1898).
[108] *Re Magarey Farlam Lawyers Trust Accounts (No 3)* [2007] SASC 9, 96 SASR 337.

3

Objections and Alternative Explanations

IT WAS EXPLAINED in Chapter 2 that the good consideration rule is best rationalised as an enrichment-based principle. This chapter addresses the objections to that explanation. It also considers some alternative explanations. Section I of this chapter responds to two main objections to the enrichment explanation. They arise from the law relating to the mistaken discharge of unenforceable obligations and the approach to valuation of debts in the law of unjust enrichment. Section II considers alternative explanations for the good consideration rule.

I. OBJECTIONS TO THE ENRICHMENT EXPLANATION

A. Unenforceable Obligations

A potential objection to the enrichment thesis arises from cases in which the 'consideration' provided by the defendant is the discharge of a valid but unenforceable obligation.

> *Example 1*: C owes D £100. That debt is time-barred. Intending to discharge the debt, but unaware that the debt is unenforceable, C pays £100 to D. C later seeks restitution from D. C's claim will not succeed.[1]

D's disenrichment is the discharge of an unenforceable debt. Since the valuation of enrichments is a factual enquiry,[2] it may be argued that D's receipt of £100 and its loss of an unenforceable debt cannot be netted off against each other. Why then does C's claim fail?

The answer is that C's claim is precluded by the obligation rule. As explained in Chapter 1, there are two distinct principles that apply in Example 1: the good consideration rule and the obligation rule. Although the good consideration rule may not apply in Example 1, the obligation rule does. It is notable that courts

[1] *Moses v Macferlan* (1760) 2 Burr 1005, 1012; 97 ER 676, 680–681; *Bize v Dickason* (1786) 1 Term Rep 285, 99 ER 1097.

[2] Andrew Burrows, *The Law of Restitution* (3rd edn, Oxford, Oxford University Press, 2011) 408.

have never applied the good consideration rule in cases resembling Example 1. The reasoning in the authorities in these circumstances is almost entirely based on the legal obligation between C and D or, in other words, the obligation rule.[3]

B. Valuation of Debts

Another objection to the enrichment explanation is based on the valuation of debts. The objection is that the enrichment explanation 'rests on the false premise that a legal right to be paid money … is worth as much as having the money in hand'.[4] In valuing a debt, it is said, a discount must be made to account for the fact that the debtor may default. Thus, the defendant's enrichment (ie the receipt of money) and its disenrichment (ie the value of the debt) do not cancel each other out. Overall, the defendant is enriched despite the discharge of the debt.

This objection does not withstand scrutiny. That is because, unless there is positive evidence to suggest that the debtor may default (for instance, as a consequence of the debtor's insolvency) the law of unjust enrichment makes no discount in valuing a debt for the purposes of quantifying the defendant's enrichment. This is apparent from at least three areas in the law of unjust enrichment where the defendant's enrichment is linked to the value of a debt. As explained below, in all three areas, the value of a debt is considered to be its face value, unless there is positive evidence as to the risk of default.

First, consider cases where the claimant (C) discharges a debt owed by the defendant (D) to a third party (X). In these cases, D is enriched by the discharge of the debt owed by D to X. D's enrichment is equal to the value of that debt. In these cases, it has never been suggested that a discount ought to be made to reflect the fact that, even if C had not discharged the debt, D may have defaulted in paying X, or indeed, X may have chosen not to pursue a claim against D. Instead, the law of unjust enrichment treats the discharge of a debt owed by D to X as an incontrovertible enrichment for D.[5] It is also well recognised that 'the measure of [D's] enrichment is the value of the discharged liability'.[6] The authorities have consistently proceeded on the basis that the value of the discharged debt is equal to its face value.

[3] *Moses* (n 1) Burr 1012, ER 680–681; *Bize* (n 1) Term Rep 286–287, ER 1098; *Larner v London County Council* [1949] 2 KB 683 (CA) 688; *Re Magarey Farlam Lawyers Trust Accounts (No 3)* [2007] SASC 9, 96 SASR 337 [168], [169], [177].

[4] James Goudkamp and Charles Mitchell, 'Denials and Defences in the Law of Unjust Enrichment' in *The Restatement Third, Restitution and Unjust Enrichment: Critical and Comparative Essays* (Oxford, Hart, 2013) 152.

[5] Burrows, *The Law of Restitution* (n 2) 49.

[6] Charles Mitchell, Paul Mitchell and Stephen Watterson, *Goff & Jones: The Law of Unjust Enrichment* (10th edn, London, Sweet & Maxwell, 2022) [4-40].

Consider, for example, *Filby v Mortgage Express*.[7] Mr and Mrs Filby held a joint development loan account with Midland bank, which had a debit balance of £194,586. The Filbys mortgaged one of their properties with the claimant. Pursuant to the mortgage, a sum of £60,801 (from the claimant) was used to bring down the debit balance in Filbys' Midland account. The claimant sought restitution from Mrs Filby, arguing that she was enriched as a consequence of being relieved of the financial burden she owed under the Midland account. Her enrichment was 'equivalent to the unsecured personal rights of Midland Bank against [Mrs Filby]'.[8] This was held to be £60,801, which is the extent to which Mrs Filby's debt to Midland was reduced by the payment.[9] This conclusion rests on the premise that the value of the debt owed to Midland by Mrs Filby is reduced by an amount equal to the monetary sum paid by Mrs Filby to Midland. This, in turn, presumes that the value of the debt is the same as its face value.

Exall v Partridge[10] is another example. In that case, the claimant had paid off rent owed by the defendants to their landlord because the landlord had taken away the claimant's carriage by way of distress. The claimant sought recoupment from the defendants. The defendants' enrichment was held to be equivalent to the value of the landlord's claim against them. No discount was made to reflect the possibility of default. The defendants were held liable to reimburse the claimant for the entirety of the sum that he had paid the landlord, ie the full amount due as rent.

Second, consider cases in which the defendant's enrichment is a claim foregone by the claimant.[11] *Gibb v Maidstone & Tunbridge NHS Trust*[12] is an example. The dispute in that case arose in the context of the termination of Ms Gibb's employment by the defendant. Under a negotiated settlement, the defendant agreed to pay Ms Gibb £250,000 as compensation. It was discovered subsequently that the compromise agreement was void. The employer was not contractually liable to compensate Ms Gibb. However, she argued that the defendant employer had been unjustly enriched at her expense. The value of the defendant's enrichment was said to consist of 'the value of the statutory unfair dismissal claim which she forewent'.[13] It was agreed that the likely award by an employment tribunal on a statutory dismissal claim in this context would have been £69,590.[14] This was said to be the value of the defendant's enrichment. No reduction was made to reflect the difference in value between the monetary value of Ms Gibb's claim and its 'true' value.

[7] *Filby v Mortgage Express (No 2) Ltd* [2004] EWCA Civ 759.

[8] ibid [64].

[9] ibid [67].

[10] *Exall v Patridge* (1799) 8 Term Reports 308, 101 ER 1405. See also, *Brook's Wharf and Bull Wharf Ltd v Goodman Brothers* [1937] 1 KB 534 (CA).

[11] See, Mitchell, Mitchell and Watterson (n 6) [4-37].

[12] *Rose Gibb v Maidstone & Turnbridge Wells NHS Trust* [2010] EWCA Civ 678.

[13] ibid [24].

[14] ibid [33].

Third, consider cases in which restitution is sought of bank transfers. Suppose that C transferred £100 to D's bank account. D's enrichment is not the receipt of £100 in cash, but rather the bank's liability to D of £100.[15] Yet, it has never been suggested that the value of D's enrichment is anything other than £100. The cases have consistently held otherwise.[16] Burrows justifies this result on the basis that a bank's creditworthiness is always 'assumed'.[17] But it is difficult to see how, on principle, this notion can be confined to banks. Default by a bank is not impossible. Nor is it inevitable that all non-bank entities will default in paying their debts. Therefore, the preferable and more principled approach is to value debts at their face value unless there is contrary evidence on the basis of which a discount ought to be made.

II. ALTERNATIVE EXPLANATIONS

This section will consider some alternative explanations for the good consideration rule. It will be suggested that none of them withstand scrutiny.

A. Change of Position Explanation

In *Lloyds Bank*, Waller LJ explained the good consideration rule as being based on the defence of change of position: 'if a payment has discharged the debt, then unless an order to return the money reinstates the debt, the payee will have changed his position in no longer having a remedy against the debtor'.[18] With respect, this explanation faces insuperable problems.[19]

First, all leading authorities on the good consideration rule treat it as a different defence from change of position. In *Barclays Bank*, Goff J identified good consideration and change of position as separate defences.[20] Thereafter,

[15] Burrows, *The Law of Restitution* (n 2) 45–46.

[16] *National Westminster Bank Ltd v Barclays Bank International Ltd* [1975] QB 654 (QB); *Chase Manhattan Bank v Israel-British Bank* [1981] Ch 105 (Ch D). See also, Andrew Burrows, Ewan McKendrick and James Edelman, *Cases and Materials on the Law of Restitution* (2nd edn, Oxford, Oxford University Press, 2006) 841; Andrew Lodder, *Enrichment in the Law of Unjust Enrichment and Restitution* (Oxford, Hart, 2012) 75–76.

[17] Burrows, *The Law of Restitution* (n 2) 45–46.

[18] *Lloyds Bank Plc v Independent Insurance Co Ltd* [2000] QB 110 (CA) 126 (Waller LJ). See also, *K&S Corp Ltd v Sportingbet Australia Pty Ltd* [2003] SASC 96, [2004] ALMD 250 [161]; Robert Goff and Gareth Jones, *Goff & Jones: The Law of Restitution* (Gareth Jones ed, 6th edn, London, Sweet & Maxwell, 2002) [41-001]–[41-002]; Robert Goff and Gareth Jones, *Goff & Jones: The Law of Restitution* (Gareth Jones ed, 7th edn, London, Sweet & Maxwell, 2007) [41-001]–[41-002].

[19] See generally, Graham Virgo, *The Principles of the Law of Restitution* (3rd edn, Oxford, Oxford University Press, 2015) 175–176; Sonja Meier, 'Mistaken Payments in Three-Party Situations: A German View of English Law' (1999) 58 Cambridge Law Journal 567, 588.

[20] *Barclays Bank Ltd v WJ Simms Son & Cooke (Southern) Ltd* [1980] QB 677 (QB) 695 (Goff J). See also, *Lloyds Bank* (n 18) 130 (Peter Gibson LJ); Andrew Burrows, 'Is There a Defence of Good

English courts have consistently maintained the distinction between these two rules.[21] The leading authorities in Australia,[22] Canada[23] and Hong Kong[24] have also recognised this distinction.

Second, the change of position explanation fails to account for the requirement that, in order for the good consideration rule to operate, the payment must have been intended to discharge the debt.[25] Change of position only requires a causal relationship between the claimant's payment and the defendant's discharge of the debt; it is immaterial whether the claimant's payment was intentional.

Third, as Waller LJ recognised in *Lloyds Bank*,[26] the change of position explanation rests on the assumption that a debt, once discharged, cannot be revived.[27] As Moore has convincingly demonstrated, that assumption rests on uncertain foundations.[28] In *Aiken v Short* – the authority upon which Goff J based the good consideration rule in *Barclays Bank* – Bramwell B proceeded on the basis that restitution may lead to the revival of debts.[29] Subsequent authorities confirm that, at least in some circumstances, a discharged debt may be revived.[30]

Fourth, as explained in Chapter 1, the good consideration rule applies regardless of the unjust factor upon which the claim is based. In particular, as the Supreme Court of New Zealand held in *Stiassny*, the good consideration rule applies to claims based on the *Woolwich* principle.[31] By contrast, the change of position defence is not available in such cases.[32]

Consideration?' in Charles Mitchell and William Swadling (eds), *The Restatement Third, Restitution and Unjust Enrichment: Critical and Comparative Essays* (Oxford, Hart, 2013) 171–172.

[21] *Stephen John Edmond Jones v Kelly Churcher, Abbey National Plc* [2009] EWHC 722 (QB), [2009] 2 Lloyd's Rep 94 [48]–[55], [56]; *Mahme Trust Reg v Nezhet Tayeb* [2002] EWHC 1543 (Ch), [2003] WTLR 21 [146], [147]; *Midland Bank Plc v Guadalupe ValeroConchita Foulis* (CA, 4 March 1991); *Deutsche Morgan Grenfell Group Plc v Inland Revenue Commissioners* [2006] UKHL 49, [2007] 1 AC 558 [84] (Lord Scott) (*DMG*); *Gulf International Bank BSC v Albaraka Islamic Bank BSC* (QB, 24 July 2003).

[22] *David Securities v Commonwealth Bank of Australia* [1992] HCA 48, (1992) 175 CLR 353, 379; *ANZ Banking Group Ltd v Westpac Banking Corporation* (1987) 164 CLR 662, 673; *Australian Financial Services & Leasing Pty Ltd v Hills Industries Ltd* [2014] HCA 14, (2014) 88 ALJR 552 [100], [101]; *Hills Industries Ltd v Australian Financial Services & Leasing Pty Ltd* [2012] NSWCA 380, (2012) 295 ALR 147 [81].

[23] *BMP Global Distribution v Bank of Nova Scotia* 2009 SCC 15 [21]–[22].

[24] *Takahashi v Shu* [2011] HKCFA 15 [40].

[25] See Chapter 1, Section II(B) above.

[26] *Lloyds Bank* (n 18) 126.

[27] Burrows, 'Is There a Defence of Good Consideration?' (n 20) 171.

[28] Jonathon Moore, 'Restitution from Banks' (DPhil thesis, University of Oxford, 2000) 306–307. See also, John Dawson, 'Erasable Enrichment in German Law' (1981) 61 Boston University Law Review 271, 289.

[29] *Aiken v Short* (1856) 1 Hurl & N 210, 216; 156 ER 1180, 1182.

[30] See *The Colonial Bank v The Exchange Bank of Yarmouth* (1885) 11 App Cas 84 (PC); *Australian Financial Services* (n 22).

[31] *Stiassny v Commissioner of Inland Revenue* [2012] NZSC 106 [67].

[32] *Test Claimants in the FII Group Litigation v Revenue & Customs Commissioners* [2008] EWHC 2893 (Ch), [2009] STC 254 [337]–[342].

B. Contractual Restriction and 'At the Expense of' Explanations

This section considers two related explanations for the good consideration rule. The first among them is the contractual restriction explanation. It suggests that the denial of restitution in cases such as *Lloyds Bank* is based on the need to protect contractual bargains.[33] The focus here is on the contract between the customer (third party) and the bank (the claimant). According to this explanation:[34]

> [T]he bank should not be entitled to restitution from [the defendant] because this would undermine the contractual risks (especially the risk of the customer's insolvency) undertaken by the bank in the contract with its customer.

Consider an example:

> *Example 2*: Under a contract, X owes £10,000 to D. X discharges this debt by making a payment from her account with C bank. C makes the payment to D overlooking the fact that X does not have sufficient funds in her account. C cannot recover the payment from D.[35]

The contractual restriction explanation suggests that allowing C to claim restitution from D will disturb the allocation of contractual risks between C and X. That is because, if C were to get restitution from D, C does not have to look to X for payment. As a result, C no longer assumes the risk of X's insolvency.

The difficulty with this explanation is that D also assumed the risk of X's insolvency under the contract between X and D. If D is entitled to retain C's payment, D does not have to seek payment from X. Following the logic of the contractual restriction explanation, this must mean that D no longer assumes the risk of X's insolvency. In short, since C and D both assumed the risk of X's insolvency, redistribution of the insolvency risk cannot explain why the law of restitution chooses to protect one of these parties over the other.

Burrows relies on *Costello*[36] in support of the contractual restriction explanation. In that case, the claimant constructed houses on the defendant's land based on a contract with a company called Oakwood. It was held that the claimant could not seek restitution from the defendant since the claimant's performance was rendered pursuant to a contract with Oakwood. By contrast to Example 2, however, there was no contract between the defendant and Oakwood. Thus, it could not be said in *Costello* that the defendant had assumed the risk of Oakwood's insolvency. As Etherton LJ noted, 'legally enforceable promises were made only between Oakwood and the claimants'.[37] This reasoning does

[33] Burrows, 'Is There a Defence of Good Consideration?' (n 20) 170; Peter Birks, *Unjust Enrichment* (2nd edn, Oxford, Oxford University Press, 2005) 90–91; Peter Birks, 'The Burden on the Bank' in Francis Rose (ed), *Restitution and Banking Law* (Oxford, Mansfield, 1998) 220.

[34] Burrows, 'Is There a Defence of Good Consideration?' (n 20) 172–173.

[35] *Lloyds Bank* (n 18).

[36] *MacDonald Dickens & Macklin v Costello* [2011] EWCA Civ 930, [2012] QB 244.

[37] ibid [21] (Etherton LJ).

not assist if, as is the case in Example 2, D had entered into valid contracts with both C and X.

A similar analysis applies to *Pan Ocean*.[38] In that case, the owner of a ship (X) had assigned the benefit of a charter (with C) to the defendant (D). C's claim against D for the restitution of overpaid hire failed, inter alia, because allowing restitution would permit C to evade the risk of X's insolvency. In *Pan Ocean*, unlike in Example 2, D had not assumed the risk of X's insolvency as regards the relevant payments, namely overpayments of hire. That is because the remedial consequences of any overpayment of hire were expressly governed by the contract between C and X.[39] As Lord Goff explained:[40]

> [T]he relevant contract imposes on the assignor [X] an obligation of repayment in the circumstances in question, and that there is nothing in the assignment which even contemplates, still less imposes, any additional obligation on the assignee [D] to repay.

The risk of non-payment as a result of X's insolvency was therefore rightly imposed on C.

Consider the 'at the expense of' explanation now. It suggests that, in cases like *Lloyds Bank*, the defendant's enrichment is not 'at the expense of' the claimant bank, but at the expense of its customer.[41] As to why the defendant's enrichment is not 'at the expense of' the claimant bank, proponents of the 'at the expense of' thesis offer two arguments.

On one view, the validity of the 'at the expense of' analysis is contingent on there being a valid contract between the claimant bank and its customer. Birks adopted this view. His analysis was that 'the party making the performance [ie the claimant bank] and thus conferring the benefit had a valid contractual right to be paid for that performance by the other party to the contract [ie the customer]'.[42] However, what about cases where the claimant was fraudulently induced to make a payment to the defendant? In such cases, the third party's fraud renders the contract with the claimant void. Thus, fraudulent procurement of the claimant's performance, an area where the good consideration rule has been routinely applied,[43] falls outside the scope of this version of the 'at the expense of' explanation.

There is another version of the 'at the expense of' explanation. That is the argument that the defendant's enrichment is not at the expense of the bank

[38] *Pan Ocean Shipping Co Ltd v Creditcorp Ltd (The Trident Beauty)* [1994] 1 WLR 161 (HL). See also, *Lumbers v W Cook Builders Pty Ltd (In Liquidation)* [2008] HCA 27, (2008) 232 CLR 635.

[39] James Goodwin, 'Contract, Unjust Enrichment, and Risk' (2012) 128 Law Quarterly Review 503, 504.

[40] *Pan Ocean* (n 38) 166 (Lord Goff).

[41] Peter Birks, 'Overview: Tracing, Claiming and Defences' in Peter Birks (ed), *Laundering and Tracing* (Oxford, Clarendon Press, 1995) 335.

[42] Birks, *Unjust Enrichment* (n 33) 89–90.

[43] *Australian Financial Services* (n 22); *Gaffner v American Finance Co* 206 P 916 (Wash 1922); *Associates Discount Co v Clements* 321 P 2d 673, 679 (Okla 1958).

because the claimant bank did not render any 'performance' to the defendant. As Stevens explains:[44]

> The payment made to the defendant was made by her debtor, through the agency of his bank. The bank had rendered its performance towards X, the debtor. The bank's performance was not for the defendant, regardless of the physical movement of cash from the bank to the defendant. The only recourse the bank ought to have had was against the party towards and for whom it had rendered its performance.

This argument derives support from civilian jurisdictions such as Germany. In Germany, Wilburg and subsequently Von Caemmerer suggested that the law of unjustified enrichment is concerned with the reversal of defective 'performances' or 'purposive transfers'.[45] In order for there to be a valid claim to reverse a defective performance, 'the transferor must be pursuing a purpose towards the enriched party'.[46] Krebs also relies on the German law notion of 'performance' to explain cases like *Lloyds Bank*. He says:[47]

> if the [customer X] decides to pay the [defendant D] by bank transfer, and for this reason requests his bank to pay [D] and debit the corresponding amount to his account, [X] is rendering his performance to [D], although he is doing so indirectly.

There are a number of difficulties with the analysis offered by Stevens and Krebs.

The critical distinction between the decisions in *Barclays Bank* and *Lloyds Bank* is that in the former case the debt owed by the customer to the defendant was discharged by the bank's payment whereas in the latter it was not. The 'performance' analysis cannot properly account for this feature. Stevens attempts to do so. He relies on the fact that, in *Barclays Bank*, the bank's payment was not authorised by its customer. According to him, this means that the bank was not performing to its client. It also means, he says, the bank's payment is governed by the 'default position', which is that the bank was rendering performance to the defendant.[48] This analysis is unpersuasive. As Meier explains, '[t]he bank intends to fulfil an obligation towards its client. This is the objective meaning of its acts. The fact that there is no valid order cannot change the direction of the performance'.[49] In other words, the bank's 'performance' is towards its client whether the bank's payment was authorised or not. The fact that the bank's payment was not authorised does not create a performance link between the bank and the defendant.

[44] Robert Stevens, *The Laws of Restitution* (Oxford, Oxford University Press, 2023) 44. See also, Robert Stevens, 'The Unjust Enrichment Disaster' (2018) 134 Law Quarterly Review 574; Duncan Sheehan, *The Scope and Structure of Unjust Enrichment* (Oxford, Hart, 2024) 44–45.

[45] Thomas Krebs, *Restitution at the Crossroads: A Comparative Study* (London, Cavendish, 2001) 208.

[46] ibid 218.

[47] ibid 208.

[48] Stevens, *The Laws of Restitution* (n 44) 45.

[49] Sonja Meier, 'Comment on the Performance Chapters of "The Laws of Restitution"' (Symposium on *Laws of Restitution*, Oxford, October 2023). I am grateful to Professor Meier for providing me with a copy of this paper.

The fact that Meier is right, and Stevens is not, is confirmed by a 1984 decision of the Bundesgerichtshof.[50] The facts were remarkably similar to *Barclays Bank*, but the Bundesgerichtshof reached the opposite result. The claimant brewery had ordered its bank to stop payments of rent to the brewery's landlords but, mistakenly, the bank continued to pay. The bank discovered its mistake and sought restitution from the defendants. Despite the stop order, it was held that there was no performance relationship between the bank and the landlord. Rather:[51]

> The performance relationship, as perceived by the defendants, was between the brewery and the defendants – the bank's involvement was merely instrumental in getting the brewery's money to the defendants.

Thus, the performance analysis, when correctly applied, is incapable of distinguishing between cases where the debt owed to the defendant is discharged and cases where it is not. For the same reason, it cannot explain the operation of the good consideration rule in English law. This is why Birks resiled from this version of the 'at the expense of' explanation. He said that if this analysis were accepted it would:[52]

> endanger the bank's right to recover from the immediate payee any mistaken payment made in the belief that it was paying on the credit of its customer, even an accidental second payment.

Moreover, even in the category of cases where the 'at the expense of' reasoning provides a valid reason for denying restitution, it is not a good *explanation* for the good consideration rule. Instead, it is best understood as an additional reason, independent of the good consideration rule, for denying restitution. As an earlier edition of Goff and Jones said:[53]

> [The 'at the expense of explanation'] is an attractive analysis, but it was not the ground of the Court of Appeal's decision [in *Lloyds Bank*] which was that the defendant-payee had given good consideration … The fact that the decision may be explained on other grounds does not mean that the Court of Appeal's reasoning was unsound.

Furthermore, the 'at the expense of' explanation cannot account for the operation of the good consideration rule in two-party cases. In those cases, the defendant's enrichment plainly *is* at the expense of the claimant.

Finally, the 'at the expense of' reasoning also cannot account for the two qualifications to the good consideration rule: the requirements that the payment must have been intentional and that the good consideration rule will not apply if the payor's mistake was induced by the payee or if the payee was aware of the

[50] BGHZ 89, 376 (19 January 1984) cited in Krebs (n 45) 225.
[51] ibid; see also, Meier (n 19) 603.
[52] Birks, 'The Burden on the Bank' (n 33) 219–20.
[53] Goff and Jones (7th edn) (n 18).

payor's mistake.[54] The state of mind of the claimant and the defendant are irrelevant to the 'at the expense of' requirement.

C. Bona Fide Purchase Explanation

It has been suggested that the good consideration rule is an application of the bona fide purchase defence. Although this view was adopted in the third edition of Goff and Jones,[55] later editions resiled from this view.[56] However, this explanation is supported in the latest edition of Goff and Jones.[57]

The scope of the bona fide purchase defence itself remains unclear, and it is impossible within the confines of this book to clear up the doctrinal controversies surrounding its application. Consequently, this section will consider in outline the major competing accounts of the bona fide purchase defence. It will demonstrate that none of them can satisfactorily account for the good consideration rule.

Virgo and Swadling argue that the bona fide purchase defence has a narrow scope. According to them, this defence is an exception to the *nemo dat* principle; it has no role to play in cases that are not concerned with the vindication of property rights.[58] Since none of the leading cases on the good consideration rule were based on subsisting property rights, this version of the bona fide purchase defence cannot explain the good consideration rule.

According to Key, the availability of the bona fide purchase defence depends on the nature of the claim. It is available if the claim is proprietary in nature, but not otherwise.[59] Almost all leading cases on the good consideration rule were *in personam* claims. Therefore, this account of the bona fide purchase defence also fails to account for the good consideration rule.

On a broader view, the bona fide purchase defence ensures consistency between unjust enrichment and property law.[60] As Birks puts it, 'the personal claim has to be killed off by the defence of bona fide purchase in order to avoid the stultification of the proprietary exception to *nemo dat*'.[61] On this view, the good consideration rule operates where the bona fide purchase defence in property

[54] *Barclays Bank* (n 20) 695; *Lloyds Bank* (n 18) 130 (Peter Gibson LJ).

[55] Robert Goff and Gareth Jones, *The Law of Restitution* (3rd edn, London, Sweet & Maxwell, 1986) 108–109.

[56] Goff and Jones (6th edn) (n 18) [41-001]; Goff and Jones (7th edn) (n 18) [41-001].

[57] Mitchell, Mitchell and Watterson (n 6) [29-24]. See also, *Lloyds Bank* (n 18) 133 (Peter Gibson LJ).

[58] Virgo, *The Principles of the Law of Restitution* (n 19) 656; William Swadling, 'Restitution and *Bona Fide* Purchase' in William Swadling (ed), *The Limits of Restitutionary Claims: A Comparative Analysis* (United Kingdom National Committee of Comparative Law 1997) 79–105.

[59] Paul Key, 'Bona Fide Purchase as a Defence in the Law of Restitution' [1994] Lloyd's Maritime and Commercial Law Quarterly 421, 426.

[60] Burrows, *The Law of Restitution* (n 2) 576–577; Burrows, 'Is There a Defence of Good Consideration?' (n 20) 168.

[61] Birks, *Unjust Enrichment* (n 33) 240–245.

law applies to exclude the *nemo dat* rule. It has never been suggested, however, that the application of the good consideration rule is linked to the application of the *nemo dat* principle. Birks himself thought that the good consideration rule was not so confined.[62] Consequently, this version of the bona fide purchase defence also fails to explain the good consideration rule.

The broadest version of the bona fide purchase defence is the one proposed by Barker.[63] He argues that this defence promotes 'transactional security'. It protects the sanctity of the contract between the defendant and a third party. This account, however, restricts the operation of the bona fide purchase defence to cases where the defendant received the benefit by way of an exchange with a party other than the claimant.[64] For this reason, Barker accepts that cases applying the good consideration rule cannot be explained on the basis of bona fide purchase:[65]

> [A]lthough the idea that D has given 'good consideration' in good faith sounds very like the defence of bona fide purchase, the latter is, to my mind, also a blind alley. This is because the policy of transactional security underpinning the bona fide purchase defence need only be invoked where the defendant has received a benefit by way of exchange with a party other than the plaintiff.

Finally, there is one objection that applies to all accounts of the bona fide purchase defence considered above: that bona fide purchase is a complete defence and applies regardless of the value of the consideration provided.[66] By contrast, the good consideration rule operates in a pro tanto manner[67] and only precludes restitution to the extent of the value of the consideration given by the defendant.

[62] Peter Birks, 'The Role of Fault in the Law of Unjust Enrichment' in William Swadling and Gareth Jones (eds), *The Search for Principle: Essays in Honour of Lord Goff of Chieveley* (Oxford, Oxford University Press, 1999) 1256.

[63] Kit Barker, 'After Change of Position: Good Faith Exchange in the Modern Law of Restitution' in Peter Birks (ed), *Laundering and Tracing* (Oxford, Clarendon, 1995) 193.

[64] *Barclays Bank Plc v Boulter* [1999] 1 WLR 1919 (HL) 1925–1926.

[65] Barker (n 63).

[66] *Lipkin Gorman v Karpnale Ltd* [1991] 2 AC 548 (HL) 580–581.

[67] *Devaux v Conolly* (1849) 8 CB 640, 137 ER 658; *Anglo-Scottish Beet Sugar Corporation, Ltd v Spalding Urban District Council* [1937] 2 KB 607 (KB).

Part II

The Obligation Rule

It was explained in Chapter 1 that the good consideration rule and the obligation rule are two different principles. Part I argued that the best explanation for the good consideration rule is based on the absence of the defendant's enrichment.

Part II will consider the obligation rule. It proceeds in four stages. Chapter 4 is devoted to understanding the obligation rule. It argues that the obligation rule is a bright-line rule, not a flexible principle that requires weighing up the unjust factor and the defendant's legal entitlement against each other. Chapter 5 critiques the prevailing academic accounts of the obligation rule. Chapters 6 and 7 advance the positive case, setting out an alternative explanation for the obligation rule which is based on equality between the claimant and the defendant. Chapter 8 outlines the doctrinal consequences of the equality thesis.

4

Bright-Line Rule or Flexible Principle?

Burrows's *Restatement of the English Law of Unjust Enrichment*[1] formulates the obligation rule in the following way:

> In general, an enrichment is not unjust if the benefit was owed to the defendant by the claimant under a valid contractual, statutory or other legal obligation.

Save for the words 'in general', that formulation is clear and uncontroversial.[2] But those two words give rise to a fundamental question regarding the nature of the obligation rule: is it a bright-line rule or a flexible principle? There is support in academic commentary[3] and judicial authority[4] for the latter view. This chapter will argue that they are incorrect. If the enrichment was received by the defendant in discharge of a valid legal obligation, the claimant is not entitled to restitution. This is a bright-line rule. It does not require courts to balance against each other the relative strengths of the unjust enrichment claim and the legal obligation.

There are four key challenges to the bright-line conception of the obligation rule: (a) the decision of the High Court of Australia in *Roxborough v Rothmans of Pall Mall Australia Ltd*;[5] (b) the House of Lords' decision in *Deutsche Morgan Greenfell Group Plc v Inland Revenue Commissioners*;[6] (c) the law relating to restitution of benefits conferred under unenforceable contracts; and (d) the decision of the Supreme Court in *International Energy Group Ltd v Zurich Insurance* ('*Zurich Insurance*').[7] It will be suggested that the first three are consistent with the bright-line conception of the obligation rule. As for the fourth, it will be argued that the reasoning of the majority judges in

[1] Andrew Burrows, *A Restatement of the English Law of Unjust Enrichment* (Oxford, Oxford University Press, 2012) [3(6)].

[2] See eg *DD Growth Premium 2X Fund v RMF Market Neutral Strategies* [2017] UKPC 36, [2018] Bus LR 1595 [62] (Lord Sumption); *Fairfield Sentry Ltd (In Liquidation) v Migani* [2014] UKPC 9, [2014] 1 CLC 611 [18] (Lord Sumption).

[3] Andrew Burrows, 'Is There a Defence of Good Consideration?' in Charles Mitchell and William Swadling (eds), *The Restatement Third, Restitution and Unjust Enrichment: Critical and Comparative Essays* (Oxford, Hart, 2013).

[4] *International Energy Group Ltd v Zurich Insurance plc* [2015] UKSC 33, [2015] 2 WLR 1471.

[5] *Roxborough v Rothmans of Pall Mall Australia Ltd* [2001] HCA 68, (2001) 208 CLR 516.

[6] *Deutsche Morgan Grenfell Group Plc v Inland Revenue Commissioners* [2006] UKHL 49, [2007] 1 AC 558 ('*DMG*').

[7] *International Energy Group Ltd v Zurich Insurance plc* [2015] UKSC 33, [2015] 2 WLR 1471.

Zurich Insurance is misconceived and that, in future cases, the scope of that reasoning must be confined to the '*Fairchild* enclave'.

I. *ROXBOROUGH*: RESTITUTION WITHIN A CONTRACT

This section asks whether the decision of the High Court of Australia in *Roxborough* suggests that the obligation rule is a flexible principle. The answer is that it does not, as explained below.

A. The Decision in *Roxborough*

The claimant and the respondent were retailers and wholesalers of tobacco respectively. They were both licensees under the New South Wales Business Franchise Licenses (Tobacco) Act 1987 ('the Act'). The contractual arrangement between the parties was that, in anticipation of the wholesaler's payment of licence fee, the retailer would advance an equivalent sum to the wholesaler. On 5 August 1997, the High Court of Australia declared the imposition of licence fee under the Act invalid.[8] As a result, the respondent was no longer liable for the licence fee. The claimant, who had already paid the wholesaler an amount attributable to that fee, sought restitution of that amount.

The High Court of Australia awarded restitution. The Court held that failure of consideration was not limited to the failure of contractual reciprocation but included the disappearance of a contemplated state of affairs; in this case, that was the wholesaler's licence fee liability.[9] The finding that there was a failure of consideration in these circumstances raised, for the first time, several difficult questions: did the retailer's obligation subsist despite the invalidity of the licence fee? Would granting restitution to the retailer in these circumstances contradict the parties' contractual bargain? The majority judgment does not provide a satisfactory answer to these questions. It merely asserts that:[10]

> [W]hile the wholesale price, exclusive of the tax, was arrived at by the operation of forces of supply and demand in the market for tobacco products, and reflected the negotiated agreement of the parties, the tax was imposed externally by government.

The conclusion of the majority judges seemingly contradicts the bright-line conception of the obligation rule. The retailer's payment was made in discharge of a contractual obligation. This suggests that the obligation rule ought to have precluded the retailer's restitution claim.[11] Academic literature offers

[8] *Ha v New South Wales* [1997] HCA 34, (1997) 189 CLR 465.

[9] *Roxborough* (n 5) [16] (Gleeson CJ, Gaudron and Hayne JJ).

[10] ibid [13].

[11] Kirby J dissented on the ground that the validity of the contract precluded restitution: ibid [166] (Kirby J).

two explanations for why restitution was awarded in *Roxborough*. Sections (B) and (C) below will explain why neither of them is persuasive. The better explanation of *Roxborough* is based on the conditional nature of the retailer's contractual obligation. On that analysis, which is set out in section (D) below, the decision in *Roxborough* is consistent with the bright-line conception of the obligation rule.

B. Negotiability Reasoning

Burrows seeks to explain *Roxborough* on the basis that the award of restitution in that case did not interfere with the parties' contractual allocation of risks. This is because, he says, the 'tax element was imposed outside the risks bargained for'.[12] Similarly, according to Birks, the 'crucial fact is that neither the payment of the tax nor the amount of that payment were viewed as negotiable'.[13]

With respect, this explanation does not withstand scrutiny. It is true that the statutory imposition of the licence fee liability was not negotiable. But it does not follow that the allocation of this liability as between the parties was also non-negotiable. This is apparent from the statutory scheme. By section 41(1)(c), the Act imposed liability for the licence fee on the wholesaler.[14] But, by virtue of the contractual arrangement between the parties, that burden had been shifted to the retailer. The claim that the licence fee was not subject to negotiation between parties is, therefore, incorrect. As O'Brien explains:[15]

> Although the payment of the tax by *someone* was non-negotiable, as between themselves the retailer and wholesaler had clearly engaged in negotiation ending in an agreement that the retailer in effect pay the tax.

The payment of the fee by either the wholesale or the retailer was not negotiable. The quantum of the licence fee was also not negotiable. But it does not follow that the allocation of the burden of that liability between the retailer and the wholesaler was also not negotiable.

> *Example 1:* C (a retailer) and D (a wholesaler) agree to engage X (a carrier) for transporting goods. The contract provides that transport charges shall be borne by C.

One of C or D must bear X's charges. But this does not mean the allocation of transport costs are not negotiable as between C and D. In this example, the contract provides that those charges shall be borne by C. But the parties

[12] Andrew Burrows, 'Restitution of Mistaken Enrichments' (2012) 92 Boston University Law Review 767, 767–777; Andrew Burrows, *The Law of Restitution* (3rd edn, Oxford, Oxford University Press, 2011) 90.

[13] Peter Birks, 'Failure of Consideration and its Place on the Map' (2002) 2 Oxford University Commonwealth Law Journal 1, 5. See also, *Roxborough* (n 5) [13].

[14] *Roxborough v Rothmans of Pall Mall Australia Ltd* [1999] FCA 107 (Emmet J).

[15] Angus O'Brien, 'The Relationship Between the Laws of Unjust Enrichment and Contract: Unpacking *Lumbers v Cook*' (2011) 32 Adelaide Law Review 83, 95 (emphasis in original).

could have agreed that D will bear that expense. The same analysis applies to *Roxborough*.

C. Allocation of Risks Reasoning

According to Beatson, the law of unjust enrichment may sometimes perform a gap-filling function within subsisting contracts:[16]

> If the reason for not allowing concurrence of action between restitutionary and contractual claims before discharge is to do with not subverting risk allocation and contractual valuation then doctrine should be directly focused on those factors … Except in the case of speculative contracts, it should not be assumed, as it has been in the past, that all risks have been distributed to one side or the other. Where all risks have not been so distributed, there will be a gap in the contractual allocation and there is room for adjustment either by applying the principle of unjust enrichment or some other principle.

On this view, the correct approach to analysing *Roxborough* is to ask whether the risk that the licence fee may be declared invalid was distributed between the parties.[17]

The 'allocation of risks' reasoning faces insuperable problems. First, it presumes that the only reason for not permitting restitution within subsisting contracts is to prevent subversion of the contractual risk allocation. As Chapter 2 demonstrated, at least in some cases, there may be other more fundamental reasons for denying restitution, such as the absence of a primary element of unjust enrichment. If that view is accepted, it is preferable to focus on the parties' contractual obligations. The more abstract question of whether certain risks were contractually allocated is vague and unhelpful.

Second, whether certain risks were contractually allocated between the parties is an indeterminate enquiry. Proponents of the allocation of risks reasoning offer no methodology for identifying 'gaps' in contractual bargains.[18] Other than by reference to obligations imposed by express or implied contractual terms, it is unclear how this exercise is meant to operate.[19] It is unsurprising, therefore, that the application of this methodology to *Roxborough* has led to radically opposite views. Beatson and Virgo argue that *Roxborough* is incorrectly decided because the burden of proving that there was no allocation of risks is on the claimant. According to them, the claimant could not have

[16] Jack Beatson, 'Restitution and Contract: Non-Cumul?' (2000) 1 Theoretical Inquires in Law 83, 94.

[17] Peter Birks, 'Failure of Consideration and its Place on the Map' (n 13); Ralph Cunnington, 'Failure of Basis' [2004] Lloyd's Maritime and Commercial Law Quarterly 234.

[18] Tang Wu, 'Unjust Enrichment Within a Valid Contract: A Close Look at Roxborough v Rothmans of Pall Mall Australia Ltd' (2007) 23 Journal of Contract Law 201.

[19] Mitchell McInnes, 'Unjust Factors, Juristic Reasons and Contracts in Anglo-Canadian Law' in Paula Giliker (ed), *Re-examining Contract and Unjust Enrichment: Anglo-Canadian Perspectives* (Leiden, Martinus Nijhoff, 2007) 31.

discharged that burden on the facts of *Roxborough*.[20] Cunnington, on the other hand, applies the same methodology to reach the opposite result.[21] Jaffey applies the same methodology to conclude that the relevant risk was 'shared' by the parties.[22]

Third, the 'allocation of risks' reasoning is based on the incorrect assumption that contractual silence as to specific eventualities equates to a gap in the parties' bargain. As Smith explains, the better analysis is as follows:[23]

> Read literally, what such contracts state is that the parties' obligations are unconditional (save as provided for in the contract) … Indeed, the claim that silence indicates a gap in a contract is inconsistent with the basic idea that contractual obligations are promissory obligations.

Smith's analysis may be illustrated with a simple example.

> *Example 2*: C entered into a contract with D under which D agreed to hire C's car. One week before the start of the hire, C realised that the market price for car hire had doubled. The rise in market price was unforeseen and not subject to negotiation between C and D.[24]

In the absence of any contractual implied term, it is incorrect to say that there was a gap in the contractual allocation of risks as to what would happen if the market price for car hire were to increase. As Chadwick LJ said in *Bromarin*:[25]

> It is not an appropriate approach to construction to hold that, where the parties had contemplated an event A, and they did not contemplate event B, their agreement must be taken as applying only in event A and cannot apply in event B.

Thus, the fact that the parties in *Roxborough* had not contemplated the invalidity of the licence fee at the time of contracting does not mean that there was a gap in their allocation of contractual risks.

D. Conditionality Reasoning

Stevens argues that the right way to analyse *Roxborough* is to ask whether the retailer's contractual obligation was conditional on the validity of the licence fee:[26]

> [W]hat would the position have been if [the retailer] had not been paid at the time when invalidity of the tax had been discovered? … Is this portion of the price earned

[20] Jack Beatson and Graham Virgo, 'Contract, Unjust Enrichment and Unconscionability' (2002) 118 Law Quarterly Review 352, 357.

[21] Cunnington (n 17) 250–251.

[22] Peter Jaffey, 'Failure of Consideration: Roxborough v Rothmans' (2003) 66 Modern Law Review 284.

[23] Stephen Smith, *Contract Theory* (Oxford, Oxford University Press, 2004) 285.

[24] ibid 285–286.

[25] *Bromarin v IMD Investments* [1999] STC 301 (CA) (Chadwick LJ).

[26] Robert Stevens, 'Is There a Law of Unjust Enrichment?' in Simone Degeling and James Edelman (eds), *Unjust Enrichment in Commercial Law* (Sydney, Thomson Reuters, 2008) 29;

> even where the purpose of charging it, payment of a tax to the state, will never be fulfilled. Precisely the same question is determinative of the issue where the price has been paid in advance.

The remainder of this section makes three claims. First, the retailer's obligation in *Roxborough* was conditional on the validity of the licence fee. Second, the conditionality of that obligation meant that in *Roxborough* there was no conflict between the retailer's unjust enrichment claim and the wholesaler's contractual entitlement. Third, on this basis, the decision in *Roxborough* is consistent with the bright-line conception of the obligation rule.

Although Burrows adopts the negotiability reasoning as the primary justification for *Roxborough*, he also argues persuasively that the retailer's obligation in that case was conditional on the wholesaler's licence fee liability:[27]

> In the *Roxborough* case, the tax element was a fixed separate element from the rest of the price ... Separated out in this way, one can see that, once the tax was held not to be owing, that part of the price could also be said not to be owing albeit that no particular clause could be struck down as void.

There is some judicial support for this view. In *Wayne County Produce*,[28] for example, Cardozo CJ considered a fact pattern very similar to *Roxborough*. On those facts, he said:[29]

> This is not a case where the item of the tax is absorbed in a total or composite price to be paid at all events ... This is a case where the promise of the buyer is to pay a stated price, and to put the seller in funds for the payment of a tax besides. In such a case the failure of the tax reduces to an equivalent extent the obligation of the promise.

123 East Fifty-Fourth Street is another illustration of the conditionality reasoning.[30] In that case, the defendant restaurant owner had paid tax which was, in fact, not due. The defendant recovered the tax amount. However, that amount had already been passed on by the defendant to its customers. The question was whether the customers could recover the tax from the defendant. The second circuit Court of Appeals held that:[31]

> [I]f, before the plaintiff had paid it, the treasury had declared that the tax was not due, the plaintiff could not have successfully resisted the guests' demand that it be turned back to them, the very purpose for which they had paid it having then become incapable of execution.

Robert Stevens, *The Laws of Restitution* (Oxford, Oxford University Press, 2023) 126–127. See also, Stephen Waddams, 'Contract and Unjust Enrichment: Competing Categories, or Complementary Concepts?' in Charles Rickett and Ross Grantham (eds), *Structure and Justification in Private Law: Essays for Peter Birks* (Oxford, Hart, 2008) 174–175.

[27] Burrows, 'Restitution of Mistaken Enrichments' (n 12) 767.

[28] *Wayne County Produce Co v Duffy-Mott Co Inc* 155 NE 669 (NY 1927).

[29] ibid 669 (Cardozo CJ). This reasoning was cited with approval in *Roxborough* (n 5) [18].

[30] *123 East Fifty-Fourth Street v United States* 157 F 2d 68 (2d Cir 1946).

[31] ibid 71.

In other words, the obligation of the customers to pay the tax component to the restaurant was conditional on the validity of the restaurant's tax liability.[32]

When one appreciates that the retailer's contractual obligation in *Roxborough* was conditional on the validity of the licence fee, it becomes apparent that granting restitution in that case did not contradict the parties' contractual obligations.[33] The invalidity of the licence fee meant that the retailer was not under a liability to pay the defendant. Nor did that payment discharge any claim the wholesaler had against the retailer. The invalidity of the statute meant that there was no such claim. On this analysis, *Roxborough* is consistent with the bright-line conception of the obligation rule.

II. *DMG*: AN 'EU ESTOPPEL' EXPLANATION

This section examines the decision of the House of Lords in *DMG*.[34] It argues that the decision in *DMG* can be reconciled with the bright-line conception of the obligation rule based on the principle of 'EU estoppel'.[35]

A. The Decision in *DMG*

The dispute concerned the claimant's obligation to pay Advance Corporation Tax ('ACT'). Under the Income and Corporation Taxes Act 1988 ('the Act') dividend distributions by UK resident companies were subject to ACT. However, ACT could later be set off against Mainstream Corporation Tax ('MCT'). The Act provided for an exemption for distributions between companies that had opted for Group Income Election ('GIE'). However, this exemption was only available if the paying company and the receiving company were both resident in the UK.[36] This provision was challenged before the ECJ. The ECJ found that the discriminatory nature of the GIE provisions breached the freedom of establishment guaranteed by the EC Treaty.[37] The remedial consequences of this conclusion were left to national courts.[38] This issue arose for consideration of the English Court in *DMG*.

[32] For the application of this reasoning in Australia, see *Commissioner of State Revenue (Vict) v Royal Insurance Australia Ltd* (1994) 182 CLR 51 (Mason CJ); *Roxborough v Rothmans of Pall Mall Australia Ltd* [1999] FCA 1535 [100] (Gyles J); *James More & Sons Ltd v University of Ottawa* 49 DLR (3d) 666 (Ont HC).

[33] For another example of restitution being awarded following the failure of conditional obligations within a subsisting contract, see *British American Continental Bank v British Bank for Foreign Trade* [1926] 1 KB 328 (CA).

[34] *Deutsche Morgan Grenfell Group plc v Inland Revenue Commissioners* [2006] UKHL 49, [2007] 1 AC 558.

[35] Terminology adopted from *Foster v British Gas Plc* [1988] ICR 584 (CA) (Lord Donaldson MR).

[36] Income and Corporation Taxes Act 1988, s 247(1).

[37] *Metallgesellschaft Ltd v Inland Revenue Commissioners* (C-397 and 410/98) [2001] Ch 620.

[38] ibid [96].

The claimants were a German holding company and its UK subsidiaries. The residence requirement denied them the opportunity to opt for GIE. Had this not been the case, they argued, a GIE would have been made, which would have meant that the subsidiary was not liable for ACT. Consequently, the claimants sought restitution from the Revenue. Two features of the claim merit attention at this stage. First, the claimant's ACT had been set off against its MCT liability. Therefore, the Revenue's enrichment consisted solely of a timing advantage. Second, to take advantage of the extension of the limitation period for claims seeking 'relief from the consequences of a mistake',[39] the claimant had to rely on the unjust factor of mistake.

At first instance, Park J granted restitution.[40] His judgment was premised on two key findings. First, the judgment in *Metallgesellschaft* did not nullify DMG's tax liability. Second, DMG's mistake was in not realising that it 'could have made group income elections ... which would have had the effect of preventing the ACT from being payable'.[41] The Court of Appeal took a different view. According to Parker LJ, ECJ's judgment nullified the claimant's obligation to pay tax.[42] Thus, DMG's mistake was its belief that ACT was payable whereas, in fact, it was not. The House of Lords reversed the Court of Appeal's decision.[43] This section focusses on two questions: was the ACT due when it was paid? If so, why was restitution granted?

None of the judges except Lord Scott properly grappled with the difficulty posed by the fact that the claimant was seeking restitution of a sum that was due to the Revenue under a valid statutory obligation. Lord Hoffmann agreed with the Court of Appeal that 'the mistake was about whether DMG was liable for ACT'.[44] He also said that the ECJ's judgment did not nullify DMG's tax liability. This conclusion, along with the fact that the claimant did not exercise GIE, should have led him to consider the implications of the fact that the claimant was seeking restitution of a sum that was due. He sought to overcome that difficulty by stating that:[45]

> The election provisions were purely machinery, which DMG would undoubtedly have used, by which it could enforce its right to exemption from liability.

Lord Walker also dismissed GIE as a 'procedural requirement'.[46] Lord Hope, by contrast, characterised the mistake differently. Agreeing with Park J, he held that the claimant's mistake was its belief that GIE was not available.[47]

[39] Limitation Act 1980, s 32(1)(c).

[40] *Deutsche Morgan Grenfell Group Plc v Inland Revenue Commissioners* [2003] EWHC 1779 (Ch), [2003] 4 All ER 645 (Park J) ('*DMG* (Ch)').

[41] ibid [21].

[42] *Deutsche Morgan Grenfell Group Plc v Inland Revenue Commissioners* [2005] EWCA Civ 78, [2006] 2 WLR 103 (Parker LJ).

[43] *DMG* (n 6).

[44] ibid [32] (Lord Hoffmann).

[45] ibid [32] (Lord Hoffmann).

[46] ibid [143] (Lord Walker).

[47] ibid [62] (Lord Hope).

Beyond this, he did not address the difficulty posed by the fact that ACT was in fact due.

Lord Scott dissented. In his view, the ECJ's judgment did not nullify the claimant's ACT liability. Accordingly, he said:[48]

> [I]f the legal obligation under which the money was paid cannot be, or has not been, invalidated, then, in my opinion, whether or not it can be shown that 'but for' the mistake in question the money would not have been paid, a restitutionary remedy for the recovery of the money would not be available.

B. Reconciling *DMG* with the Obligation Rule

The decision in *DMG* seemingly contradicts the bright-line conception of the obligation rule. The claimant's payment in that case discharged a statutory obligation. Yet, restitution was granted. This section will argue that the decision in *DMG* can be reconciled with the obligation rule. That claim is based on three propositions. First, the ACT was owed to the Revenue when it was paid. Second, the relevant mistake in *DMG* was DMG's belief that it was not eligible to make a GIE. Third, the decision to grant restitution is explicable on the basis that the principle of 'EU estoppel' precluded the Revenue from relying on its statutory entitlement as against DMG.

i. Statutory Liability and Characterisation of the Mistake

The ECJ's decision in *Metallgesellschaft* did not automatically nullify DMG's ACT liability. The contrary view is based on a misunderstanding of the relationship between EU norms and national legislation.[49] The European Communities Act 1972 incorporates obligations created by the European Union into the English legal system.[50] They take precedence over domestic norms in cases of conflict. However, the appropriate remedy to rectify national legislations that contravene EU norms is the process of 'disapplication' by national courts.[51] Non-compliance with an EU norm does not automatically nullify a primary legislation. This was the view adopted in *Thoburn*.[52] As Craig explains:[53]

> What Lord Justice Laws said in *Thoburn* was that the constitutional impact of EU law on national law was not going to be dictated top-down by the European Court

[48] ibid [85] (Lord Scott).

[49] Robert Stevens, 'Justified Enrichment' (2005) 5 Oxford University Commonwealth Law Journal 141, 143; Stevens, *The Laws of Restitution* (n 26) 87–88.

[50] European Communities Act 1972, s 2(1).

[51] *Regina v Secretary of State for Transport, Ex parte Factortame Ltd & Others (No 2)* [1991] 1 AC 603 (HL).

[52] *Thoburn v Sunderland City Council* [2002] EWHC 195 (Admin), [2003] QB 151.

[53] House of Commons European Scrutiny Committee, *The EU Bill and Parliamentary Sovereignty*, vol 1 (10th Report 2010–11) [21] www.publications.parliament.uk/pa/cm201011/cmselect/cmeuleg/633/633i.pdf accessed 22 September 2014.

> of Justice on our courts ... So it is for our courts to decide what they believe to be the impact of EU law within our national constitutional order.

The fact that the decision in *Metallgesellschaft* did not nullify DMG's liability to pay ACT is apparent from the judgment of the ECJ. The ECJ did not hold that the levy of ACT was invalid. Rather, the decision was that the discriminatory nature of the taxation regime contravened the EC Treaty:[54]

> [W]hat is contrary to Community law ... is not the levying of a tax in the United Kingdom on the payment of dividends by a subsidiary to its parent company but the fact that subsidiaries, resident in the United Kingdom, of parent companies having their seat in another Member State were required to pay that tax in advance whereas resident subsidiaries of resident parent companies were able to avoid that requirement.

It follows that there were at least two ways in which the breach of the EC Treaty could have been rectified: by making GIE available to all companies regardless of residence or by making it inapplicable to UK resident companies. Either would have ensured that the taxation regime was non-discriminatory. The choice between these two methods was a matter for the UK.

The analysis set out above suggests that the ACT was due when it was paid. It follows that the Court of Appeal's characterisation of the mistake was incorrect. The claimant's belief that it was liable to pay ACT was true.[55] Rather, the relevant mistake was DMG's belief that it was not eligible to make a GIE. On the true state of the law, that was false.

ii. EU Estoppel: Reconciling DMG *and the Bright-Line Obligation Rule*

The principle of 'EU estoppel' was first evolved by the ECJ in the context of 'direct effect' of unimplemented directives.[56] Its first authoritative formulation is in Advocate General Warner's opinion in *Enka*:[57]

> A member state that fails fully to give effect to a directive is in breach of the Treaty ... to allow it ... to rely upon that fact as against a private person in proceedings in its own Courts would be to allow it to plead its own wrong.

Within a span of two years, 'EU estoppel' was adopted as a full-fledged rationale for giving direct effect to unimplemented directives.[58] In *Ratti*,[59] for example,

[54] *Metallgesellschaft* (n 37) [83]. See also, Robert Chambers, '*Deutsche Morgan Grenfell Group Plc v IRC*' (2006) 6 Oxford University Commonwealth Law Journal 227, 228; Stevens, 'Justified Enrichment' (n 49) 143.

[55] *DMG* (Ch) (n 40) [231].

[56] Sacha Prechal, *Directives in EC Law* (2nd rev edn, Oxford, Oxford University Press, 2005) 218–223.

[57] Case 38/77 *Enka BV v Inspecteur der Invoerrechten en Accijnzen* [1977] ECR 2203, 2226 (Opinion of AG Warner). See also, Alan Dashwood, 'The Principle of Direct Effect in European Community Law' (1978) 16 Journal of Common Market Studies 229.

[58] Paul Craig and Gráinne Búrca, *EU Law: Text, Cases, and Materials* (5th edn, Oxford, Oxford University Press, 2011) 280.

[59] Case 148/78 *Pubblico Ministero v Tullio Ratti* [1979] ECR 1629.

criminal proceedings had been initiated against Mr Ratti under an Italian law which required manufacturers of chemical products to affix labels identifying the substances present in them and their volume. At the time of prosecution, the charging legislation ought to have been amended to ensure compliance with Directive 73/173. This required the repeal of the provision under which Mr Ratti was charged. The ECJ concluded that the proceedings against Mr Ratti were unlawful because:[60]

> [A] member State which has not adopted the implementing measures required by the Directive in the prescribed periods may not rely, as against individuals, on its own failure to perform the obligations which the Directive entails.

Subsequent case law of the ECJ affirms the 'EU estoppel' principle. The ECJ's decision in *Faccini Dori*,[61] for instance, explained that the *Ratti* line of cases were intended to 'prevent a State from taking advantage of its own failure to comply with Community law'.[62] A State's failure to comply with EU norms must not deprive individuals of the benefit of those norms. This reasoning was subsequently reiterated by the ECJ in the context of directives intended to ensure equality of working conditions between men and women,[63] social security benefits[64] and employment in the armed forces.[65]

As explained in sub-section (i) above, the claimant's mistake in *DMG* was its belief that it was not eligible to make a GIE. That mistake led to the Revenue's enrichment. This establishes a prima facie case for restitution. But there are two complications. First, it may be suggested that the claimant did not make a mistake as to the availability of GIE. Even if the claimant had applied to exercise GIE, the Revenue would have rejected that claim, relying on the residence requirement in section 247.[66] Second, it may be argued that the claimant's valid statutory obligation to pay ACT ought to have precluded restitution, as the claimant's liability to pay ACT subsisted as long as the claimant did not exercise GIE. As Stevens puts it, 'the election was like a lever which, when pulled, could prevent liability from arising'.[67] In *DMG*, the claimant never pulled the lever.

[60] ibid [22].

[61] Case C-91/92 *Faccini Dori v Recreb Srl* [1994] ECR I-3325. See also, Case C-316/93 *Nicole Vaneetveld v SA Le Foyer* [1994] ECR I-763, Opinion of AG Jacobs [20].

[62] *Faccini Dori* (n 61) [2].

[63] Case 152/84 *Marshall v Southampton & South West Hampshire Area Health Authority (Teaching)* [1986] ECR 723.

[64] Case 286/85 *Norah McDermott & Ann Cotter v Minister for Social Welfare & the Attorney General* [1987] ECR 1453.

[65] Case 222/84 *Johnston v Chief Constable of the Royal Ulster Constabulary* [1986] ECR 1651. For the application of the EU estoppel doctrine by English Courts, see *Foster v British Gas Plc* [1991] 2 AC 306 (HL) 315; *Marks & Spencer Plc v Customs & Excise Commissioners (No 1)* [2000] 1 CMLR 256 (CA); *Rolls Royce Plc v Mrs D Doughty* [1988] 1 CMLR 569 (UKEAT).

[66] Graham Virgo, 'Deutsche Morgan Grenfell: Restitution of Tax Paid by Mistake' [2004] British Tax Review 8, 10–11.

[67] Stevens, 'Justified Enrichment' (n 49) 142–143; Stevens, *The Laws of Restitution* (n 26) 87.

Both these arguments are incorrect for the same reason. Both of them permit the Revenue to rely on the discriminatory and unlawful residence requirement in section 247 against the claimant. The first objection states that, even if the claimant had attempted to make a GIE, the Revenue would have rejected that claim. However, any such rejection would have to have been based on the discriminatory residence requirement in section 247. The 'EU estoppel' principle prevents the Revenue from relying on its (hypothetical) unlawful rejection of DMG's application to make a GIE.

The same analysis applies to the second contention. The crux of the second objection is that, since the claimant did not in fact exercise a GIE, its ACT payment was made in pursuance of a valid statutory obligation. But it is important to bear in mind that, as Park J found at first instance, the only reason the claimant chose not to exercise the GIE was because section 247 – which breached the EC Treaty – precluded that option.[68] For the Revenue to rely on the liability of the claimant that arose solely by virtue of its failure to exercise the GIE, therefore, amounts to the Revenue relying on its own unlawful act to deny the claimant a restitutionary remedy that it would otherwise have had.[69] The principle of EU estoppel precludes this result.

On this analysis, there is no inconsistency between *DMG* and the obligation rule. *DMG* was simply a case in which the Revenue was estopped from relying upon the relevant legal obligation.

The 'EU estoppel' analysis explains why the decision in *DMG* is different from, and has no application to, two commonly proposed variations of the facts in that case:

> *Example 3A*: C seeks restitution of tax from the Revenue. C argues that she would not have had to pay the tax had she not mistakenly failed to exercise an election in a deed of variation.[70]
>
> *Example 3B*: C seeks restitution of tax from the Revenue. C argues that, had she not used up her tax reliefs against an earlier unlawful exaction by the Revenue, she would have been able to offset those reliefs against the later levy of lawful tax.[71]

In both cases, the tax was received by the Revenue in discharge of C's statutory liability. Unlike in *DMG*, however, that liability was not procured by any wrong committed by the Revenue. Therefore, the Revenue may rely on the claimant's

[68] *DMG* (Ch) (n 40).

[69] See, Charles Mitchell and Monica Chowdry, 'Tax Legislation as a Justifying Factor' [2005] Restitution Law Review 1, 18 ('*Deutsche Morgan Grenfell* was anomalous, in that the infringing statutory section did not impose a liability, but rather denied the claimants an opportunity which it gave other taxpayers to escape from a liability or, more accurately, to defer their liability to a later date').

[70] *Test Claimants in the FII Group Litigation v Revenue & Customs Commissioners* [2008] EWHC 2893 (Ch), [2009] STC 254 [257].

[71] *Test Claimants in the FII Group Litigation v Revenue & Customs Commissioners* [2010] EWCA Civ 103, [2010] STC 1251 [181] (Arden LJ).

legal obligation to preclude restitution. The decision in *DMG* does not assist C in either case.

III. UNENFORCEABLE CONTRACTS

The previous sections demonstrated that the decisions in *Roxborough* and *DMG* are compatible with the bright-line conception of the obligation rule. This section will consider the law governing restitution of benefits conferred pursuant to unenforceable contracts. It will explain that this area of the law is also consistent with that conception.

The restitution of benefits conferred under an unenforceable contract is sometimes characterised as an 'exception' to the bright-line nature of the obligation rule. For example, Burrows says:[72]

> When a contract is unenforceable … the contractual obligations under it are probably best viewed as valid … however, there can be restitution of money paid or for services rendered under an unenforceable contract; and the best justification for that is that restitution does not conflict with the contractual allocation of risk given that the contract is unenforceable.

Although Burrows cites no authority in support of this proposition in his commentary, in the *Restatement*[73] he relies on the Canadian Supreme Court's decision in *Deglman v Guaranty Trust Co of Canada*[74] ('*Deglman*') and the Australian High Court's decision in *Pavey & Mathews Pty Ltd v Paul* ('*Pavey*').[75]

This section will argue that cases granting restitution in respect of payments made or services rendered under an unenforceable contract are consistent with the bright-line nature of the obligation rule. They are not an exception to that conception. Sub-section A will examine the key authorities, sub-section B will consider and reject Burrows's explanation for these cases and sub-section C will defend an alternative approach.

A. The Cases

The authorities that Burrows relies upon to support the 'unenforceable contracts exception' – *Deglman* and *Pavey* – were also the first decisions to recognise unjust

[72] Andrew Burrows, *The Law of Restitution* (3rd edn, Oxford, Oxford University Press, 2011) 90. See also, Rohan Havelock, 'A Taxonomic Approach to Quantum Meruit' (2016) 132 Law Quarterly Review 470, 484.

[73] Andrew Burrows, *A Restatement of the English Law of Unjust Enrichment* (Oxford, Oxford University Press, 2012) 34–35.

[74] *Deglman v Guaranty Trust Co of Canada* [1954] SCR 725 (Supreme Court of Canada).

[75] *Pavey & Mathews Pty Ltd v Paul* [1987] HCA 5, (1987) 162 CLR 221.

enrichment as a unified legal concept in Canada[76] and Australia[77] respectively. However, the potential problem posed by the subsisting, albeit unenforceable, contract passed by unnoticed in both cases.[78]

In *Deglman*, the plaintiff lived with his aunt for 6 months. During that time, she requested him to run errands and perform services for her, which he did. In return, she promised him that she would make adequate provision for him in her will. In particular, she offered to leave him a piece of property she owned. Before the Supreme Court of Canada, it was common ground that this constituted a valid oral contract and that the contract had been fully performed by the plaintiff. However, section 4 of the Statute of Frauds posed a difficulty. It provided that 'no action shall be brought' based on a contract in respect of 'any interest in or concerning' 'lands', unless 'the agreement ... or some memorandum or note thereof' was 'in writing'. As a result, the oral contract was valid but unenforceable.[79] Could the plaintiff nevertheless bring a claim based on quantum meruit for the value of services he provided his aunt?

The Supreme Court of Canada unanimously held that the answer to this question was 'yes'. Rand J recognised that the plaintiff's claim was for restitution of his aunt's unjust enrichment.[80] This was not an action based on her contractual promise. Consequently, the Statute of Frauds did not pose an impediment to this claim. However, the claimant had rendered his services pursuant to a valid oral contract. As Duggan, Ziegel and Girgis put it, 'when the plaintiff did the work, he had a legal, contractual obligation to do so'.[81] Under the Canadian law of restitution, this constituted a valid 'juristic basis' for the defendant's enrichment. Why then did the obligation rule not preclude the claim?

Pavey raises a similar question. In that case, the claimants were builders who had carried out building work for the defendant under an oral contract. After the work was completed and the defendant took possession, the builders brought a claim for the balance they were due to be paid. The defendant argued that the oral contract was unenforceable pursuant to section 45 of the New South Wales Builders Licensing Act 1971. Section 45 provided that a 'building contract' was unenforceable unless it 'is in writing signed by each of the parties'.

[76] GHL Fridman, *Restitution* (2nd edn, Toronto, Carswell, 1992) 303.

[77] Michael Bryan, 'Peter Birks and Unjust Enrichment in Australia' (2004) 28 Melbourne University Law Review 724.

[78] Peter Maddaugh and John McCamus, *The Law of Restitution* (looseleaf edn, Toronto, Thomson Reuters, 2016) [13-4]–[13-5]. Fridman (n 76) 303.

[79] On this point, the Supreme Court reversed the Ontario Court of Appeal. The Court of Appeal had found that 'the part-performance exception' took this case out of the purview of the Statute of Frauds: see, *Deglman v Guaranty Trust Co of Canada* [1953] OWN 665 (Ontario Court of Appeal) [3].

[80] *Deglman* (Supreme Court of Canada) (n 74) [7] (Rand J).

[81] Anthony Duggan, Jacob S Ziegel and Jassmin Girgis, 'The State Of The Law of Unjust Enrichment in Common Law Canada' (2009) 59 Canadian Business Law Journal 39, 39.

The question for the court was whether section 45 also precluded the claimant from seeking quantum meruit for the value of services he rendered.

The majority held that the plaintiff's claim had a 'different foundation in law'[82] from the oral contract between the parties. It did not depend on an implied contract between the parties. It turned instead on the need to reverse the unjust enrichment that the defendant derived from the claimant's services. Accordingly, the statutory requirement of formality did not stand in the way of the restitution claim.[83]

B. Burrows's Reasoning

As mentioned earlier, Burrows argues that these cases were right in granting restitution despite the presence of a subsisting contractual relationship between the parties. That is because, he says, 'restitution does not conflict with the contractual allocation of risk given that the contract is unenforceable'.[84] With respect, this reasoning does not withstand scrutiny.

First, contractual obligations remain valid despite their unenforceability. Unenforceability affects the remedy, not the right.[85] As Birks explains, 'the word "unenforceable" is by convention reserved for a good contract on which no action can be brought'.[86] Burrows appears to agree with this proposition. He notes that 'an unenforceable contract is a valid contract but is simply unenforceable in the courts by one or both parties'.[87]

Second, contrary to Burrows's reasoning, the unenforceability of a valid and subsisting contract does not mean that there was no contractual allocation of risks.[88] The common reasons for unenforceability do not relate to the substance of the contract. For example, the Limitation Act 1980 bars claims based on a

[82] *Pavey* (n 75) 228.

[83] For other examples of cases granting restitution of the value of services rendered under unenforceable contracts, see *Mavor v Pyne* (1825) 3 Bingham 285, 130 ER 522; *Pulbrook v Lawes* (1876) 1 QBD 284; *Scarisbrick v Parkinson* (1869) 20 LT 175; *Scott v Pattison* [1923] 2 KB 723 (KB). See also, David Ibbetson, 'Implied Contracts and Restitution: History in the High Court of Australia' (1988) 8 Oxford Journal of Legal Studies 312, 319–325; George Palmer, *The Law of Restitution*, vol 3 (Toronto, Little, Brown, 1978) 326.

[84] Burrows, *The Law of Restitution* (n 72) 90. See also, Havelock (n 72) 484.

[85] HG Beale and AS Burrows, *Chitty on Contracts* (32nd edn, London, Sweet & Maxwell, 2015) [1-112]; Tariq A Baloch, 'The Unjust Enrichment Pyramid' (2007) 123 Law Quarterly Review 636, 643. See also, *Leroux v Brown* (1852) 12 Common Bench Reports 801, 138 ER 1119; *Anthony McIntyre v Gentoo Group Limited* [2010] EWHC 5 (Admin).

[86] Peter Birks, *Unjust Enrichment* (2nd edn, Oxford, Oxford University Press, 2005) 126.

[87] Burrows, *The Law of Restitution* (n 72) 105.

[88] AT Denning, 'Quantum Meruit and the Statute of Frauds' (1925) 41 Law Quarterly Review 79, 81 ('The work was done under an express contract, and although that contract was not enforceable it was a valid, subsisting and unrescinded contract and, in accordance with the third proposition stated above, no action in those circumstances should have been allowed on an implied contract').

contract after the expiry of six years from the cause of action.[89] The reasons for this rule are based on policy and relate to the unfairness of defendants being harassed[90] with 'stale claims',[91] the difficulties posed by the deterioration of evidence over time[92] and the need to incentivise claimants to bring their actions relatively quickly.[93] These reasons have nothing to do with the parties' contractual allocation of risks. Indeed, it is difficult to see why the passage of time *after* a breach of contract should have any consequence for an otherwise valid risk-allocation. The same point may be made about contracts that fall foul of the Statute of Frauds. It is commonly accepted that the purpose of such a legislative provision is to 'protect against false claims'.[94] It is unsurprising, therefore, that both the Limitation Act and the Statute of Frauds only prohibit the bringing of an action.[95] They do not invalidate contractual obligations.

Third, there are a number of areas of the law that demonstrate that the validity of the parties' risk allocation is unaffected by contractual unenforceability. Consider a debtor who owes a number of debts to the creditor. Suppose that one of the debts is time-barred. If the debtor does not specify the debt that it intended to discharge, the creditor is free to appropriate a payment made by the debtor to the time-barred debt.[96] Another example is the creditor's lien. A creditor who is entitled to exercise a lien on goods belonging to the debtor may exercise that right even though the underlying debt is unenforceable.[97] These examples demonstrate that the parties' allocation of risks remains in place despite the unenforceability of the contract.

C. An Alternative Explanation

The previous section argued that Burrows's explanation for cases such as *Deglman* and *Pavey* is unconvincing. This section will offer an alternative explanation. As with *Roxborough*, the explanation offered here is based on the conditional nature of the defendant's contractual entitlement.

[89] Limitation Act 1980, s 5.

[90] Andrew McGee, *Limitation Periods* (7th edn, London, Sweet & Maxwell, 2014) 14; Andrew Burrows, 'Some Recurring Issues in Relation to Limitation of Actions' in James Goudkamp, Andrew Dyson and Frederick Wilmot-Smith (eds), *Defences in Tort* (Oxford, Hart, 2015) 311–312.

[91] *AB v Ministry of Defence* [2012] UKSC 9, [2013] 1 AC 78 [164] (Lady Hale).

[92] Tang Hang Wu, 'Natural Obligations and the Common Law of Unjust Enrichment' (2015) 6 Oxford University Commonwealth Law Journal 133, 139; Burrows, 'Some Recurring Issues in Relation to Limitation of Actions' (n 90) 311–312.

[93] McGee (n 90) 14; Burrows, 'Some Recurring Issues in Relation to Limitation of Actions' (n 90) 311–312.

[94] Keith Turner QC, 'The Law of Restitution by George E Palmer' (1979) 9 Manitoba Law Journal 335, 339.

[95] Statute of Frauds 1677 (England), s 4; Statute of Frauds 1990 (Canada), s 4; Limitation Act 1980, s 5.

[96] *Friend v Young* [1897] 2 Ch 421 (Ch); Beale and Burrows (n 85) [28-129].

[97] *Spears v Hartly* (1800) 3 Espinasse 81, 170 ER 545.

In cases like *Deglman* and *Pavey*, the claimant was under a valid contractual obligation to render services to the defendant. As a logical corollary, the defendant had a valid contractual right to the claimant's services. However, this was not an unconditional right. The defendant's contractual right to the claimant's services was premised on the defendant's obligation to remunerate or reward the claimant. In *Deglman*, the defendant aunt's contractual right to the claimant's services was conditional on her obligation to make adequate provision for the claimant in her will. This was clear from the parties' oral contract. Both the Ontario Court of Appeal[98] and the Canadian Supreme Court[99] found that the claimant had rendered the services based on the aunt's promise to leave him property under her will. In *Pavey*, the claimant builders provided services to the defendant on the basis that the defendant would remunerate them for their work.[100] The defendant's contractual entitlement was not a right to gratuitous services from the claimant. It was an entitlement to the claimant's services subject to remuneration.

In other words, the defendant's obligation to remunerate was a condition-precedent for the defendant's entitlement to services. The defendant's failure to remunerate defeats that entitlement. As McInnes puts it, in *Deglman*, 'while [the claimant] initially intended to confer the benefit upon his aunt, her right to retain the value of that enrichment was ultimately premised upon her conveyance of the house'.[101]

On this view, cases like *Deglman* and *Pavey* are not exceptions to the obligation rule. They are cases where the defendant's entitlement was defeated by the conditionality associated with the contractual obligation. In both cases, a condition precedent to the defendant's entitlement was not satisfied. The claimant's services were, therefore, not 'earned' by the defendant.[102]

[98] *Deglman* (Ontario Court of Appeal) (n 79) [1].

[99] *Deglman* (Supreme Court of Canada) (n 74) [2].

[100] *Pavey* (n 75) 224–225.

[101] Mitchell McInnes, 'The Measure of Restitution' (2002) 52 The University of Toronto Law Journal 163, 204–205. The conditionality reasoning also applies to cases where services are rendered by a claimant to the defendant pursuant to a statutory duty: see Daniel Friedmann, 'Valid, Voidable, Qualified, and Non-Existing Obligations: An Alternative Perspective on the Law of Restitution' in Andrew Burrows (ed), *Essays on the Law of Restitution* (Oxford, Clarendon, 1991) 254–255; *Matheson v Smiley* [1932] 2 DLR 787 (Manitoba Court of Appeal).

[102] Robert Stevens, 'Is There a Law of Unjust Enrichment?' (n 26) 24–30; Stephen Waddams, 'Contract and Unjust Enrichment: Competing Categories, or Complementary Concepts?' in Peter Birks, Charles Rickett and Ross Grantham (eds), *Structure and Justification in Private Law: Essays for Peter Birks* (Oxford, Hart, 2008) 173–175; James Edelman and Elise Bant, *Unjust Enrichment* (2nd edn, Oxford, Hart, 2016) ('There are a number of situations in which a defendant has a juristic reason for receipt, but no juristic reason to retain an enrichment ... Consider the facts of the famous English case of *Fibrosa Spolka Akcyjna v Fairbairn Lawson Combe Barbour Ltd* ... the contract provided for a juristic reason for the receipt of the money, but once the contract had been terminated without the counter-performance upon which the payment depended, there was no accrued right to retain the payment. This is why Lord Wright said that the payment was conditional and the right to retain it fell away when the condition failed'); McInnes (n 101) 175 ('Despite fully intending the

There are a number of reasons why this conditionality explanation is preferable to Burrows's analysis. First, there is considerable support for the conditionality reasoning in the academic literature. For example, Weinrib adopts the conditionality reasoning to rationalise *Deglman*:[103]

> The relevant question is not whether the plaintiff was obligated to do certain acts, but whether he was obligated to transfer value – that is, to do those acts without receiving their quantitative equivalent in return. Although the nephew was contractually obligated to provide the services, he was not contractually obligated to provide them for nothing, as if he had made a gratuitous promise under seal.

Similarly, according to McInnes, the decisive feature in *Deglman* was the conditionality of the defendant's enrichment. 'Despite fully intending the defendant to receive an enrichment', he says, 'the plaintiff may intend for him to retain it only if a certain condition is met.'[104] That condition was never satisfied and, consequently, the plaintiff was entitled to restitution.[105]

Second, Burrows's reasoning cannot reconcile *Deglman* and *Pavey* with decisions that deny restitution of enrichments conferred under valid but unenforceable contracts. Indeed, the general rule is that enrichments conferred under unenforceable contracts are irrecoverable.[106] Support for that view goes as far back as *Moses v Macferlan*.[107] In that case, Lord Mansfield identified the mistaken 'payment of a debt barred by the Statute of Limitations'[108] as a case where an action for recovery would fail. Lord Mansfield reiterated that view in *Bize v Dickason*.[109] In that case, the defendant had underwritten insurance policies issued by the claimant insurer. After paying out the claims, the claimant sought reimbursement from the defendant. Overall, the claimant was owed £662. However, the claimant owed the defendant the much larger sum of £1,356 as insurance premium. The claimant paid off the premium owed to the defendant while mistakenly believing that it was not entitled to deduct £662. In this context, Lord Mansfield said (*obiter*),[110]

defendant to *receive* an enrichment, the plaintiff may intend for him to *retain* it only if a certain condition is met').

[103] Ernest Weinrib, 'Unjust Enrichment', in *Corrective Justice* (Oxford, Oxford University Press, 2012) 219.

[104] McInnes (n 101) 175.

[105] See also, Lionel Smith, 'Demystifying Juristic Reasons' (2007) 45 Canadian Business Law Journal 281, 292–293.

[106] Graham Virgo, *The Principles of the Law of Restitution* (3rd edn, Oxford, Oxford University Press, 2015) 144; Graham Virgo, 'Demolishing the Pyramid – the Presence of Basis and Risk-Taking in the Law of Unjust Enrichment' in Andrew Robertson and Tang Wu (eds), *The Goals of Private Law* (Oxford, Hart, 2009) 491.

[107] *Moses v Macferlan* (1760) 2 Burr 1005, 97 ER 676.

[108] ibid 680–681.

[109] *Bize v Dickason* (1786) 1 Term Rep 285, 99 ER 1097.

[110] ibid 286–287. See also, Gerhard Dannemann, 'Unjust Enrichment as Absence of Basis: Can English Law Cope?' in Andrew Burrows and Alan Rodger (eds), *Mapping the Law: Essays in Memory of Peter Birks* (Oxford, Oxford University Press, 2006) 369.

> [W]here a man has paid a debt, which would otherwise have been barred by the Statute of Limitations ... though the law would not have compelled the payment, yet the money being paid, it will not oblige the payee to refund it.

On Burrows's analysis, the unenforceability of the contracts in these cases should have meant that there was no conflict between the restitution claim and the contractual allocation of risks. On that approach, the denial of the restitution is inexplicable. By contrast, on the analysis offered here, the result in these cases is unsurprising. In both *Moses* and *Bize*, the defendant was unconditionally entitled to the enrichment. This meant that restitution could not be awarded despite the unenforceability of the underlying obligation.

Third, the explanation offered here has the merit of ensuring coherence across a number of different areas. For instance, the conditionality explanation aligns cases that grant restitution within unenforceable contracts with the decision of the High Court of Australia in *Roxborough*. As explained earlier in this chapter, restitution was granted in that case because the retailer's contractual obligation was conditional. The same analysis applies to cases where restitution is sought within an unenforceable contract. The relevant question is: does the defendant have an unconditional right to the enrichment in respect of which the claimant seeks restitution? In *Deglman* and *Pavey*, the answer was 'no'. As Ibbetson explains in his insightful analysis of the early cases in this area, 'the fact that the contract might have been unenforceable is in the first place analytically irrelevant' to the restitution claim.[111]

IV. *ZURICH INSURANCE*: THE OBLIGATION RULE IN THE 'FAIRCHILD ENCLAVE'[112]

In *International Energy Group Ltd v Zurich Insurance* ('*Zurich Insurance*'),[113] by a majority of 4 to 3, the Supreme Court preferred to characterise the obligation rule as a flexible principle as opposed to a bright-line rule. This section examines the decision in *Zurich Insurance*. It argues that the reasoning of the majority judges in that case is incorrect.[114] For the future, it is preferable to confine the scope of that reasoning to the '*Fairchild* enclave'.

[111] David Ibbetson, 'Implied Contracts and Restitution: History in the High Court of Australia' (1988) 8 Oxford Journal of Legal Studies 312, 322.

[112] This section is based on a case note published at (2017) 80 Modern Law Review 1150. The tort and insurance issues arising from *Zurich Insurance* have been extensively examined elsewhere: Sarah Green, 'Between a Rock of Uncertainty and a Hard Case' (2016) 132 Law Quarterly Review 25; James Goudkamp, 'The Insurance Law Legacy of *Fairchild*' [2015] Lloyd's Maritime Commercial Law Quarterly 443; Jonathan Morgan, 'Reinterpreting the Reinterpretation of the Reinterpretation of Fairchild' (2015) 74 Cambridge Law Journal 395; Rob Merkin, 'Insurance and reinsurance in the *Fairchild* enclave' (2016) 36 Legal Studies 302.

[113] *International Energy Group Ltd v Zurich Insurance plc* [2015] UKSC 33, [2015] 2 WLR 1471.

[114] See Stevens, *Laws of Restitution* (n 26) 88–89.

A. The Decision in *Zurich Insurance*

Alan Carré was employed by the Guernsey Gas Light Company Ltd ('GGCL') for a little more than 27 years. During that period, GGCL negligently exposed him to asbestos. This caused Mr Carré to contract mesothelioma of which he subsequently died. As the successor to GGCL's liabilities, International Energy Group Ltd (the claimant) settled Mr Carré's claim.

The claimant then brought proceedings against GGCL's insurers. However, GGCL was only insured for eight of the 27 years during which it employed Mr Carré. Six of those years were covered by a policy from Midland Assurance. Zurich Insurance (the defendant) had taken over Midland's liabilities. The defendant contended that it could not be held liable for *all* of GGCL's liability to Mr Carré. It was only liable, it argued, for a part of GGCL's liability, namely a share reflecting the proportion of the period during which GGCL was insured to the total duration of Mr Carré's employment (roughly, 6/27).

At first instance, Cooke J accepted the defendant's argument.[115] The defendant's liability was governed by Guernsey law. Thus, the Compensation Act 2006[116] was inapplicable. Cooke J therefore applied the special rule in *Fairchild v Glenhaven Funeral Services Ltd*[117] as interpreted in *Barker v Corus UK Ltd* ('*Barker*').[118] In *Barker*, the House of Lords had held that an employer was only liable for their aliquot contribution to the claimant employee's risk of contracting mesothelioma. Cooke J held that the defendant insurer's liability to the claimant employer must similarly be proportionate.

The Court of Appeal reversed that decision.[119] It was bound by the Supreme Court's decision in *Durham v BAI (Run off) Ltd* ('*Trigger*'),[120] which was decided about two months after Cooke J's decision. In *Trigger*, the Supreme Court held that the 'weak' or 'broad' causal rule in *Fairchild* carried over to insurers' liability.[121] On that basis, the Court of Appeal concluded that Mr Carré's mesothelioma was 'caused' during the insurance period as long as he was negligently exposed to asbestos during that period, thereby materially increasing his risk of contracting the disease.

The Supreme Court agreed with Cooke J. All seven judges held that the defendant's liability must be confined to reflect the period of Mr Carré's employment during which GGCL was insured. The Court's reasoning may be analysed in three stages.

[115] *International Energy Group Limited v Zurich Insurance plc* [2012] EWHC 69 (Comm).

[116] Compensation Act 2006, s 3 provides for joint and several liability among employers who negligently expose their employees to asbestos resulting in the employees contracting mesothelioma.

[117] *Fairchild v Glenhaven Funeral Services Ltd* [2002] UKHL 22, [2003] 1 AC 32.

[118] *Barker v Corus UK Ltd* [2006] UKHL 20, [2006] 2 AC 572.

[119] *International Energy Group Ltd v Zurich Insurance Plc* [2013] EWCA Civ 39.

[120] *Durham v BAI (Run off) Ltd* [2012] UKSC 14, [2012] 1 WLR 867 ('*Trigger*'). *Trigger* was decided two months after Cooke J's decision.

[121] ibid [66] (Lord Mance).

First, the Court considered the liability of GGCL (the employer) to Mr Carré.[122] This was uncontroversial. Mr Carré was never employed by anyone other than GGCL.[123] Therefore, GGCL was liable for all of Mr Carré's loss. However, the point of contention was whether GGCL's liability to Mr Carré was 'solidary' (each exposure resulting in GGCL's liability for all of Mr Carré's loss) or 'proportionate' (GGCL's liability being proportionate to the extent of its contribution to Mr Carré's exposure).[124] This was relevant because the defendant relied on GGCL's proportionate liability as the basis for its further submission that the defendant insurer's liability must also be proportionate.

On GGCL's liability, the defendant's contention was unanimously upheld. The Compensation Act 2006 was inapplicable in Guernsey and, therefore, this question was governed by the common law. The common law rule, as laid down in *Barker*, provided for proportionate liability of GGCL to Mr Carré.

This led to the 'second main question', namely the defendant insurer's liability to GGCL. In theory, it was open to the defendant to argue that, despite GGCL's solidary liability to Mr Carré, the defendant's liability to GGCL must be proportionate. The former is a question of tort law whereas the latter is a question of interpretation of the insurance policy. However, the defendant conceded this point. Despite being invited to withdraw that concession,[125] the defendant maintained that if GGCL's liability to Mr Carré was solidary the defendant's liability to GGCL must also be solidary.[126]

On the issue of the insurer's liability, the Court did not speak with one voice. Lord Mance, with whom Lord Clarke, Lord Carnwath and Lord Hodge agreed, constituted the majority. According to Lord Mance, although GGCL's liability to Mr Carré was proportionate, the Court was bound by *Trigger* to hold that the defendant insurer's liability to GGCL was solidary. Thus, even if GGCL was only insured for one year during Mr Carré's employment, GGCL's insurer would be liable for all of Mr Carré's claim. This result followed from the conclusion in *Trigger* that mesothelioma was 'caused' in the *Fairchild* sense during each policy period.

Lord Sumption, with whom Lord Neuberger and Lord Reed agreed, disagreed with this analysis. According to Lord Sumption, the defendant's liability to GGCL depended on the construction of the insurance policy. That exercise had to account for a fundamental limitation on the scope of an insurer's liability, namely the period of insurance.[127] The defendant's liability to GGCL could not extend beyond the insurance period. Therefore the defendant's liability had to be proportionate to the period of GGCL's insurance.

[122] *Zurich Insurance (UKSC)* (n 113) [25]–[35] (Lord Mance).

[123] ibid [141] (Lord Sumption).

[124] This terminology is borrowed from Goudkamp (n 112) 445–446.

[125] *Zurich Insurance (UKSC)* (n 113) [147] (Lord Sumption).

[126] It appears that this concession was motivated by the insurers' apprehension of Parliamentary intervention: ibid [203] (Lord Neuberger and Lord Reed).

[127] ibid [151] (Lord Sumption).

Left as it is, the majority's conclusion on the second question would have led to the anomalous result that the defendant insurer was liable for all of Mr Carré's claim against GGCL although GGCL was only insured for a part of Mr Carré's employment. Lord Mance sought to avoid this result by proposing a novel right of 'equitable recoupment'. In respect of the period of Mr Carré's employment during which GGCL was *not* insured, he said, GGCL must be treated as a 'self-insurer'.[128] The defendant insurer was entitled to recoupment from GGCL in respect of that period. This meant that, although the defendant insurer was prima facie liable to GGCL for all of Mr Carré's claim, the defendant could seek recoupment from GGCL of a sum reflecting the period for which GGCL was not insured. The remainder of this section examines this right of recoupment.

B. The Nature of the Right of Recoupment

The right to recoupment recognised by Lord Mance is best analysed as being based on the need to reverse GGCL's unjust enrichment at the expense of the defendant insurer. There is overwhelming support for this view in the cases[129] and commentaries.[130] Lord Mance also appears to have proceeded on this basis.[131] Moreover, during oral argument, Lord Reed and Lord Neuberger suggested that the right of recoupment was best conceptualised as being based on the law of unjust enrichment.[132]

On the unjust enrichment approach, the injustice that generates restitution in the form of recoupment may be illustrated through an example:

> *Example 4*: C guarantees a debt of £100 owed by D to X. On D's default, X claims £100 from C. C pays and then seeks recoupment of £100 from D.

[128] ibid [65] (Lord Mance).

[129] *Westdeutsche Landesbank Girozentale v Islington LBC* [1996] AC 669 (HL) 727 (Lord Woolf); *Societe Eram Shipping Company Ltd v Compagnie Internationale De Navigation* [2001] EWCA Civ 1317 [46] (Mance LJ); *Kuwait Oil Tanker Co SAK & Another v Qabazard* [2002] EWCA Civ 34 [5] (Longmore LJ); *Alan Robert Lumley v Melvin Edward Riddell Robinson* [2002] EWCA Civ 94 [12] (Aldous LJ). See also, *Caledonia North Sea Ltd v London Bridge Engineering Ltd* [2000] SLT 1123, 1141 (Lord Rodger) (Scotland); *Burke and Another v Lfot Pty Limited* [2002] HCA 17 [38] (Gaudron A-CJ and Hayne J) (Australia); *County of Carleton v City of Ottawa* [1965] SCR 663 [8]–[11] (Hall J) (Canada); *Cosmic Insurance Corp Ltd v Ong Kah Hoe* [1997] SGHC 237 [28]–[33] (Rubin J) (Singapore).

[130] Charles Mitchell, Paul Mitchell and Stephen Watterson, *Goff & Jones: The Law of Unjust Enrichment* (10th edn, London, Sweet & Maxwell, 2022) [19-03]; Andrew Burrows, *The Law of Restitution* (3rd edn, Oxford, Oxford University Press, 2011) ch 17; Graham Virgo, *The Principles of the Law of Restitution* (3rd edn, Oxford, Oxford University Press, 2015) 231; James Edelman and Elise Bant, *Unjust Enrichment* (2nd edn, Oxford, Hart, 2016) 293–298; Keith Mason, John Carter and Gregory Tolhurst, *Mason & Carter's Restitution Law in Australia* (2nd edn, Melbourne, LexisNexis Butterworths, 2008) 228–229; Charles Mitchell, *The Law of Contribution and Reimbursement* (Oxford, Oxford University Press, 2003) [3.01]–[3.03]. See also, Law Commission, *Report on Limitation of Actions* (LC270, 10 July 2001) [2.49]; Law Commission, *Report on Contribution* (Law Com No 79, 1977) [13].

[131] *Zurich Insurance (UKSC)* (n 113) [68]–[72] (Lord Mance).

[132] Merkin (n 112) 314.

As between C and X, C was liable to pay £100 to X. However, as between C and D, D is 'primarily' liable for the debt. The function of the recoupment claim is to shift the liability from C (whose liability is 'secondary') to D (whose liability is primary).[133] C's recoupment right against D ensures that the burden of D's liability ultimately falls on D. This understanding of the justification for a recoupment right leads to two objections to Lord Mance's reasoning.

First, for the unjust enrichment justification for recoupment to operate, D must have been under a pre-existing 'liability'. It is the cost of that liability that the law seeks to shift from C to D. However, this was not the case in *Zurich Insurance*. In respect of the period during which the employer was uninsured, the employer was not under a liability to the defendant insurer or, indeed, to any third party. Lord Mance attempted to overcome this difficulty by treating the employer as a 'self-insurer'[134] in respect of the uninsured periods. This may have been intended as an articulation of the fact that the employer is at risk for periods during which it was not insured.[135] However, characterising the employer as 'self-insured' does not meet the objection that, in respect of the periods during which the employer was uninsured, the employer was under no liability at all.[136] Therefore, as between the employer and its insurer, there was no liability that called for readjustment by the law of unjust enrichment.

Second, the justification for the recoupment right is premised on the proposition that, as between C and D, there are good reasons why the burden must fall on D instead of C. But what if C had contractually undertaken the burden of the debt from D? In that case, it is not 'unjust' for C to bear that liability.

Morris v Breaveglen Ltd[137] illustrates this. Mr Morris was employed by B Ltd. Under a sub-contract, B had agreed to supply labour to S Ltd. Under that contract, Mr Morris was working under the instructions of S's foremen when he was injured. Although Mr Morris was working with S, he continued to be B's employee and, therefore, B was held liable to compensate Mr Morris. B then sought contribution from S. B's claim was dismissed on the basis that it was inconsistent with the contract between B and S. Under that contract, B had agreed that S would not be liable for 'any claim arising out of an accident to an employee' of B. In the normal course, the primary liability for Mr Morris's injury would have fallen on S. But B had contractually undertaken that liability from S. It was therefore not 'unjust' for that burden to fall on B.[138]

[133] Burrows, *The Law of Restitution* (n 130) 436; Charles Mitchell, 'Unjust Enrichment' in Peter Birks (ed), *English Private Law* (3rd edn, Oxford, Oxford University Press, 2013) [18.114]; Mitchell, Mitchell and Watterson (n 130) [19-01]; Mitchell, *The Law of Contribution and Reimbursement* (n 130) [3.27]. For a different explanation based on 'powerlessness' see Edelman and Bant (n 130) 293.

[134] *Zurich Insurance (UKSC)* (n 113) [65] (Lord Mance).

[135] ibid [75] (Lord Mance).

[136] Merkin (n 112) 318–319.

[137] *Morris v Breaveglen Ltd* [1993] PIQR P294 (CA).

[138] See, *Mawson v Cassidy* (CA, 26 January 1995); *Belger v Belger* (CA, 17 July 1989). See also, Merkin (n 112) 318 (critiquing the recoupment right based on insurance principles).

Against that background, let us return to *Zurich Insurance*. According to Lord Mance, the defendant insurer was liable to GGCL (the employer) for all of Mr Carré's claim. The basis of that liability was the insurance policy. The fact that the parties did not foresee the decisions in *Fairchild* and *Trigger* at the time of entering into the insurance contract is immaterial to this analysis. As Lord Mance explained in *Trigger*,[139] 'if the common law during or even after the currency of an insurance develops in a manner which increases employers' liability' – as it did in *Zurich Insurance* – 'that is a risk which the insurers must accept'.[140] Lord Collins made the same point in *Wasa International Insurance Co Ltd v Lexington Insurance Co*, where he said that 'an insurer under the original insurance takes the risk of changes in the law'.[141] In short, on Lord Mance's analysis, the defendant insurer had contractually agreed that it would be liable to GGCL on a solidary basis.

In these circumstances, what 'injustice' is the right of recoupment in *Zurich Insurance* responding to? In other words, in what sense is the imposition of solidary liability on the defendant insurer – an obligation it voluntarily undertook – 'unjust'? The majority judges offer no convincing answer. The correct position is that the insurance contract under which the defendant had voluntarily agreed to indemnify the employer removes any basis or reason for there being a right of recoupment by the insurer against GGCL. As Lord Sumption put it, it is difficult to understand 'by what standard it is said to be unjust when the parties have agreed that it should be so.'[142]

C. The Obligation Rule

The insurance contract also posed a second hurdle for the recoupment right. It had the consequence that the enrichment in respect of which the insurer was seeking recoupment was owed to the employer under a valid legal obligation. Accordingly, restitution ought to have been precluded by the obligation rule.

Lord Mance sought to overcome this difficulty in two ways. First, he suggested that the recoupment claim did not contradict the insurance contract. Second, he said that the obligation rule was not a bright-line rule.[143] I will consider each of these points in turn.

[139] *Trigger* (n 120) [69] (Lord Mance).

[140] ibid [69]–[70] (Lord Mance).

[141] *Wasa International Insurance Co Ltd v Lexington Insurance Co* [2009] UKHL 40, [2010] 1 AC 180 [110].

[142] ibid [183] (Lord Sumption).

[143] Lord Mance also cited with approval Lord Mansfield's decision in *Moses v Macferlan* (1760) 2 Burr 1005, 97 ER 676 as a 'cornerstone of common law restitution': see *Zurich Insurance (UKSC)* (n 113) [70]. That was a case where restitution was granted despite the defendant's valid entitlement to retain the enrichment. Thus, it contradicts the obligation rule. However, on this point,

i. The 'No Inconsistency' Reasoning

According to Lord Mance, recognising a recoupment right in these circumstances 'does not involve contradicting or acting inconsistently with [the insurance contract]. On the contrary, it is accepting their implications, and relying on matters independent of them'.[144]

In order to evaluate this reasoning it is necessary to look closely at the nature of the 'inconsistency' or 'contradiction' that the obligation rule responds to. What matters is an inconsistency or contradiction of *result*. The question is whether permitting restitution will undo the *effect* of the defendant's legal entitlement. The obligation rule applies when, as a result of the restitution claim, the defendant will be deprived of the benefit of its entitlement. Although the term 'nullify'[145] has sometimes been used to describe the relationship between restitution claims and the defendant's legal entitlements, it is clear that these two private law obligations cannot 'nullify' each other except in the sense described above.

> *Example 5*: C owes £100 each to D and X under two separate contracts. C intends to pay X but mistakenly pays D. C seeks restitution from D. C's claim will fail.[146]

This is often treated as an archetypal instance of the operation of the obligation rule.[147] It is materially indistinguishable from *Zurich Insurance*. Just as in Example 5, the defendant insurer in *Zurich Insurance* owed GGCL an amount equivalent to Mr Carré's claim. Even if that payment prima facie generated an unjust enrichment claim, as C's mistake in Example 5 does, that claim is precluded by GGCL's contractual entitlement to the enrichment. Just as Lord Mance reasoned in *Zurich Insurance*, it is possible to argue in Example 5 that C's restitution claim is based on 'accepting [the] implications' of the contract between C and D, ie D's entitlement to £100, and 'relying on matters independent of them', ie C's mistake. That does not justify C's claim in Example 5. With respect, it should not have justified the defendant insurer's recoupment claim

Moses v Macferlan has been discredited both judicially and in academic writing: see, *Marriot v Hampton* (1797) 7 Term Reports 269, 101 ER 969; *Phillips v Hunter* [1795] 2 Hy Bl 402; *Brisbane v Dacres* 5 Taunt 160, 128 ER 641; Mitchell, Mitchell and Watterson (n 130) [2-33]–[2-34]; Daniel Friedmann, 'Unjust Enrichment, Pursuance of Self-Interest and the Limits of Free Riding' (2003) 36 Loyola of Los Angeles Law Review 831, 833–834; Ernest Weinrib, *Corrective Justice* (Oxford, Oxford University Press, 2016) 202.

[144] *Zurich Insurance (UKSC)* (n 113) [67] (Lord Mance).

[145] Daniel Friedmann, 'Valid, Voidable, Qualified, and Non-Existing Obligations: An Alternative Perspective on the Law of Restitution' in Andrew Burrows (ed), *Essays on the Law of Restitution* (Oxford, Clarendon Press, 1991) 248.

[146] Based on dicta in *Platt v Bromage* (1854) 24 LJ Ex 63, 65.

[147] Andrew Burrows, 'Is There a Defence of Good Consideration?' in Charles Mitchell and William Swadling (eds), *The Restatement Third, Restitution and Unjust Enrichment: Critical and Comparative Essays* (Oxford, Hart, 2013) 174.

in *Zurich Insurance* either. As Leggatt LJ observed in *Equitas Insurance Ltd v Municipal Mutual Insurance Ltd*:[148]

> giving an insurer an equitable right to recoup part of the insured loss from its insured is not just close to inconsistent, but is clearly inconsistent, with the contract between the parties as it was interpreted by the majority in [*Zurich Insurance*].

ii. Not a Bright-Line Rule

In order to justify the right of recoupment, Lord Mance also denied the existence of any bright-line rule precluding restitution claims that contradict contractually dictated results. On this point, he adopted Burrows's analysis.

This approach consists of a general rule and flexible exceptions. The general rule denies restitution when the enrichment is owed by the claimant to the defendant under a valid legal obligation.[149] The exceptions operate when there is no 'policy inconsistency'[150] between the restitution claim and the defendant's entitlement. In determining whether the exception applies, the question 'at the root of the issue is whether the legal entitlement of D to the payment from C is outweighed by the injustice constituted by D receiving a payment that C mistakenly did not mean to make'.[151] When it is, C's restitution claim will succeed despite D's legal entitlement. There are two main objections to this approach.

First, Burrows's approach requires courts to weigh up against each other the unjust factor upon which the restitution claim is based and the defendant's legal entitlement. According to Burrows, the exception applies when the legal entitlement is 'easily outweighed'.[152] According to Burrows, therefore, in the context of unjust enrichment claims, some legal entitlements of the defendant are less secure than others. However, it is not clear what it is about these entitlements that render them more susceptible to reversal through restitution. Legal entitlements are conclusions reached by a legal system after a reconciliation of competing interests.[153] As Scott explains, their normative force is 'not transparent'.[154] This suggests that it is not easy to proceed on the basis that legal entitlements are normatively inferior to others.

In any case, it is not the relative normative weight of the unjust factors and the legal entitlement that motivated the results in Burrows's exception cases.

148 [2019] EWCA Civ 718 [143] (Leggatt LJ).
149 Burrows, *The Law of Restitution* (n 130) 88.
150 ibid 90.
151 Burrows, 'Is There a Defence of Good Consideration?' (n 147) 177.
152 ibid 177.
153 John Gardner, 'Obligations and Outcomes in the Law of Torts' in Peter Cane and John Gardner (eds), *Relating to Responsibility* (Oxford, Hart, 2001) 1–2; Joseph Raz, *The Morality of Freedom* (Oxford, Clarendon Press, 1986) 172.
154 Helen Scott, 'Defence, Denial or Cause of Action? 'Enrichment Owed' and the Absence of a Legal Ground' in Andrew Dyson, James Goudkamp and Frederick Wilmot-Smith (eds), *Defences in Unjust Enrichment* (Oxford, Hart, 2016) 59.

Consider *DMG*.[155] As explained earlier in this chapter, in that case, the Advance Corporation Tax in respect of which the claimant sought restitution was due to the Revenue when it was paid.[156] Why did this not preclude restitution? According to Burrows, this is because,[157]

> [T]he statutory obligation was undermined by the legislature's failure contrary to EU law, to provide a group income election for companies such as the claimants.

As explained earlier in this chapter, the consequence of the legislature's contravention of EU law was that the principle of 'EU estoppel' precluded the Revenue from relying on an obligation procured by its own breach of EU law.[158] This analysis does not require any evaluation of the relative normative weights of the legal obligation and the unjust factor. Rather, the Revenue is simply precluded from relying on the relevant legal obligation.

It was also explained in Section I of this chapter that *Roxborough*[159] is not inconsistent with the bright-line nature of the obligation rule. In that case, the retailer's contractual obligation to the wholesaler was conditional on the validity of the licence fee. As Burrows explains, 'once the tax was held not to be owing, that part of the price was not, in substance, owing, albeit that no particular clause could be struck down as void'.[160] This had the consequence that there was no countervailing legal entitlement in respect of the tax component. The invalidity of the tax rendered the defendant wholesaler's entitlement to that sum inoperative.[161]

A second objection to the analysis of Burrows and Lord Mance is the indeterminacy of the 'weighing up' process that it involves. Scott's incommensurability objection focuses on this issue.[162] She argues that the unjust factor is a primary fact whereas the legal entitlement is 'a purely legal institution'.[163] They are incommensurable considerations.

In general, incommensurability objections rely on the unavailability of a common metric to measure or compare two values.[164] In the absence of a

[155] *Deutsche Morgan Grenfell Group Plc v Inland Revenue Commissioners* [2006] UKHL 49, [2007] 1 AC 558 ('*DMG*').

[156] Robert Stevens, 'Justified Enrichment' (2005) 5 Oxford University Commonwealth Law Journal 141, 142–145.

[157] Burrows, *The Law of Restitution* (n 130) 91 (emphasis added).

[158] This point was considered in greater detail in Section II of this Chapter.

[159] *Roxborough v Rothmans of Pall Mall Australia Ltd* [2001] HCA 68, (2001) 208 CLR 516.

[160] Burrows, 'Is There a Defence of Good Consideration?' (n 147) 177.

[161] Stephen Waddams, 'Contract and Unjust Enrichment: Competing Categories, or Complementary Concepts?' in Peter Birks, Charles Rickett and Ross Grantham (eds), *Structure and Justification in Private Law: Essays for Peter Birks* (Oxford, Hart, 2008) 174–175; Robert Stevens, 'Is There a Law of Unjust Enrichment?' in Simone Degeling and James Edelman (eds), *Unjust Enrichment in Commercial Law* (Sydney, Thomson Reuters, 2008) 29.

[162] Scott (n 154).

[163] ibid 59.

[164] Andrew Dyson, James Goudkamp and Frederick Wilmot-Smith, 'Defences in Unjust Enrichment: Questions and Themes' in Andrew Dyson, James Goudkamp and Frederick Wilmot-Smith (eds),

common measure, it is said that it is conceptually impossible to 'weigh' or 'balance' things against each other.[165] Incommensurability does not mean that it is impossible to make a rational choice between two vales.[166] Waldron's distinction between 'weak' and 'strong' incommensurability explains this. 'Strong incommensurability' arises when two considerations are 'genuinely incomparable';[167] neither overrides the other, nor are they of equal weight. In cases of 'weak commensurability', although there is no common metric to weigh up the competing values, they are linked by a 'priority rule'. There is an ordering between them that permits rational choice, although that choice is not reached through commensuration.

This analysis explains why Burrows's methodology is objectionable in a way that the bright-line rule is not. The latter is a rule of priority pursuant to which the legal obligation overrides the restitution claim.[168] By contrast, an approach that requires the unjust factor and the legal entitlement to be 'balanced' or 'weighed' against each other demands the identification of a common benchmark against which they can be compared. No such criterion has been identified so far. This renders the weighing up exercise an indeterminate process. Some examples may illustrate this point further.

Consider restitution claims based on duress. According to Burrows, even duress claims are precluded by the defendant's entitlement.[169] This view is consistent with authority.[170] For the bright-line rule, this result is unproblematic. However, it is difficult to see how it can be justified by weighing the unjust factor and the legal obligation against each other. On the balancing methodology, when, if ever, does the normative force of duress prevail over the legal obligation? Does the result differ depending on how objectionable the defendant's conduct is?

> *Example 6*: C owes £100 to D. D puts a gun to C's head and demands payment. Under threat, C pays. D accepts the payment in discharge of the debt. Is C entitled to restitution?

Defences in Unjust Enrichment (Oxford, Hart, 2016). See also, Raz (n 153) 322; Webber Grégoire, *The Negotiable Constitution* (Cambridge, Cambridge University Press, 2009) 90.

[165] See, Robert Stevens, 'Contributory Fault – Analogue or Digital?' in Andrew Dyson, Frederick Wilmot-Smith and James Goudkamp (eds), *Defences in Unjust Enrichment* (Oxford, Hart, 2016) 259. For examples of commensurability objections in public law see, Grégoire (n 164) 90–91; Stavros Tsakyrakis, 'Proportionality: An Assault on Human Rights?' (2009) 7 International Journal of Constitutional Law 468.

[166] Francisco Urbina, 'Incommensurability and Balancing' (2015) 35 Oxford Journal of Legal Studies 575; Cass Sunstein, 'Incommensurability and Valuation in Law' (1994) 92 Michigan Law Review 779.

[167] Jeremy Waldron, 'Fake Incommensurability: A Response to Professor Schauer' (1993) 45 Hastings Law Journal 813, 816.

[168] ibid 817.

[169] Andrew Burrows, *A Restatement of the English Law of Unjust Enrichment* (Oxford, Oxford University Press, 2012) 33.

[170] *Flower v Sadler* (1882) 10 QBD 572 (CA); *Ward v Lloyd* (1843) 6 Man & G 785, 134 ER 1109. This point is considered in more detail at Chapter 8(II).

Another example of the indeterminacy of the balancing methodology may be found in claims for the restitution of performance rendered under valid but unenforceable contracts. According to Burrows, restitution is permissible in these cases despite the validity of the underlying contract. As explained earlier in this Chapter, he identifies this category of case as an exception to the general rule.[171] Yet, it is unclear how the balancing methodology can account for this result. Burrows accepts that obligations that are valid but unenforceable (for example, a time-barred debt) are capable of denying restitution generally.[172] Why, then, is the result different in cases involving restitution for money paid or services rendered under unenforceable contracts?

A third illustration of the indeterminacy of Burrows's approach is the majority's reasoning in *Zurich Insurance*. On behalf of the majority judges, Lord Mance said:[173]

> [T]here is no policy inconsistency between recognising that the terms of the insurances … make [the defendant] answerable in the first instance for [the employer's] liability towards Mr Carré and recognising an equity, based on consideration of the wider circumstances – in particular GGLCL/IEG's exposure of Mr Carré for further periods when it was not insured by Midland – requiring IEG itself to contribute towards Zurich's cost of meeting such liability.

With respect, the assertion that there is no 'policy inconsistency' between the terms of the contract and the recoupment right is incorrect. As a matter of contractual construction, Lord Mance had found that the defendant insurer was liable for all of Mr Carré's claim, including in respect of periods during which the employer was uninsured. On this construction, the contract imposed solidary liability upon the insurer. The very purpose of the recoupment right was to modify that result. As Lord Sumption said, the recoupment right seeks to 'undo in part what the contract has done'.[174] Indeed, without acting inconsistently with the contract, the recoupment claim cannot achieve that purpose. Therefore, it is unclear why Lord Mance considered that there was no 'policy inconsistency' between the restitution claim and the insurance contract.

For the reasons set out above, the decision of the majority judges in *Zurich Insurance* is incorrect. The preferable view is that its value as precedent ought to be confined to the '*Fairchild* enclave'. Some support for this view may be derived from post-*Zurich Insurance* cases that have considered the operation of the obligation rule.

The first among them is *DD Growth Premium 2X Fund v RMF Market Neutral Strategies (Master) Limited*.[175] In that case, Lord Sumption pointed out

[171] See Section III of this Chapter.
[172] Burrows, *The Law of Restitution* (n 130) 88.
[173] *Zurich Insurance (UKSC)* (n 113) [72] (Lord Mance).
[174] ibid [184] (Lord Sumption).
[175] [2017] UKPC 36 [62].

that there was 'more than a century and a half of authority' for the proposition that a restitution claim is not available if the enrichment was owed to the defendant by the claimant under a valid legal obligation. He did not suggest that this was anything other than a bright-line rule. Nor did he make reference to any exceptions to this principle.

Subsequently, in *ICICI Bank UK Plc v Assam Oil Co Ltd*,[176] Andrew Burrows QC (sitting as a Judge of the High Court) referred to the good consideration rule and the obligation rule in the following terms:

> it is a well-established proposition of law that a mistaken payer is not entitled to restitution of payments that were owed by the payer under a valid contract between the payer and the payee … it is also the law that a mistaken payer is not entitled to restitution 'if the money is paid to discharge, and does discharge, a debt owed to the payee … by a third party by whom [the payer] is authorised to discharge the debt'

Although the majority in *Zurich Insurance* had relied on Burrows's academic work to characterise the obligation rule as a flexible principle it appears that, sitting as a judge, Andrew Burrows QC did not characterise the obligation rule in that way.

Finally, in *Equitas Insurance*, Leggatt LJ expressed 'concern' about the majority's reasoning in *Zurich Insurance*.[177] He observed that the equitable right of recoupment was 'clearly inconsistent' with the contract between the parties. Citing with approval the academic criticism of the majority's reasoning,[178] he concluded that allowing a restitutionary claim to override a valid contract ought to be 'an absolutely last resort, if not a counsel of despair'.[179] Similarly, in *Dargamo Holdings Ltd*, the Court of Appeal held that any flexibility the obligation rule offers must be confined to 'rare cases'.[180]

In summary, this chapter considered four challenges to the bright-line conception of the obligation rule. It was explained that three of these – namely *Roxborough*, *DMG* and the law relating to restitution of mistaken benefits conferred under unenforceable contracts – do not in fact support the idea that the obligation rule is a flexible principle rather than a bright-line rule. As for the fourth, the decision in *Zurich Insurance*, it was suggested that the reasoning of the majority judges is misconceived and best understood as a judicial response to the difficulties that arise within the '*Fairchild* enclave'. That decision should not be understood as qualifying generally the bright-line nature of the obligation rule.

[176] [2019] EWHC 750 (Comm) [38(ii)].
[177] *Equitas Insurance Ltd v Municipal Mutual Insurance ltd* [2019] EWCA Civ 718.
[178] Including a version of this section published in (2017) 80 Modern Law Review 1150.
[179] *Equitas Insurance Ltd* (n 177) [145].
[180] *Dargamo Holdings Ltd v Avonwick Holdings Ltd* [2021] EWCA Civ 1149, [2022] 1 All ER (Comm) 1244 [128] (Carr LJ).

5

The Subsidiarity of Unjust Enrichment

THIS CHAPTER CONSIDERS the academic literature that seeks to explain the obligation rule. It suggests that almost all such academic accounts rely on the 'subsidiarity' of unjust enrichment (Section I). They presume that unjust enrichment claims are subsidiary to other legal events and must therefore give way to those in cases of conflict. It then argues that a general doctrine according to which unjust enrichment claims are hierarchically inferior to other private law obligations is indefensible in English law (Section II).[1]

I. ACADEMIC EXPLANATIONS

Subsidiarity has only rarely been expressly articulated as an explanation for the relationship between unjust enrichment claims and countervailing legal obligations. However, many accounts of that relationship presume subsidiarity. Academic literature features four prominent examples of this, which I will call the 'contradiction explanation', the 'circularity explanation', the 'absence of basis explanation' and the 'consent explanation'. They are examined in turn below.[2]

A. The Contradiction Explanation

Example 1: C owes D £100. The debt is time-barred. Intending to discharge the debt, although unaware that the debt is no longer enforceable, C pays £100 to D. D accepts

[1] See generally, Brice Dickson, 'Contract and Restitution: A Few Comparative Remarks' in Francis Rose (ed), *Failure of Contracts: Contractual, Restitutionary and Proprietary Consequences* (Oxford, Hart, 1997) 246; Stephen Swann, 'The Structure of Liability for Unjustified Enrichment: First Proposals of the Study Group on a European Civil Code' in Reinhard Zimmermann (ed), *Grundstrukturen eines Europäischen Bereicherungsrechts* (Tübingen, Mohr Siebeck, 2005) 277; Daniel Visser, *Unjustified Enrichment* (Cape Town, Juta, 2008) 57; Stephen Waddams, *Dimensions of Private Law: Categories and Concepts in Anglo-American Legal Reasoning* (Cambridge, Cambridge University Press, 2003) 170.

[2] Burrows has made a significant contribution to this debate: see Andrew Burrows, 'Is There a Defence of Good Consideration?' in Charles Mitchell and William Swadling (eds), *The Restatement Third, Restitution and Unjust Enrichment: Critical and Comparative Essays* (Oxford, Hart, 2013). His analysis was adopted by the Supreme Court in *International Energy Group Ltd v Zurich*

the payment in discharge of the debt. Realising the mistake, C seeks restitution from D. C's claim will not succeed.[3]

On one view, denying restitution in Example 1 is necessary to protect the integrity of D's legal entitlement. According to Friedmann, C's claim is in 'direct conflict with the very concept that [C] was under an obligation to make the payment in the first place'.[4] Permitting restitution will therefore 'nullify'[5] that obligation, which is impermissible. Beatson echoes this view.[6] According to Barker, similarly, it would be a 'self-contradiction'[7] for the law to permit restitution in Example 1.

With respect, none of these claims withstand scrutiny. They simply raise the question: why is D's legal entitlement to the enrichment normatively superior to C's unjust enrichment claim? Consider Friedmann's reasoning first. He contends that C's claim for restitution will 'nullify' D's legal entitlement. But would the denial of restitution not amount to D's legal entitlement 'nullifying' C's claim for restitution? It is unclear why that is thought to be less problematic.

Similarly, although Barker's claim of self-contradiction is correct, there are two ways of untying that knot. The assertion that this must be done by prioritising the defendant's entitlement over the claimant's restitution claim requires additional justification. Beatson admits this difficulty when he observes that 'a restitution claim in this situation would *either* nullify the contractual obligation, *or* if subject to a contractual defence, be pointless'.[8] The critical question is why the law must prioritise the legal obligation over the restitution claim. The contradiction explanation does not answer that question. Instead, it simply presumes that the unjust enrichment claim is subsidiary to the legal obligation.

B. The Circularity Explanation

Example 2: C owes £100 each to D and X. C intended to pay X but mistakenly paid D. C's claim for restitution from D will fail.[9]

Insurance plc [2015] UKSC 33, [2015] 2 WLR 1471. Burrows's approach was examined in Chapter 4, Section IV.

[3] *Moses v Macferlan* (1760) 2 Burr 1005, 97 ER 676; *Bize v Dickason* (1786) 1 Term Rep 285, 99 ER 1097.

[4] Daniel Friedmann, 'Valid, Voidable, Qualified, and Non-Existing Obligations: An Alternative Perspective on the Law of Restitution' in Andrew Burrows (ed), *Essays on the Law of Restitution* (Oxford, Clarendon, 1991) 248.

[5] ibid.

[6] Jack Beatson, 'The Temptation of Elegance: Concurrence of Restitutionary and Contractual Claims' in William Swadling and Gareth Jones (eds), *The Search for Principle: Essays in Honour of Lord Goff of Chieveley* (Oxford, Oxford University Press, 1999) 153.

[7] Kit Barker, 'Bona Fide Purchase as a Defence to Unjust Enrichment Claims: A Concise Restatement' [1999] Restitution Law Review 75, 88.

[8] Beatson (n 6) 153 (emphasis added).

[9] Based on dicta in *Platt v Bromage* (1854) 24 LJ Ex 63, 65. See also, Andrew Burrows, *A Restatement of the English Law of Unjust Enrichment* (Oxford, Oxford University Press, 2012) 32–33.

In response to C's claim for restitution of £100, D may demand £100 from C based on the debt owed by C to D. This is the basis of the circularity reasoning. It suggests that the denial of restitution in Example 2 is 'required in order to break the circularity of holding a party contractually liable to confer a benefit which the law of restitution requires the other party to return'.[10] There are two potential objections to this reasoning.

First, as Stevens argues, the circularity reasoning 'does not explain at which point the circle should be broken'.[11] As Webb says, 'if the problem is merely one of circularity, it could just as well be solved by denying the initial obligation to make the transfer'.[12] In order to assess whether this objection is fatal to the circularity explanation, it is necessary to formulate the circularity explanation more precisely.

In Example 2, the circularity argument may be made in one of two ways. One of those is as follows:

> *Circularity 1*: The restitution claim requires D to pay C £100. The debt owed by C to D means that C must pay D £100. Unless C's claim is denied, these claims will go on in endless circles.

The rejection of Circularity 1 by Stevens and Webb is persuasive. The infinite circle of claims between C and D may equally be cut at the point where C receives restitution of £100 from D. Circularity 1 does not explain why the law must stop the circle by prioritising C's debt to D.

However, the circularity explanation may be formulated in a different way:

> *Circularity 2*: Even if C's claim for restitution of £100 from D succeeds, C will immediately be required to restore £100 to D by virtue of D's entitlement. C's claim is, therefore, pointless. Hence, it must be dismissed.

According to Circularity 2, there are no endless circles in Example 2. There are only two claims. Step 1 is a claim by C against D for restitution of £100. If this claim succeeds, step 2 is a claim by D against C for £100 based on C's debt to D. The existence of D's counter-claim renders C's claim redundant.

Lord Hope's speech in *Deutsche Morgan Grenfell Group Plc* supports Circularity 2.[13] Lord Hope said:[14]

> At what point can it be said that the payee has been unjustly enriched? The answer … will depend on the facts of the case. One can leave on one side cases where there

[10] Andrew Burrows, 'Solving the Problem of Concurrent Liability' (1995) 48 Current Legal Problems 103, 111. See also, Niamh Connolly, 'A Common Law Perspective on the Concurrence of Claims in Contract and Unjust Enrichment' (2014) 22 European Review of Private Law 1005, 1015.

[11] Robert Stevens, 'Is There a Law of Unjust Enrichment?' in Simone Degeling and James Edelman (eds), *Unjust Enrichment in Commercial Law* (Sydney, Thomson Reuters, 2008) 23.

[12] Charlie Webb, *Reason and Restitution: A Theory of Unjust Enrichment* (Oxford, Oxford University Press, 2016) 151–152.

[13] *Deutsche Morgan Grenfell Group Plc v Inland Revenue Commissioners* [2006] UKHL 49, [2007] 1 AC 558 ('*DMG*').

[14] ibid [65] (Lord Hope) (emphasis added).

is another ground on which the payee was entitled to be paid: *frustra petis quod mox restiturus es*.

'*Frustra petis quod mox restiturus es*' is the maxim that one ought not to seek in vain that which one must immediately restore.[15] The decision in *Post Office v Hampshire County Council*[16] illustrates its application. In that case, the employees of the defendant council were engaged in draining water off the road when they plunged a crowbar into a grass-verge and damaged the claimant post office's underground cables. The claimant sought compensation for the damaged cables. The claim was based on the defendant's employees' negligence. The Council contended that its employees' decision to dig over the grass-verge was based on negligent advice from the claimant's employees who had incorrectly informed the workers that the cables lay under the carriageway, not on the grass-verge. Rejecting the post office's claim, Ormrod LJ held:[17]

> I accept without hesitation … that on the authorities this is a classic example of the circuity of action situation and that consequently a defendant to a claim … can rely by way of defence on facts which indicate that had he brought a counterclaim he would have been entitled in law to recover from the Post Office as damages for negligence the sum claimed against him by the Post Office. Consequently I accept … that Hampshire County Council has not only a valid counterclaim but a valid defence to the claim in this case.

When viewed against this backdrop, it is apparent that Stevens and Webb's reasoning is not a persuasive objection to Circularity 2. Circularity 2 suggests that the correct analysis of Example 2 is as follows. Just as in *Hampshire County Council*, there is no possibility of an endless circle of claims in Example 2. Example 2 may be analysed in two steps. Step 1 is a claim by C against D based on C's mistake. Step 2 is a claim by D against C based on the debt owed by C to D. There is no possibility of a further claim by C against D. This is because C's payment in step 2 was not mistaken. Nor is there any other unjust factor that would support a further claim by C against D.

The same analysis applies even if C's restitution claim was based on failure of consideration.

> *Example 3*: C contracted to buy 100 widgets from D. The price, £100, was to be paid in advance. C paid this sum. Subsequently, D failed to deliver the widgets. C seeks restitution of £100 from D.

In this example, step 1 is a claim by C for restitution of £100 from D. In step 2, D claims £100 from C based on D's contractual entitlement.[18] There is no unjust factor justifying a further claim by C. C may argue that it has a further

[15] John Trayner, *Trayner's Latin Maxims* (4th edn, London, Sweet & Maxwell, 1993) 232.

[16] *Post Office v Hampshire County Council* [1980] QB 124 (CA).

[17] ibid 136 (emphasis added).

[18] Whether £100 is due to D despite the non-delivery of the widgets is a question of contractual construction. For the present purposes, it is assumed that it is.

failure of consideration claim. But this is incorrect. The 'consideration' for C's primary payment was C's expectation that D will deliver the widgets. However, that is not the basis for C's second payment. The second payment was made to fulfil C's contractual obligation to D. That basis never failed and, consequently, no further failure of consideration claim is available to C.

Thus, although Stevens and Webb's rejection of Circularity 1 is correct, their reasoning does not withstand scrutiny as an objection to Circularity 2. However, there is a second objection which is persuasive, and fatal, to both Circularity 1 and Circularity 2. That objection is that neither formulation can explain why the rule denying restitution in Example 2 operates when D's legal entitlement is valid but unenforceable.[19] Consider Example 1 again:

> *Example 1:* C owes D £100. The debt is time-barred. Intending to discharge the debt, although unaware that the debt is no longer enforceable, C pays £100 to D. D accepts the payment in discharge of the debt. Realising the mistake, C seeks restitution from D.

There is no possibility of an endless of circle of claims here. Nor can D assert a counterclaim against C so as to attract the *frustra petis* rule. Thus, the circularity explanation cannot explain why C's restitution claim fails. It must therefore be rejected.

C. The Absence of Basis Explanation

It has been suggested that absence of basis is a necessary, though not sufficient, condition for restitution.[20] On this analysis, the presence of a valid basis has been offered as an explanation for the obligation rule. As Virgo puts it, the argument is that:[21]

> [I]f there is a lawful basis for the defendant's receipt of an enrichment, restitution should be denied because there is no reason why the law of restitution should undermine a lawful transfer. It is consequently preferable to recognize that if there is a legally effective basis for the transfer of a benefit to the defendant a claim in unjust enrichment should be denied.

Virgo calls this the 'presence of basis' bar.[22] On this account, the presence of a legal basis operates by denying a primary element that constitutes the defendant's unjust enrichment.[23]

[19] Stevens (n 11) 23.

[20] Whether a full-fledged absence of basis model can explain the obligation rule is considered in Conclusion, Section II.

[21] Graham Virgo, *The Principles of the Law of Restitution* (3rd edn, Oxford, Oxford University Press, 2015) 133.

[22] Graham Virgo, 'Demolishing the Pyramid – the Presence of Basis and Risk-Taking in the Law of Unjust Enrichment' in Andrew Robertson and Tang Wu (eds), *The Goals of Private Law* (Oxford, Hart, 2009) 488–504.

[23] Virgo, *The Principles of the Law of Restitution* (n 21) 133.

Virgo's reasoning fails to resolve a fundamental issue. Assuming (as Virgo does[24]) that the English law of unjust enrichment operates on the basis of unjust factors, why is the presence of a valid basis normatively relevant? With respect, Virgo's analysis neglects this issue entirely. Edelman and Bant consider this question in their commentary. They say:[25]

> There is a simple reason in principle why the law requires, in addition to an unjust factor, a lack of juristic reason for a plaintiff to retain an enrichment. That reason is the coherence of the law … [T]he law would be internally contradictory if one branch of the law held that a defendant had a right to an enrichment and another held that the defendant must give back the enrichment.

This reasoning suffers from the same flaw as the contradiction explanation and the circularity explanation. There is no doubt that the law must be internally coherent. But what is needed to explain the obligation rule is a justification for why coherence is achieved by prioritising the defendant's legal entitlement over the claimant's unjust enrichment claim. It is equally possible to achieve coherence by prioritising the unjust enrichment claim. As Stevens observes, 'appeals to coherence take us no further as they do not explain why the apparent contradiction should be resolved one way and not the other'.[26] To rely on the need for consistency in the law to deny a restitution claim is, therefore, to presume the subsidiarity of unjust enrichment without justifying it.

D. The Consent Explanation

Smith offers yet another explanation for the obligation rule. On his account, consent plays a number of different roles within the law of unjust enrichment.[27] It plays a negative role when it impugns transactions that require reversal. Sometimes, however, consent plays a positive role:[28]

> Mistake is about consent, and voluntarily assumed obligations are a way of freezing consent so that it cannot be withdrawn. My earlier voluntary promise to pay $100, so long as it stands, now debars me from deploying any argument based on voluntariness at the time of the payment. I cannot raise my mistake as showing that I did not mean to enrich you, when I have voluntarily and irrevocably bound myself to enrich you. In a case like this, the mistake would have to be one that undermines the earlier promise, a principle with which everyone is familiar.

[24] ibid ch 6.

[25] James Edelman and Elise Bant, *Unjust Enrichment* (2nd edn, Oxford, Hart, 2016) 134.

[26] Robert Stevens, *The Laws of Restitution* (Oxford, Oxford University Press, 2023) 85.

[27] Lionel Smith, 'Unjust Enrichment: Big or Small?' in Simone Degeling and James Edelman (eds), *Unjust Enrichment in Commercial Law* (Pyrmont, Lawbook Co, 2008) 36–46.

[28] ibid 39. See also, Webb (n 12) 152 ('in obligatory enrichments, the claimant no longer has a choice').

This reasoning suffers from two flaws. First, Smith's explanation presupposes an antecedent positive manifestation of the claimant's consent. This confines its explanatory scope to cases where the claimant voluntarily assumed the obligation it owed the defendant. However, as demonstrated below,[29] the scope of the obligation rule is not restricted in this way. It applies even if the legal obligation was not voluntarily assumed by the claimant.

Second, Smith fails to explain why the voluntarily assumed countervailing obligation gets priority over the unjust enrichment claim. Smith accepts that the law of unjust enrichment is concerned with protection of the claimant's consent against dispositions that are not supported by its fully effective consent. In substance, therefore, Smith is pitting one consent-based obligation (the restitution claim) against another (the defendant's entitlement) and asserting the superiority of the latter. In doing so, he, like many other academic commentators, is presuming the subsidiarity of unjust enrichment without justifying that assumption.

II. SUBSIDIARITY IN THE ENGLISH LAW OF UNJUST ENRICHMENT

Section I demonstrated that most explanations for the obligation rule presume the subsidiarity of unjust enrichment. This section will examine whether a general doctrine of subsidiarity is defensible in English law. It will be suggested that it is not.

One of the biggest hurdles in the way of a clear examination of subsidiarity is terminology.[30] In the context of unjust enrichment, subsidiarity has been used in many different senses.[31] In particular, two distinct uses of that term are prominent in academic writing. In their influential work on the subject, Grantham and Rickett define subsidiarity as:[32]

> the relationship between two claims or doctrines where the scope and operation of one claim are constrained by another claim, even where all the elements of the former claim are made out. At its weakest, subsidiarity denotes the subordination of one claim where another claim in fact offers the plaintiff a basis of recovery. At its strongest, subsidiarity denies the availability of a claim because another claim is in principle available, even though on the facts it does not avail the plaintiff.

[29] See Chapter 5, Section II(A) above.

[30] Charles Mitchell, Paul Mitchell and Stephen Watterson, *Goff & Jones: The Law of Unjust Enrichment* (10th edn, London, Sweet & Maxwell, 2022) [2-04]; Visser, *Unjustified Enrichment* (n 1) 57; Daniel Visser, 'Unjustified Enrichment' in Jan Smits (ed), *Elgar Encyclopedia of Comparative Law* (Cheltenham, Edward Elgar 2012) 951–952; Steve Hedley, 'Unjust Enrichment: A Middle Course?' (2002) 2 Oxford University Commonwealth Law Journal 181, 190.

[31] John Dawson, *Unjust Enrichment: A Comparative Analysis* (Buffalo, William S Hein, 1999) 106.

[32] Ross Grantham and Charles Rickett, 'On the Subsidiarity of Unjust Enrichment' (2001) 117 Law Quarterly Review 273.

The authors appear to have in mind cases where the claimant has two avenues for recovery, one of which is based on unjust enrichment. There is an obvious difference between these cases and the cases in which the obligation rule operates. In the former, the competing claims are both available to the claimant against the defendant. By contrast, in cases where the obligation rule operates, the potential claims oppose each other. The claimant has an unjust enrichment claim against the defendant and the defendant has a (non-restitution) claim against the claimant.

The terminology of subsidiarity has also been employed to characterise the relationship between such opposing claims. *Goff and Jones* uses subsidiarity in this sense.[33] For the present purposes, we are only concerned with the second meaning of subsidiarity ie as a rule of priority between opposing claims. The remainder of this section will use subsidiarity in that sense.

The academic literature suggests that the positive case for subsidiarity rests on two considerations: (a) the primacy of individual autonomy over unjust enrichment claims; and (b) insights from other legal systems where unjust enrichment is a subsidiary doctrine. On analysis, neither consideration offers a proper basis for a doctrine of subsidiarity in English law.

A. Primacy of Individual Autonomy

Grantham and Rickett rely on the need to protect individual autonomy and choice to justify the subsidiarity of unjust enrichment in English law:[34]

> The Anglo-American liberal democratic political tradition accords primacy to individual autonomy and choice. The fundamental consequence of that tradition, for the legal system, is that various interests are positively protected ... while unjust enrichment is shown to be operative only in a negative sense ... That distinction makes unjust enrichment necessarily a subsidiary legal standard.

This analysis suffers from two flaws. First, this reasoning only applies if the countervailing obligation arose out of a voluntary arrangement such as a contract. However, it will be demonstrated below that the operation of the obligation rule is not confined in this way. Second, even where the countervailing legal obligation arises out of a contract, subsidiarity faces insuperable problems.

Taking the second objection first, the notion of hierarchy between legal obligations does not accurately describe the relationship between contractual obligations and unjust enrichment.[35] As Waddams convincingly demonstrates,

[33] Mitchell, Mitchell and Watterson (n 30) [2-01]–[2-06].

[34] Grantham and Rickett, 'On the Subsidiarity of Unjust Enrichment' (n 32) 274. See also, Joachin Dietrich, 'Quantum Meruit for Services Rendered in a Three-party Context: (Implied) Contract, Restitution, or Unjust Enrichment?' [2009] Restitution Law Review 98, 102; Ross Grantham and Charles Rickett, *Enrichment and Restitution in New Zealand* (Oxford, Hart, 2000) 52.

[35] Mitchell, Mitchell and Watterson (n 30) [2-04].

contract and restitution perform a complementary rather than a subsidiary role.[36] This is illustrated by cases that have awarded restitution within subsisting contracts. The decision of the High Court of Australia in *Roxborough v Rothmans of Pall Mall Australia Ltd*[37] is an example. As explained in Chapter 4 of this book, in that case, the existence of an agreed regime of allocation of risks between the parties did not preclude restitution.[38]

Consider another illustration:

> *Example 4*: C contracts with D for the supply of oil. The contract provides that: (a) D will supply 10 barrels of oil each month at the rate of £10,000 for each barrel; (b) payment is due on the 5th of each month; (c) oil is to be delivered on the 15th of each month. C paid on 5 September, but D failed to deliver oil on 15 September. C wishes to recover the payment but is keen to continue the contract for future months.[39]

The preferable view is that C may bring a claim for restitution of one month's payment. The best explanation for this result is that, although C's payment was due on 5 September, D did not earn an accrued right to that payment until she rendered counter-performance.[40] Whether this is the case is a question of contractual construction. But, generally, D's counter-performance will be a condition precedent for D to earn the payment.[41] Whether or not the contract is subsisting or terminated, it is this analysis that determines whether restitution is available.[42] The notions of subsidiarity and primacy are too simplistic to capture the complex relationship between restitution and contractual obligations. As Smith explains:[43]

> It begins to appear that unjustified enrichment is not actually subsidiary to contract law ... To say that there can be no claim in unjustified enrichment so long as there is a subsisting contract is to make a slightly inaccurate generalization by aiming at a false target.

In response to this analysis, proponents of subsidiarity may argue that the problems outlined above arise from a misguided focus on the contract as a whole.

[36] Stephen Waddams, 'Contract and Unjust Enrichment: Competing Categories, or Complementary Concepts?' in Peter Birks, Charles Rickett and Ross Grantham (eds), *Structure and Justification in Private Law: Essays for Peter Birks* (Oxford, Hart, 2008) 172.

[37] *Roxborough v Rothmans of Pall Mall Australia Ltd* [2001] HCA 68, (2001) 208 CLR 516.

[38] See Chapter 4, Section I above.

[39] Andrew Tettenborn, 'Subsisting Contracts and Failure of Consideration: A Little Scepticism' [2002] Restitution Law Review 1, 3. See also, Stevens (n 11) 29.

[40] Edelman and Bant articulate this point slightly differently. According to them, D may have a right to *receive* the payment, but not a right to *retain* it: see Edelman and Bant (n 25) 135.

[41] For a contrary example see, *Ministry of Sound (Ireland) Limited v World Online Limited* [2003] EWHC 2178 (Ch), [2003] 2 All ER (Comm) 823 [33].

[42] Stevens (n 11) 24–30; Waddams, 'Contract and Unjust Enrichment: Competing Categories, or Complementary Concepts?' (n 36) 173–175.

[43] Lionel Smith, 'Property, Subsidiarity, and Unjust Enrichment' in David Johnston and Reinhard Zimmermann (eds), *Unjustified Enrichment: Key Issues in Comparative Perspective* (Cambridge, Cambridge University Press, 2010) 615.

One must, it may be said, focus on the specific contractual obligation. Let us now consider that possibility by comparing two examples.

> *Example 5.1*: C contracts to buy 1000 widgets from D. Under the contract, £1000, a part of the purchase price, was payable in advance. C paid this sum. Subsequently, before delivery, D repudiated the contract. C accepts D's repudiation and seeks restitution of £1000.[44]
>
> *Example 5.2*: C contracts to buy 1000 widgets from D. C pays £1000 as advance purchase price. Subsequently, before delivery could take place, C repudiated the contract. D declines to accept C's repudiation.[45]

D's termination does not retrospectively wipe away C's contractual obligations in Example 5.1. Yet, it is clear that C's claim for restitution will succeed in that example.[46] Why is C entitled to restitution of £1,000 although that payment was made based on C's contractual obligation? In response, Burrows suggests that termination has the effect of rendering the contractual allocation of risks ineffective. Consequently, after termination in Example 5.1, he argues, there is no conflict between C's restitution claim and the contract.[47] The better view is that termination does not retrospectively disturb the parties' allocation of risks.[48] In any event, Burrows's explanation does not apply to Example 5.2. In that case, C's termination is not accepted by D. Accordingly, C's termination is legally ineffective[49] and the parties' contractual obligations remain on foot. But should D be able to preclude C's restitution claim infinitely by simply refusing to put an end to the contract? The answer must surely be 'no'. In the end, therefore, we are forced to conclude that restitution may operate despite the subsistence of C's contractual obligations.

Now consider the first objection, which concerns the explanatory scope of the personal autonomy reasoning. The authorities make it clear that the obligation rule is not confined to cases where the countervailing obligation is voluntarily assumed. Consider, for instance, Lord Hope's dictum in *Kleinwort Benson*:[50]

> The third question arises because the payee cannot be said to have been unjustly enriched if he was entitled to receive the sum paid to him. The payer may have been mistaken … but his mistake will not provide a ground for its recovery if the payee can show that he was entitled to it on some other ground.

[44] For a similar illustration see, Example 8 in Burrows, *A Restatement of the English Law of Unjust Enrichment* (n 9) 34.

[45] Tettenborn (n 39) 2.

[46] *Giles v Edwards* (1797) 7 Term Reports 181, 101 ER 920; *Fibrosa Spolka Akcyjna v Fairbairn Lawson Combe Barbour Ltd* [1943] AC 32 (HL).

[47] Andrew Burrows, *The Law of Restitution* (3rd edn, Oxford, Oxford University Press, 2011) 90.

[48] John Carter, 'Restitution and Contract Risk' in Mitchell McInnes (ed), *Restitution: Developments in Unjust Enrichment* (LBC Information Services, 1996) 157.

[49] *Howard v Pickford Tool Co Ltd* [1951] 1 KB 417 (CA).

[50] *Kleinwort Benson Ltd v Lincoln City Council* [1998] UKHL 38, [1999] 2 AC 349, 408.

Lord Hope did not suggest that this analysis was confined to contractual entitlements. On the contrary, his reasoning in *DMG* confirms that he did not intend to restrict the application of this rule in that way:[51]

> At what point can it be said that the payee has been unjustly enriched? The answer to [this] question will depend on the facts of the case. One can leave on one side cases where there is another ground on which the payee was entitled to be paid: *frustra petis quod mox restiturus es*.

An earlier section of this chapter identified an important limitation of Lord Hope's reasoning based on the *frustra petis* rule.[52] However, his reliance on this analysis suggests that he did not intend to confine the application of the obligation rule to countervailing legal obligations that have a consensual origin.

Burrows's *Restatement* also affords a wide scope to the obligation rule. It says that the rule applies to 'valid contractual, statutory or other legal obligations'.[53] Similarly, Friedmann considers the rule applicable 'irrespective of whether the obligation arises under a statute or was imposed by the common law or the rules of equity'.[54]

There is ample support in authority for the view that the defendant's contractual right to receive the enrichment precludes restitution.[55] Statutory entitlements have the same effect.[56] On principle, the same must be true of obligations owed to the defendant that arise out of civil wrongs.[57] This is confirmed by the decision of the South Australian Supreme Court in *Re Magarey Farlam*.[58]

The claimants were partners of a solicitors' firm. One of the firm's employees had misappropriated funds from the firm's trust account. When the partners found out about the defalcations they paid $93,000 into the account. This was intended to replenish funds belonging to eight clients of the firm who were thought to be victims of the misappropriation. Subsequently, it turned out that the claimants had underestimated both the quantum of misappropriation as well as the number of its victims. Upon discovering this, they sought restitution of the amount that they had paid into the firm's account. It was argued

[51] *DMG* (HL) (n 13) [65].

[52] See Chapter 5, Section I(B) above.

[53] Burrows, *A Restatement of the English Law of Unjust Enrichment* (n 9) 31. See also, Keith Mason, John Carter and Gregory Tolhurst, *Mason & Carter's Restitution Law in Australia* (2nd edn, Melbourne, LexisNexis Butterworths, 2008) 439–440; Carter (n 48) 143.

[54] Friedmann (n 4) 248. See also, *David Securities v Commonwealth Bank of Australia* [1992] HCA 48, (1992) 175 CLR 353, 388–389 (Brennan J) ('If a defendant has a right to receive a payment, whether under a statute, in discharge of a liability owing to him or pursuant to a contract a mistake by the plaintiff in making the payment does not convert the receipt into an unjust enrichment.').

[55] *Steam Saw Mills Company Ltd v Baring Brothers* [1922] 1 Ch 244 (CA); *Fairfield Sentry Ltd (In Liquidation) v Migani* [2014] UKPC 9, [2014] 1 CLC 611.

[56] *Test Claimants in the FII Group Litigation v Revenue & Customs Commissioners* [2010] EWCA Civ 103, [2010] STC 1251 [181] (Arden LJ).

[57] The legal entitlements that may preclude a claim in restitution through the operation of the obligation rule are considered in Chapter 8.

[58] *Re Magarey Farlam Lawyers Trust Accounts (No 3)* [2007] SASC 9, 96 SASR 337.

that this payment was caused by a mistake as to the extent of the fraud. Among other grounds, the Court denied restitution on the basis that the payment was owed to the defendants. The defendants' legal entitlement to those sums was said to be based on the claimants' vicarious liability for the defaulting employee's wrongdoing. Debelle J held:

> [A] payment cannot be recovered if, in fact, the payer is liable to the payee … Mr Howard submitted that the partners of Magarey Farlam were vicariously liable to the eight clients who had together lost $93,000.[59]
>
> [T]he partners are vicariously liable for the fraudulent activities of [the defaulting employee]. That liability is a further bar to the claim by the partners to recover the sum of $93,000.[60]

Debelle J's reasoning confirms that the obligation rule operates even if the countervailing entitlement is not a contractual obligation. However, the explanatory scope of the personal autonomy reasoning is confined to cases where the defendant's entitlement has a consensual origin. It cannot explain the application of the obligation rule in cases where the legal obligation was not voluntarily assumed by the claimant. The personal autonomy reasoning is, therefore, an insufficient basis upon which to conclude that the English law of unjust enrichment is a subsidiary doctrine.

B. Subsidiarity in Other Jurisdictions

Subsidiarity of unjust enrichment has been expressly adopted in at least three legal systems: France, Italy and Scotland.[61] This section examines the law in these jurisdictions. In broad terms, there are two reasons why English law must not follow them. First, in all three jurisdictions, subsidiarity is used in the first sense, ie as a rule of priority between two alternative claims available to a claimant. Subsidiarity in that sense does not assist in explaining the obligation rule. Second, the operation of subsidiarity in these jurisdictions is attributable to unique features of those legal systems that are not reflected in English law.

Subsidiarity originated in France. It was a judicial creation, first adopted by the *Cour de cassation* in the *Clayette* case.[62] In that case, the Court held:[63]

> The action de in rem verso … should be allowed whenever the patrimony of one person is enriched at the expense of that of another person without legitimate cause

[59] ibid [177].

[60] ibid [183].

[61] For a general survey of the application of subsidiarity in Eastern Europe, see Ewa Łętowska, 'Unjust Enrichment in Eastern European Countries' in Ernst Caemmerer and Peter Schlechtreim (eds), *International Encyclopedia of Comparative Law*, vol X (The Hague, Martinus Nijhoff, 1995) 22–31.

[62] *Clayette case* S1918141, 12 May 1914 (French Court of Cassation).

[63] ibid cited in J Beatson and EJH Schrage, *Cases, Materials and Texts on Unjustified Enrichment* (Oxford, Hart, 2003) 427.

> and ... that other person does not have at his disposal, to obtain what is due to him, any action arising from a contract, a quasi-contract, a delict or a quasi-delict.

Academic opinion in France largely mirrors this view. The subsidiary status of restitution is often justified on the basis of the need to prevent the 'subversion of the legal order'.[64] Unless tightly confined, it is feared, unjustified enrichment would undermine the 'normal legal rules' of the system.[65] Nicholas goes so far as to say that subsidiarity is necessary to prevent unjustified enrichment from perpetrating a 'fraud on the law'.[66]

When viewed through the common law lens, this analysis seems unpersuasive. Why is unjustified enrichment treated as an external legal event? Why does it 'subvert' rather than contribute to the 'normal' rules of the legal system? As Smith points out, what is missing is an account of why other legal obligations receive precedence over unjustified enrichment.[67] For this, one must look elsewhere.

When one does so, it is apparent that the subsidiary status of unjustified enrichment in French law is based on its 'extra-codal nature'.[68] There is no direct basis for a general doctrine of unjustified enrichment in the French Civil Code.[69] It was created and evolved almost entirely by the courts. This is remarkable in a civilian jurisdiction such as France where, as a general rule, judges are required to base their decisions upon legislation, not precedents.[70] This is especially so since almost all other private law obligations find their genesis in the French Civil Code. Therefore, French judges felt that unjustified enrichment should be invoked only if no remedy was available within the Civil Code.[71] The real concern appears to have been that an action in unjustified enrichment would subvert the structure of the Civil Code.

This view is confirmed by an examination of the small pockets of the law of unjustified enrichment that *are* provided for in the French Civil Code.

[64] CM Jooste, 'Compensation for Improvements by Tenants in South African Law' in EJH Schrage (ed), *Unjust Enrichment and the Law of Contract* (Alphen aan den Rijn, Kluwer Law International, 2001) 270. See also, Aimite Jorge, 'The Subsidiarity Rule: The Unjust Enrichment Doctrine in Construction Law' (2013) 5 International Journal of Law in the Built Environment 253, 253.

[65] Gerrit F Van Maanen, 'Subsidiarity of the Action for Unjustified Enrichment – French Law and Dutch Law: Different Solutions for the Same Problem' (2006) 14 European Review of Private Law 409, 414.

[66] Barry Nicholas, 'Unjustified Enrichment in the Civil Law and Loiusiana Law' (1962) 36 Tulane Law Review 605, 610.

[67] Smith, 'Property, Subsidiarity, and Unjust Enrichment' (n 43) 609. See also, Daniel Visser, 'Concurrence of Enrichment and Contractual Claims' (2000) 117 South African Law Journal 173, 175.

[68] Hector MacQueen, 'Unjustified Enrichment, Subsidiarity and Contract' in Vernon Palmer and Elspeth Reid (eds), *Mixed Jurisdictions Compared: Private Law in Louisiana and Scotland* (Edinburgh, Edinburgh University, 2009) 323. See also, Nicholas (n 66) 639.

[69] Beatson and Schrage (n 63) 423.

[70] Albert Tate, 'The Loiusiana Action for Unjustified Enrichment: A Study in Judicial Process' (1976–1977) 51 Tulane Law Review 446, 457–458.

[71] ibid.

The 'action for a thing not due' is an example. It is revealing that subsidiarity is inapplicable to this category of cases.[72] In short, subsidiarity in French law is best understood as a doctrine that stands for the 'superiority of the written law over the unwritten law'.[73] Clearly, this cannot justify subsidiarity of the English law of unjust enrichment.

There is a further reason why we must not transplant the doctrine of subsidiarity from France to England. Its application in practice has led to numerous difficulties in France.[74] These difficulties have led French commentators to suggest that the doctrine should be abandoned altogether. Viney, for instance, has argued that:[75]

> [S]hould one conclude that the principle of subsidiarity of this action has disappeared or that it survives in an attenuated form? If one opted for the second thesis, one would have to propose a new criterion, which might be inspired by the idea that the action de in rem verso should not be an obstacle to the application of the normal rules applicable to the situation envisaged. But what are these 'normal rules'? It would take the devil to answer that question. It seems better simply to abandon this hazy notion of subsidiarity which was only invented to reduce the scope of the innovation introduced by the *arret Boudier*.

The doctrine of subsidiarity has followed a similar trajectory in Italy. The Italian Civil Code expressly provides for the subsidiarity of unjustified enrichment.[76] This is unsurprising since, on this issue, the draftsmen of the Italian Civil Code were heavily inspired by judicial developments in France.[77] Moreover, even in Italy, the doctrine of unjustified enrichment evolved extra-codally.[78] Subsequently, when it was codified, it retained its subsidiary nature.

The general trend in jurisdictions such as Italy and France stands in stark contrast to the law in some other civilian jurisdictions, such as Germany and Netherlands. Germany does not adopt a notion of priority between unjust enrichment claims and other private law obligations.[79] Although the position is less clear in Dutch law, the predominant view is against subsidiarity.[80]

[72] Smith, 'Property, Subsidiarity, and Unjust Enrichment' (n 43) 622.

[73] George Challies, *The Doctrine of Unjustified Enrichment in the Law of the Province of Quebec* (2nd edn, Montreal, Wilson & Lafleur, 1952) 125.

[74] See Beatson and Schrage (n 63) 428–429.

[75] 'Viney's Note' cited in ibid 438 (emphasis added). See also, Maanen (n 65) 416.

[76] Italian Civil Code, art 2042 cited in Beatson and Schrage (n 63) 452.

[77] Konrad Zweigert and Hein Kötz, *Introduction to Comparative Law* (Tony Weir trs, 3rd rev edn, Oxford, Clarendon Press, 1998) 550; Francesco Giglio, 'A Systematic Approach to "Unjust" and "Unjustified" Enrichment' (2003) 23 Oxford Journal of Legal Studies 455, 464.

[78] Smith, 'Property, Subsidiarity, and Unjust Enrichment' (n 43) 622. See also, Stewart McCaa Thomas, 'Conditions for the Application of Actio De In Rem Verso' (1975) 36 Louisiana Law Review 312, 313 (explaining that the same analysis applies to the doctrine of subsidiarity in the law in Louisiana).

[79] Reinhard Zimmermann and Jacques Du Plessis, 'Basic Features of the German Law of Unjustified Enrichment' [1994] Restitution Law Review 14, 37. See also, Beatson and Schrage (n 63) 424.

[80] Beatson and Schrage (n 63) 458, 459; Eltjo Schrage, '*Cellcorps v ETE*: A Dutch Perspective' (2014) 22 European Review of Private Law 1039, 1047.

As explained above, in France and Italy, subsidiarity is based on the extra-codal nature of unjustified enrichment. By contrast, in both Germany[81] and in the Netherlands,[82] the respective Civil Codes provide for a general action based on unjustified enrichment.

Courts in Scotland have also adopted subsidiarity. The leading decision is *Varney v Lanark Town Council*.[83] In that case, the claimants were building contractors. The defendant local authority was under a statutory duty to provide sewers for buildings. In breach of this duty, the defendant failed to construct a drainage system. The claimants constructed the sewers themselves and sued the defendants for recompense. Had the claimants not constructed them, it was argued, the defendant would have had to incur the expenditure for their construction. Thus, it was said, the defendants were enriched. The claim failed. It was held that the claimants should have first exercised their statutory remedy to compel the defendant to perform its duty. In reaching that conclusion two judges relied on subsidiarity. The subsidiarity of unjust enrichment was said to be based on its 'equitable' character:[84]

> [I]n principle, I cannot see how an equitable remedy can be invoked when another remedy given by statute or, indeed, by common law was available and was not used.[85]

> Recompense is an equitable doctrine. That being so, it becomes a sort of court of last resort … If a legal remedy is available at the time when the action which gives rise to the claim for recompense has to be taken, then normally that legal remedy should be pursued to the exclusion of a claim for recompense.[86]

This reasoning was subsequently discredited in Scotland. Unlike England, Scotland does not distinguish between legal and equitable obligations and remedies.[87] The suggestion that the supplementary character of unjust enrichment is based upon its 'equitable'[88] character is, therefore, unpersuasive. This analysis is also inconsistent with the understanding of unjust enrichment in English law where unjust enrichment cuts across the boundary between common law and equity.[89] It is difficult, therefore, to justify the subsidiarity of unjust enrichment based on its equitable nature. The Scottish authorities that

[81] Bürgerliches Gesetzbuch (BGB) §812.
[82] Dutch Civil Code, art 6:212, paragraph 1.
[83] *Varney (Scotland) Ltd v Lanark Town Council* 1974 SC 245 (Second Division).
[84] See also, Dietrich (n 34) 29; Douglas Laycock, 'The Scope and Significance of Restitution' (1988–1989) 67 Texas Law Review 1277, 1278; WDH Sellar, 'Unjust Enrichment' in *The Laws of Scotland: Stair Memorial Encyclopaedia*, vol 15 (Edinburgh, Law Society of Scotland, 1996) [68].
[85] *Varney* (n 83) 257 (Lord Kissen).
[86] ibid 252–253 (Wheatly LJ).
[87] Beatson and Schrage (n 63) 470; MacQueen (n 68) 340; Niall Whitty, '*Transco plc v Glasgow City Council*: Developing Enrichment Law after *Shilliday*' (2006) 10 Edinburgh Law Review 112, 124.
[88] See, Mitchell McInnes, 'The Equitable Action in Unjust Enrichment: Ambiguity and Error' (2007) 45 Canadian Business Law Journal 253.
[89] Burrows, *The Law of Restitution* (n 47) 25–26; Edelman and Bant (n 25) 25–26.

seemingly support the subsidiarity of unjust enrichment are therefore not a good reason for adopting that doctrine in English law.

This chapter explained that most academic accounts of the relationship between unjust enrichment claims and countervailing legal obligations are based on the assumption that unjust enrichment is a subsidiary doctrine. However, a general doctrine according to which the law of unjust enrichment is subsidiary to other private law obligations is indefensible in English law.

6

The Obligation Rule and the Entitlement Thesis

IT WAS EXPLAINED in Chapter 4 that the obligation rule is a bright-line rule rather than a flexible principle. Chapter 5 argued that the prominent academic explanations for the obligation rule do not withstand scrutiny. This chapter and the next advance the positive case. They offer an alternative explanation for the obligation rule.

It will be apparent to the reader from Chapter 5 that the critical challenge is to explain why the defendant's legal entitlement gets precedence over the claimant's unjust enrichment claim. Most academic accounts simply presume that these obligations are ordered hierarchically in favour of the defendant's entitlement. They fail to justify that conclusion.

This book takes the view that the process of explaining the obligation rule must proceed in two steps. First, we must ask: what are the normative reasons that justify a claim based on unjust enrichment? This enquiry can then pave the way for the further question: does the presence of a countervailing legal obligation defeat any of those reasons?

There is no unanimity of views on the normative justification(s) for claims based on unjust enrichment. Nor can this book resolve that issue. Therefore, the approach adopted here is to consider two most prominent accounts of the normative bases for the law of unjust enrichment: the entitlement thesis and the corrective justice theory. It will be considered whether the presence of a countervailing obligation denies the justification for restitution on these accounts.

This chapter will account for the obligation rule by using the framework of the entitlement thesis. Chapter 7 will offer an explanation based on corrective justice theory.

I. THE ENTITLEMENT THESIS

In this book the phrase 'entitlement thesis' is used to refer to a category of normative theories of unjust enrichment. In broad terms, these theories suggest that, in order for an unjust enrichment claim to be normatively justifiable, the defendant's enrichment must have been derived from a pre-existing entitlement of the claimant. Some entitlement theorists consider that the claimant's pre-existing rights must be proprietary in nature, while others do not. This book uses the term 'entitlement thesis' to refer to both categories of theory.

This chapter proceeds in two parts: Section II will outline the positive case for the entitlement thesis and Section III will develop an entitlement-based explanation for the obligation rule. The explanation offered here is based on the need to maintain equality between the claimant and the defendant.

II. THE POSITIVE CASE FOR THE ENTITLEMENT THESIS

> *Example 1*: C mistakenly believed that she owed D £100. Intending to discharge the debt, she paid £100 to D. C is entitled to restitution from D.[1]

Birks considered this the 'core case' of unjust enrichment.[2] 'The law of unjust enrichment', he wrote, 'is the law of all events materially identical to the mistaken payment of a non-existent debt'.[3] What is the normative explanation for C's claim in Example 1?

On one view, the answer is the claimant's defective consent. For example, Birks considered that an enrichment was unjust 'when the claimant had not intended the recipient to have it'.[4] According to Burrows, 'the reason why a mistaken payment ... may be recoverable in unjust enrichment is because the claimant's mistake vitiates his or her intention to benefit [the defendant]'.[5] Similarly, Virgo traces the basis for unjust enrichment claims to individuals' right to self-determination. According to him, restitution is necessary when 'the claimant's decision to act can be considered to have been impaired in some way'.[6]

In *The Law and Ethics of Restitution*,[7] Dagan offers a legal realist's explanation for restitution. Even on that account, the claimant's autonomy occupies the centre-stage:[8]

> [M]istaken payments ... prompt restitution because, and to the extent that, the retention of the wealth by the recipient would undermine the claimant's autonomy and restitution would not unduly infringe on the autonomy of the recipient.

[1] *Kelly v Solari* (1841) 9 M&W 54, 152 ER 24; *Barclays Bank Ltd v WJ Simms Son & Cooke (Southern) Ltd* [1980] QB 677 (QB).

[2] Peter Birks, *Unjust Enrichment* (2nd edn, Oxford, Oxford University Press, 2005) ch 1.

[3] ibid 3.

[4] Birks, *Unjust Enrichment* (n 2) 105; Peter Birks, *An Introduction to the Law of Restitution* (Oxford, Clarendon Press, 1985) 140.

[5] Andrew Burrows, *The Law of Restitution* (3rd edn, Oxford, Oxford University Press, 2011) 87. See also, Lionel Smith, 'Unjust Enrichment: Big or Small?' in Simone Degeling and James Edelman (eds), *Unjust Enrichment in Commercial Law* (Pyrmont, Lawbook Co, 2008) 36, 45; Gerard McMeel, *The Modern Law of Restitution* (London, Blackstone, 2000) 43.

[6] Graham Virgo, *The Principles of the Law of Restitution* (3rd edn, Oxford, Oxford University Press, 2015) 37.

[7] Hanoch Dagan, *The Law and Ethics of Restitution* (Cambridge, Cambridge University Press, 2004) 18. See also, Hanoch Dagan, 'Mistakes' (2001) 79 Texas Law Review 1795.

[8] Dagan, *The Law and Ethics of Restitution* (n 7) 9.

The entitlement thesis challenges the centrality of the claimant's consent. It suggests that, by itself, the claimant's defective consent is normatively inconclusive. It is only determinative when combined with a further element, namely the claimant's entitlement from which the defendant's enrichment is derived. The entitlement theory has a long pedigree. Following Stoljar's pioneering work in the 1960s,[9] Watts,[10] Jaffey,[11] Botterell,[12] Fitzgerald[13] and Webb[14] have defended different versions of this central idea.

This chapter does not aim to defend the entitlement thesis.[15] However, a brief outline of the positive case for the entitlement theory is provided here. This is because, as explained earlier, the reasoning based on the claimant's defective consent is orthodox among the writers of textbooks on unjust enrichment. However, the theoretical writing on unjust enrichment reveals a different trend. The entitlement analysis is, as Wilmot-Smith puts it, 'statistically, the theoretical orthodoxy'.[16] It is necessary therefore to understand how the entitlement thesis differs from the consent analysis.

The positive case for the entitlement thesis may be advanced in two steps: (1) the argument based on principle and (2) the argument based on the cases.

A. The Argument Based on Principle

As mentioned above, the entitlement thesis suggests that the claimant's vitiated consent is, by itself, normatively inert. That proposition may be analysed from two perspectives: (a) why is C entitled to 'reconstitution'[17]? ('The claimant-sided enquiry'); and (b) why does D come under an obligation[18] to give up her enrichment? ('The defendant-sided enquiry').[19]

[9] SJ Stoljar, *The Law of Quasi-Contract* (Sydney, Law Book Co, 1964). See also, Samuel Stoljar, 'Unjust Enrichment and Unjust Sacrifice' (1987) 50 Modern Law Review 603.

[10] Peter Watts, 'Restitution – A Property Principle and a Services Principle' [1995] Restitution Law Review 49.

[11] Peter Jaffey, 'Two Theories of Unjust Enrichment' in Jason Neyers, Mitchell McInnes and Stephen Pitel (eds), *Understanding Unjust Enrichment* (Oxford, Hart, 2004).

[12] Andrew Botterell, 'Property, Corrective Justice, and the Nature of the Cause of Action in Unjust Enrichment' (2007) 20 Canadian Journal of Law and Jurisprudence 275.

[13] Brian Fitzgerald, 'Ownership as the Proximity or Privity Principle in Unjust Enrichment Law' (1994–1995) 18 University of Queensland Law Journal 167.

[14] Charlie Webb, *Reason and Restitution: A Theory of Unjust Enrichment* (Oxford, Oxford University Press, 2016).

[15] For criticisms of the entitlement thesis, see Burrows, *The Law of Restitution* (n 5) 30; Zoë Sinel, 'Through Thick and Thin: The Place of Corrective Justice in Unjust Enrichment' (2011) 31 Oxford Journal of Legal Studies 551, 551–552.

[16] Frederick Wilmot-Smith, 'Should the Payee Pay?' (2017) 37 Oxford Journal of Legal Studies 844, 849.

[17] Terminology borrowed from ibid 845. As Wilmot-Smith suggests, in this context, 'reconstitution' is preferable to 'restitution' because the latter pre-supposes relief *from the payee*.

[18] For the debate about whether the onus on D is better understood as a 'liability' or an 'obligation', see Stephen Smith, 'The Restatement of Liabilities in Restitution' in Charles Mitchell and William Swadling (eds), *The Restatement Third, Restitution and Unjust Enrichment: Critical and Comparative Essays* (Oxford, Hart, 2013). Both terms are used interchangeably in this book.

[19] For examples of other theoretical enquiries that pursue the methodology of splitting up these enquiries, see Jules Coleman, *Markets Morals and the Law* (Oxford, Oxford University Press, 2002) 185; AP Simester, 'Correcting Unjust Enrichment' (2010) 8 Oxford Journal of Legal Studies 579, 594.

This chapter will not consider the defendant-sided enquiry in any detail but, in summary, the question is: why is the payee the appropriate person to provide reconstitution to the payor? As Wilmot-Smith points out,[20] there are other alternatives. A legal system could socialise the claim. The claimant could be reconstituted from a publicly-funded insurance pool. In order to answer the defendant-sided question, what is required is a justification for singling out the recipient of a mistaken enrichment as the bearer of the liability for restitution.

The focus of this chapter is on the claimant-sided enquiry. Is the claimant's defective consent a normatively sufficient justification for her right to reconstitution? Proponents of the entitlement thesis suggest that it is not. In support of that contention, they rely on the fact that not all unintended benefits give rise to restitution claims.

> *Example 2*: C opened a cinema hall adjacent to an ice-cream stall. The stall is owned by D. C dislikes D and would never want to benefit D. Had C known that the stall was owned by D, C would have chosen an alternative location for the cinema hall. But C's customers buy ice-cream from D's stall on their way to the movies. D's sales soar.[21]

C made a 'mistake'.[22] D was enriched. There is a causal connection between the two in that 'but for' C's mistake D would not have received the benefit. Yet, on these facts, C has no claim against D.[23] If C's vitiated consent was a sufficient reason for restitution, why is there no claim in Example 2? This is because, proponents of the entitlement thesis say, C's defective consent is only a part of the principle that explains claims based on unjust enrichment.

They do not seek to argue that the claimant's mistake is irrelevant. On one view, mistakes are relevant because they infringe upon one's 'capacity to act in accordance with one's own rationally determined norms'.[24] Mistakes violate the claimant's interest in acting 'only for the reason she takes herself to have'.[25] Consider Example 1. On the orthodox view, C's intention was vitiated by

[20] Wilmot-Smith, 'Should the Payee Pay?' (n 16) 845.

[21] Based on Daniel Friedmann, 'Unjust Enrichment, Pursuance of Self-Interest and the Limits of Free Riding' (2003) 36 Loyola of Los Angeles Law Review 831, 840. See also, Ernest Weinrib, 'The Normative Structure of Unjust Enrichment' in Charles Rickett and Ross Grantham (eds), *Structure and Justification in Private Law: Essays for Peter Birks* (Oxford, Hart, 2008) 30–31.

[22] It may be argued that C's state of mind is better described as a misprediction since it concerned a future state of affairs where a benefit would accrue to D. But that objection can be easily overcome. C believed that the ice-cream stall was owned by someone other than D whereas, in fact, it was owned by D. C was therefore 'mistaken' in the relevant sense.

[23] Friedmann, 'Unjust Enrichment, Pursuance of Self-Interest and the Limits of Free Riding' (n 21); Ernest Weinrib, 'Unjust Enrichment' in *Corrective Justice* (Oxford, Oxford Univeristy Press, 2012) 119.

[24] Aruna Nair, '"Mistakes of Law" and Legal Reasoning: Interpreting *Kleinwort Benson v Lincoln City Council*' in Robert Chambers, Charles Mitchell and James Penner (eds), *Philosophical Foundations of the Law of Unjust Enrichment* (Oxford, Oxford University Press, 2009) 389.

[25] Frederick Wilmot-Smith, 'Retrospective Mistakes of Law' in Paul Davies and Justine Pila (eds), *The Jurisprudence of Lord Hoffmann* (Oxford, Hart, 2015) 305.

her mistake;[26] that is to say, C's consent to the payment was deficient.[27] On an alternative view, C's intention is not 'vitiated', but was 'conditional'.[28] When making the payment, C *did* intend to transfer £100 to D. But C intended to do so in order to achieve the goal of discharging a debt. Thus, C's intention was 'conditional' on the debt being due. C had no relevant intention in the event that the debt was not due.[29] C's payment was therefore not covered by her intention to pay.

On either view, mistakes are normatively relevant because they violate one's capacity to be a 'self-legislating autonomous agent'.[30] The entitlement thesis suggests that one's capacity for self-legislation is only relevant with respect to the resources at one's own disposal. I cannot claim to have an interest in determining the disposition of someone else's wealth. In Example 1, C's interest in acting according to her own rationally-determined norms is relevant because C had a prior entitlement to the £100. It is that entitlement that justifies C's right to determine the disposition of £100. Thus, on the account that treats mistakes as normatively relevant because they infringe on one's capacity to act for their own reasons, C's defective consent is an important part of the explanation for C's right to restitution. But, by itself, it is not a sufficient justification.

In short, according to the entitlement thesis, the claimant's defective consent is only a part of the explanation for claims based on unjust enrichment. In order to be normatively defensible, it must be supplemented by an account of the claimant's pre-existing entitlements from which the defendant's enrichment was derived.[31]

B. The Argument from the Cases

The significance of the claimant's entitlement may be illustrated by three categories of cases: (i) cases where restitution is denied because C had no exclusive entitlement; (ii) cases where C's entitlement performs an inclusive role by conferring on C a claim that C would not otherwise have had; and (iii) cases concerned with the restitution of spill-over benefits.

[26] Burrows, *The Law of Restitution* (n 5) 87.

[27] Frederick Wilmot-Smith, 'Reasons? For *Restitution*?' (2016) 79 Modern Law Review 1116, 1125.

[28] Webb, *Reason and Restitution* (n 14) 129.

[29] Charlie Webb, 'Intention, Mistake and Resulting Trusts' in Charles Mitchell (ed), *Constructive and Resulting Trusts* (Oxford, Hart, 2010) 323–326. See also, Webb, *Reason and Restitution: A Theory of Unjust Enrichment* (n 14) 129.

[30] Duncan Sheehan, 'Mistake, Failure of Consideration and the Planning Theory of Intention' (2015) 28 Canadian Journal of Law and Jurisprudence 155, 165.

[31] See, Daniel Friedmann, 'The Protection of Entitlements via the Law of Restitution – Expectancies and Privacy' (2005) 121 Law Quarterly Review 400, 420 ('The law of restitution deals with the recovery of benefits derived from a legally protected interest that belongs to another when the benefit was acquired in a way that is not sanctioned by the law. Hence, the award of … restitution is predicated upon the existence of a legally protected interest').

i. C has No Exclusive Entitlement

> *Example 3*: X owns a water-tank. The tank is designed such that when a valve is opened, it irrigates D's neighbouring farmland. X charges D a fee for this service. C, a passer-by, mistakenly opens the valve. As a consequence, D's land is irrigated. C seeks restitution from D.

C made a 'mistake'. D was enriched as a consequence. There is a clear causal link between the two. Nevertheless, C's claim should fail. That is because C had no prior entitlement to the water-tank or, indeed, to the water from the use of which D benefitted.

There is considerable support for this view in the cases. In *Warman v Southern Counties Car Finance Corporation*[32] the claimant entered into an agreement with the defendant for the hire-purchase of a motorcar. Three months later, the claimant discovered that the car did not belong to the defendant, returned the car to its real owner and sued the defendant for damages for breach of the hire-purchase agreement. The defendant counterclaimed for the value that the claimant derived from the use of the car until it was returned. The counterclaim failed. The Court's reasoning in reaching that conclusion was based on the fact that the defendant did not have title to the car. Finnemore J said:[33]

> This car was not, at any time, the property of the defendants. I do not think that the plaintiff in any circumstances could be called on to pay to the defendants hiring money for a car which belonged to somebody else.

The defendant's counterclaim is best analysed as being based on failure of consideration. The basis – that the defendant would transfer use of the car to the claimant and that the claimant would pay for it – was shared between the claimant and the defendant. That basis failed. Yet, the restitution claim did not succeed because the defendant did not have a prior entitlement to the car from which the claimant's benefit was derived.

This is also the best explanation for *Rowland v Divall*.[34] The facts were similar to *Warman*. The defendant sold a car to the claimant who used it for a few months. The claimant subsequently discovered that the defendant did not have title to the car. The defendant then claimed the value of the claimant's use of the car. That claim failed. As Burrows explains, the best explanation for this decision is that:[35]

> as between the defendant and the car's true owner, the enrichment comprising the use of the car was not at the expense of the defendant but rather at the expense of the true owner.

[32] *Warman v Southern Counties Car Finance Corporation* [1949] 2 KB 576 (KB). See also, Andrew Tettenborn, *The Law of Restitution in England and Ireland* (3rd edn, London, Cavendish, 2002) 18–19.

[33] *Warman* (n 32) 582–583.

[34] *Rowland v Divall* [1923] 2 KB 500 (CA). See also, *Stiassny v Commissioner of Inland Revenue* [2012] NZSC 106 [69].

[35] Burrows, *The Law of Restitution* (n 5) 75. See also, Virgo (n 6) 106.

Eighty Second Vocation Pty Ltd v Parere Investments Pty Ltd is another example.[36] The claimants were Eighty Second Vocation Pty Ltd (ESV), a computer consulting company and Mr Fox, its owner and manager. ESV had a significant shareholding in H-W Vic, a Victoria incorporated company, of which Mr Fox was also the director. Pursuant to a restructuring agreement, H-W Vic's business was taken over by the defendant company. According to the claimants, they consented to the restructuring based on the defendant's promise that they would be compensated for the loss of H-W Vic's goodwill. However, they were not compensated for that loss. The claimants alleged that there was a failure of consideration. On that basis, the claimant sought restitution of the value of HW-Vic's goodwill, a benefit that the defendant enjoyed after the restructure. The claim failed. Weinberg J said:[37]

> The short answer to this claim is that it is essentially misconceived … Any goodwill that existed through Mr Fox's endeavours on behalf of H-W Vic, belonged to that company, and to that company alone. It did not belong to the shareholders. If [the defendant] did "misappropriate" the goodwill of H-W Vic, the only party that has standing to recover damages arising from that conduct in a claim for restitution is H-W Vic. However, that company is not a party to this proceeding.

The defendant did benefit from the restructuring. The claimants' consent to that process was conditional on being compensated for their loss of goodwill. In the event, that condition was not satisfied. Consequently, the claimants' intention was impaired. However, that was not sufficient for a restitution claim. The decisive factor was that the claimants had no prior right to HW-Vic's goodwill, the entitlement from which the defendant's benefit was derived.

ii. *C's Exclusive Entitlement Performs an Inclusive Role*

> *Example 4A*: C mistakenly believed that she owed X £100. Intending to discharge the debt, she paid X. Believing himself to be £100 better off, but unaware of C's mistake, X gifted a different £100 note to D. C seeks restitution from D.

C's claim will fail.[38] Now consider a slightly modified example.

> *Example 4B*: X stole £100 from C. X then gifted *the same* £100 note to D. C seeks restitution from D.

In this example, C's claim will succeed.[39] *Lipkin Gorman* illustrates this.[40] In that case, Cass was a partner in the claimant firm of solicitors. Cass gambled

[36] *Eighty Second Vocation Pty Ltd v Parere Investments Pty Ltd* [2005] FCA 844, (2005) 144 FCR 88. See also James Edelman and Elise Bant, *Unjust Enrichment* (2nd edn, Oxford, Hart, 2016) 93–94.

[37] *Eighty Second Vocation Pty Ltd* (n 36) [106] (Weinberg J) (emphasis added).

[38] *In Re Byfield* [1982] Ch 267 (Ch D); Burrows, *The Law of Restitution* (n 5) 70; Virgo (n 6) 110; Ben McFarlane, 'Unjust Enrichment, Property Rights and Indirect Recipients' [2009] Restitution Law Review 37.

[39] Burrows, *The Law of Restitution* (n 5) 75; Virgo (n 6) 110.

[40] *Lipkin Gorman v Karpnale Ltd* [1991] 2 AC 548 (HL).

away money belonging to the claimant at the Playboy Club. The claimant proceeded against the Club. The claim succeeded. The Court's reasoning was based on 'tracing'. It was held that the claimant continued to retain a proprietary interest in the money when it was received by the defendant Club. Lord Goff said:[41]

> It is well established that a legal owner is entitled to trace his property into its product, provided that the latter is indeed identifiable as the product of his property.
>
> There is in my opinion no reason why the solicitors should not be able to trace their property at common law in that chose in action, or in any part of it, into its product, i.e. cash drawn by Cass from their client account at the bank. Such a claim is consistent with their assertion that the money so obtained by Cass was their property at common law.

In *Lipkin Gorman*, it proved crucial that the claimant had a proprietary interest in the enrichment when it was received by the defendant. As Burrows explains,[42]

> Provided C retains title it does not matter how many hands the £100 banknote or bicycle passes through before reaching D: C, by reason of his title to the property, can establish that D's gain was at C's expense.

Similarly, in Example 4B, C's entitlement from which D's enrichment is derived performs an inclusive role. It confers on C a claim that C would otherwise not have had. As McFarlane explains,[43]

> D's acquisition of a factual gain, which could be said to come at C's expense, was insufficient to trigger any duty to D, even in the absence of a specific legal ground for the transfer of value from C to D. On the model proposed here, however, the absence of liability in such cases is easily explained: in each of those cases, C lost no right.

iii. Spill-Over Benefits

> *Example 5A*: D lives in the flat above C. C heats her flat during winter. The rising heat warms up D's flat. As a consequence, D saves on her fuel bill. C seeks restitution from D.[44]

[41] ibid 574.

[42] Burrows, *The Law of Restitution* (n 5) 76.

[43] Ben McFarlane, 'Unjust Enrichment, Rights and Value' in Donal Nolan and Andrew Robertson (eds), *Rights and Private Law* (Oxford, Hart, 2012) 601.

[44] Based on Birks, *Unjust Enrichment* (n 2) 158–159.

C's claim will fail. This result is supported by the authorities from England,[45] France[46] and the United States.[47] But why does C's claim fail?

According to Birks, this is because D's enrichment was a 'gift' from C, 'although possibly not warmly wished'.[48] With respect, this reasoning is incorrect. C's heating of her own flat was not accompanied by a donative intent.[49] It was certainly not accompanied by a donative intent towards D.[50] Birks's analysis is merely 'conclusory'.[51]

It has also been suggested that C's claim in Example 5A fails because there is no unjust factor in Example 5A.[52] This reasoning is also unconvincing. First, it is unclear why 'ignorance'[53] or 'powerlessness'[54] are inapplicable. Second, consider a modified version of Example 5A:

> *Example 5B*: D lives in the flat above C. C forgot to turn off her heater when she went away for Christmas. The heat from C's flat warms up D's flat. As a consequence, D saves on his fuel bill. C seeks restitution from D.[55]

The claim will fail here too, as it did in Example 5A. But, unlike in Example 5A, there *is* an unjust factor here. C was mistaken and did not intend to heat her

[45] *Investment Trust Companies v Revenue and Customs Commissioners* [2017] UKSC 29; [2018] AC 275 [52]–[58] (Lord Reed). See also, *Edinburgh and District Tramways Co Ltd v Courtenay* 1909 SC 99, 105; *Ruabon Steamship Co Ltd v London Assurance* [1900] AC 6 (HL); Andrew Burrows, *A Restatement of the English Law of Unjust Enrichment* (Oxford, Oxford University Press, 2012) 8, 54. See also, Adam Kramer and Adrian Beltrami QC, 'A Note on Incidental Benefit and Multi-Party Situations' [2013] Restitution Law Review 46. In *TFL Management Services Ltd v Lloyds TSB Bank plc* [2013] EWCA Civ 1415, [2014] 1 WLR 2006 (CA) an application to strike out a claim was made, based on the rule against restitution for 'incidental benefits'. The English Court of Appeal rejected the application. Although at the stage of a strike out application the Court refused to formulate, for the first time, a general 'incidental benefits' exception in the law of restitution it did recognise that the claimant in an incidental benefits case would face 'a high and possibly insurmountable hurdle' ([79]). Further, the Court said that such claims are unlikely to satisfy one or more of the elements of an unjust enrichment claim ([37]).

[46] See Friedmann, 'Unjust Enrichment, Pursuance of Self-Interest and the Limits of Free Riding' (n 21) 845–846.

[47] *Ulmer v Farnsworth* 80 Me 500 (Supreme Judicial Court of Maine); *Pierson v Post* 3 Cai R 175 (Supreme Court of New York).

[48] Birks, *Unjust Enrichment* (n 2) 158.

[49] Zoë Sinel, 'The Methods and Madness of Unjust Enrichment' in Andrew Robertson and Michael Tilbury (eds), *Divergences in Private Law* (Oxford, Hart, 2016) 196–197.

[50] Burrows, *The Law of Restitution* (n 5) 111.

[51] Peter Watts, 'Publication Review: Unjust Enrichment' (2005) 121 Law Quarterly Review 163, 166. See also, Robert Stevens, *The Laws of Restitution* (Oxford, Oxford University Press, 2023) 32.

[52] Burrows, *The Law of Restitution* (n 5) 108; Virgo (n 6) 115; James Edelman, 'The Meaning of "Unjust" in the English Law of Unjust Enrichment' [2006] European Review of Private Law 309, 321.

[53] Tariq A Baloch, 'The Unjust Enrichment Pyramid' (2007) 123 Law Quarterly Review 636, 653.

[54] Eli Ball, 'Abandonment and the Problem of Incidental Gains in the Law of Restitution of Unjust Enrichment' [2011] Restitution Law Review 49, 53.

[55] Based on Webb, *Reason and Restitution: A Theory of Unjust Enrichment* (n 14) 62.

own flat. Nor did she intend to heat D's flat. But this should make no difference to the result.[56]

Example 5B also proves that the 'abandonment' explanation for claims based on spill-over benefits is incorrect.[57] The abandonment explanation suggests that restitution is denied in Example 5A because C had 'freely given up the benefit received by the defendant'.[58] However, the principle of abandonment requires an intention to abandon. Did C intend to abandon the benefit of her heating in Example 5B? The answer is 'no'. In Example 5B, C did not even intend the primary act of heating her own flat. Can C's intention to abandon be objectively presumed? Ball argues that, where heating D's flat was a foreseeable consequence of C's own actions, it can.[59] However, in Example 5B, C could not have foreseen that her action would lead to the consequence of heating D's flat.

Thus, just like Example 2 and Example 3, Example 5B is yet another illustration that the claimant's vitiated consent is by itself insufficient for there to be a restitution claim. The entitlement thesis suggests that the results in Examples 5A and 5B are explicable on the basis that D's enrichment was not derived from any of C's entitlements. C could attempt to base her restitution claim on a number of her entitlements. They are considered in turn below.

Consider C's entitlement to property. C may assert that the heat from which D benefitted was generated from her property. C does have a legally protected entitlement to her property. However, the difficulty is that the extent of that protection is limited; it does not extend to spill-overs from one's property that third-parties may benefit from.

> *Example 6*: C and D live across the street. When C switches on her light, it shines into D's study. Consequently, D can read without turning on her light. D thus saves on her electricity bill.[60]

C has no claim for restitution of D's enrichment. This is because C does not have an exclusive entitlement to the light that spills-over from C's property.[61] As Meier puts it, the spill-over benefit 'belongs to no one'.[62]

Victoria Park Racing v Taylor[63] illustrates this point. The claimant owned a racecourse where spectators were charged for admission. The defendant viewed

[56] Stevens, *The Laws of Restitution* (n 51) 32.

[57] Ball (n 54).

[58] ibid 49.

[59] ibid 67.

[60] Sonja Meier, 'No Basis: A Comparative View' in Andrew Burrows and Alan Rodger (eds), *Mapping the Law: Essays in Memory of Peter Birks* (Oxford, Oxford University Press, 2006) 356.

[61] Friedmann, 'Unjust Enrichment, Pursuance of Self-Interest and the Limits of Free Riding' (n 21) 846.

[62] Meier (n 60).

[63] *Victoria Park Racing & Recreation Grounds Co Ltd v Taylor* [1937] HCA 45, (1937) 58 CLR 479. See also, Charlie Webb, 'Property, Unjust Enrichment, and Defective Transfers' in Robert Chambers, Charles Mitchell and James Penner (eds), *Philosophical Foundations of the Law of Unjust Enrichment* (Oxford, Oxford University Press, 2009) 348–349.

the races from a raised platform built on a neighbouring land. The defendant also broadcasted the event on radio. Consequently, attendance at the claimant's racecourse dropped and the claimant suffered a loss. The claimant sought an injunction to restrain the defendant's broadcasting. The injunction was not granted. The Court recognised the claimant's exclusive interest in their property. It was also acknowledged that this includes the right to exclude others from the property. However, Dixon J said:[64]

> So far as freedom from view or inspection is a natural or acquired physical characteristic of the site … it is a characteristic which is not a legally protected interest.

Further, he said:[65]

> the right to exclude the defendants from broadcasting a description of the occurrences they can see upon the plaintiff's land is not given by law. It is not an interest falling within any category which is protected at law or in equity.

Alternatively, C may rely upon her entitlement to 'value'. It may be suggested that D was enriched as a consequence of value that was derived from C. However, the law does not recognise an abstract entitlement to value in this way.

> *Example 7*: C and D each own one of only two specimens of a rare collectible stamp. C accidentally destroys her stamp. This causes D's stamp to double in value.[66]

C's claim will fail. This result is also explicable based on C's entitlements. Before its destruction, the stamp was C's property. Consequently, she had a valid entitlement to it. However, C's entitlement to the stamp does not extend so far as to protect her against market fluctuations resulting in a shift in its value. This is relevant because, in Example 7, 'the change in value occurs through the operation of a market'.[67] As Friedmann says:[68]

> there is no unjust enrichment where property increases in value as a result of market fluctuation. This rule applies irrespective of whether the increase in value results from natural causes, from lawful transactions in property belonging to others, or from some other activity of the market participants.

Finally, can C attempt to justify her claim in Example 5B based on her entitlement to her own labour? Can C argue that she mistakenly provided a service that benefitted D? Compare Example 5B with the following illustration.

> *Example 5C*: D lives in the flat above C. Under a contract, C agreed with D that C would leave her heater on when she goes away for Christmas. As agreed, C did so. The

[64] *Victoria Park Racing* (n 63) 508.
[65] ibid 510.
[66] Based on Stevens (n 51) 30.
[67] Frederick Wilmot-Smith, 'Taxing Questions' (2015) 131 Law Quarterly Review 531, 534.
[68] Friedmann, 'Unjust Enrichment, Pursuance of Self-Interest and the Limits of Free Riding' (n 21) 840.

heat from C's flat warmed up D's flat. Later, it turned out that the contract was void because it failed to comply with a statutory formality requirement. C seeks restitution from D.

Unlike in Example 5B, C has a valid claim against D here. Proponents of the entitlement thesis would say that, in Example 5C, the entitlement upon which C's claim is based is her entitlement to her own labour.[69] Why, then, is C's entitlement to her own labour insufficient to support the restitution claim in Example 5B? The answer is that, in Example 5B (unlike in Example 5C), C did not render the performance of a service to D. As Stevens explains, the reason there is no restitution claim is 'the absence of either a payment by the plaintiff to the defendant, or a service rendered by the plaintiff accepted by the defendant'.[70]

The decision of the Supreme Court of New York in *Pierson v Post*[71] illustrates this further. In that case, the claimant was chasing a fox with his hounds. The defendant, knowing fully well that the claimant was pursuing the fox, killed it and carried it off. Although the defendant had benefitted from the claimant's prior pursuit, the Court held that the claimant had no valid claim against the defendant. This is explicable on the basis that, as in Example 5B, the claimant had not performed a service to the defendant. Like in Example 5C, the result in *Pierson* would have been different if, for instance, the defendant had engaged the claimant under a contract that later turned out to be void.

In summary, according to the entitlement thesis, the best explanation for the unavailability of restitution in cases concerned with the restitution of spill-over benefits is that, in these cases, the claimant did not have an exclusive entitlement from which the defendant's enrichment was derived.[72]

III. THE ENTITLEMENT EXPLANATION

This section considers whether the obligation rule can be explained using the framework of the entitlement thesis. Sub-section (A) considers and rejects Webb's account of the obligation rule. Sub-section (B) offers an alternative preferable explanation.

[69] See Botterell (n 12); Nicholas McBride and Paul McGrath, 'The Nature of Restitution' (1995) 15 Oxford Journal of Legal Studies 33; Fitzgerald (n 13).

[70] Stevens (n 53) 29.

[71] *Pierson* (n 47).

[72] See Charles Mitchell, Paul Mitchell and Stephen Watterson (eds), *Goff & Jones: The Law of Unjust Enrichment* (8th edn, London, Sweet & Maxwell, 2011) [4–53]. See also, Charles Mitchell, Paul Mitchell and Stephen Watterson, *Goff & Jones: The Law of Unjust Enrichment* (9th edn, London, Sweet & Maxwell, 2016) [1–31]; Friedmann, 'Unjust Enrichment, Pursuance of Self-Interest and the Limits of Free Riding' (n 21); Webb, 'Property, Unjust Enrichment, and Defective Transfers' (n 65) 351, 352; Webb, *Reason and Restitution: A Theory of Unjust Enrichment* (n 14) 65; Reinhard Zimmermann, *The Law of Obligations: Roman Foundations of the Civilian Tradition* (Oxford, Oxford University Press, 1996) 890; Watts, 'Publication Review: Unjust Enrichment' (n 51) 166.

A. Webb's Explanation

Webb has sought to explain the obligation rule based on the entitlement thesis:[73]

> [A]ny claim in unjust enrichment is rightly foreclosed by the determination that that, or some such, transfer was obligatory. By designating an action as obligatory, it is made non-optional. When I have an obligation to transfer a particular asset to you, the option to deal with that asset in some other way is one no longer open to me. So the answer to my complaint that I did not properly authorize and so did not truly choose that transfer is that the law gave me no choice not to make that transfer.

This reasoning does not withstand scrutiny. This is because Webb's reasoning is based on an inaccurate description of the nature of the obligation owed to the defendant.

> *Example 8:* C owed £100 each to D and X. C intended to pay X but mistakenly paid D. C's claim for restitution from D will fail.[74]

C was under an obligation to pay £100 to D. But C was not under an 'obligation to transfer a particular asset to [D]', as Webb claims. C was not obliged to transfer a particular £100 note to D. C may discharge its debt from *any* of its resources. Thus, contrary to Webb's assertion, 'the option to deal with that asset' – namely, the particular £100 note that C paid D – *was* open to C.[75]

Webb further suggests that '[i]f I am under an obligation to give you this laptop, I am no longer at liberty to dispose of it elsewhere'.[76] Here, again, Webb's reasoning appears to presume that a legal obligation attaches to particular assets of the claimant. It does not, as demonstrated by the fact that C could have discharged her debt from any of her resources. Webb appears to pre-empt this objection in the following passage:[77]

> If I am under an obligation to pay you £1,000, though this obligation doesn't attach to any specific fund or moneys I presently hold, when the time for payment comes, I must find that sum from the resources at my disposal. If I don't, and you obtain judgment against me, that judgment will be enforced by the sale of my assets. Indeed obligations such as these presuppose some such set of private holdings; my obligation to transfer this laptop or pay this money assumes that I have, or ought to have, such items to dispose of to you.

This analysis fails to meet the objection. Webb is right in saying that, as the claimant debtor, I must satisfy the debt out of the 'resources at my disposal'. But I am at liberty to decide which resource(s) I use for that purpose. Therefore, contrary to Webb's analysis, the fact that C owes a debt to D does not deprive C of her freedom to determine the disposition of any of her assets. Webb's analysis

[73] Webb, *Reason and Restitution: A Theory of Unjust Enrichment* (n 14) 152.

[74] Based on dicta in *Platt v Bromage* (1854) 24 LJ Ex 63, 65. See also, Andrew Burrows, *A Restatement of the English Law of Unjust Enrichment* (Oxford, Oxford University Press, 2012) 32–33.

[75] Stevens, *Laws of Restitution* (n 51) 85.

[76] Webb, *Reason and Restitution: A Theory of Unjust Enrichment* (n 14) 152.

[77] ibid 153 (emphasis added).

is based on an inaccurate conception of the impact of C's legal obligation to D on C's freedom to deal with her resources. For that reason, it is unpersuasive.

B. The Equality Thesis

This section will advance an alternative explanation for the obligation rule based on the entitlement theory. I will call it the 'equality thesis'. In summary, the equality thesis is as follows. According to the entitlement theory, the normative justification for restitution depends on the claimant's pre-transactional entitlements. For a restitution claim to succeed, the defendant's enrichment must have been derived from those entitlements. Thus, in substance, the function the restitution claim performs is to protect the claimant's entitlements from being transferred away without her fully effective consent. Equality between the parties demands that the law must afford a similar protection to the defendant. Consider Example 8, where the defendant has a valid entitlement to receive £100 from C. Granting C's restitution claim will deprive D of that entitlement other than through D's consent. Therefore, granting C restitution in Example 8 would deny D the very right upon which C's claim is based. This is impermissible.

The key point the equality thesis makes is that a claim should fail if it requires the Court to protect an interest of the claimant whilst denying similar protection to the defendant. This reasoning derives support from a number of sources.

The first among them is Kant's 'Universal Principle of Right'.[78] It stands for the idea that:[79]

> [A]n action is *right* if it can coexist with everyone's freedom in accordance with a universal law, or ... the freedom of choice of each can coexist with everyone's freedom in accordance with a universal law.

In other words, one's exercise of free choice must be consistent with a similar choice by others.[80] Kant's principle forbids us from 'making exceptions of ourselves'.[81] In Example 8, by asserting a restitution claim against D, that is what C does. On the entitlement analysis, C's claim is based on her freedom

[78] Immanuel Kant, *The Metaphysics of Morals* (Mary Gregor tr, Cambridge, Cambridge University Press, 1996) 24. Rawls has proposed a similar idea in the context of liberties: see John Rawls, *A Theory of Justice* (Oxford, Oxford University Press, 1999) 53 ('Each person is to have an equal right to the most extensive scheme of equal liberties compatible with a similar scheme of liberties for others').

[79] Dennis Klimchuk, 'Unjust Enrichment and Corrective Justice' in Jason Neyers, Mitchell McInnes and Stephen Pitel (eds), *Understanding Unjust Enrichment* (Oxford, Hart, 2004) 124 (emphasis in original). See also, George Fletcher, 'Law and Morality: A Kantian Perspective' (1987) 87 Columbia Law Review 533, 540.

[80] Matthew Doyle, 'Corrective Justice and Unjust Enrichment' (2012) 1 The University of Toronto Law Journal 229, 236–237.

[81] Klimchuk, 'Unjust Enrichment and Corrective Justice' (n 79); Peter Cane, 'Corrective Justice and Correlativity in Private Law' (1996) 16 Oxford Journal of Legal Studies 472, 473.

to choose the disposition of her entitlements. However, if C's claim were to succeed, that freedom would be denied to D.

The equality thesis also derives support from a number of normative accounts that seek to explain why a claim in unjust enrichment exists in the first place. The analysis adopted by McBride and McGrath is an example. Their thesis is premised on the idea that 'in invoking [a] right, one must concede it to everyone else similarly placed'.[82] Consider a defendant who is the recipient of an asset that was mistakenly transferred to her. The defendant may invoke a right of ownership over that asset. However, in doing so, the defendant must afford the same right to the claimant. The defendant's retention of the asset is not consistent with the claimant's right to autonomy in the disposition of her assets. Indeed, the fact that the claimant's transfer to the defendant was mistaken suggests that the claimant did not validly exercise her right to choose the disposition of her assets. Therefore, if the defendant were to deny the claimant's right to restitution, the defendant would be acting inconsistently. According to McBride and McGrath, this puts the defendant in a position where she cannot legitimately deny the normative force of the claimant's restitution claim.[83]

Similarly, according to Drassinower, the normative basis for a restitution claim is based on equality between the parties. According to him, the claimant and the defendant are equally entitled to their resources until they part with them freely:[84]

> [T]he defendant cannot claim to retain what was not given to him as a gift because such a claim is simultaneously inconsistent with the defendant's own entitlement to what is his until he freely parts with it. In denying the other's right, the defendant denies his own. In so doing, he undermines his own claim to retain the benefit.

McInnes makes a similar argument to justify restitution claims based on the claimant's mistake:[85]

> By resisting liability, the defendant broadly asserts the right to retain his … enrichment until he freely chooses to part with it. Contrary to the Kantian imperative, however, he thereby claims for himself a right that he is unwilling to extend to others.

The need for equal treatment of the parties to a restitution claim has also been emphasised in a number of analogous contexts.[86] Consider, for example,

[82] McBride and McGrath (n 69) 40.

[83] ibid 38–40.

[84] Abraham Drassinower, 'Unrequested Benefits in the Law of Unjust Enrichment' (1998) 48 The University of Toronto Law Journal 459, 468.

[85] Mitchell McInnes, 'The Measure of Restitution' (2002) 52 The University of Toronto Law Journal 163, 188. See also, Mitchell McInnes, 'Unjust Enrichment: A Reply to Professor Weinrib' [2001] Restitution Law Review 29, 36.

[86] See Weinrib (n 23) 203 ('In dealing with the defectiveness of a transfer of value, the law has to observe a strict equality in its treatment of plaintiff and defendant').

Edelman's justification of the change of position defence. He argues that change of position protects the defendant's autonomy.[87] In determining the nature and extent of that protection, equality plays a crucial role:[88]

> The degree of protection that the courts have chosen [for the defendant] is the same protection as is given to the autonomy of the claimant. This ought to be the minimum protection given to a defendant. A claimant should not be entitled to insist upon a right to protection of his autonomy in a primary claim without affording the same protection to the autonomy of the defendant in a defence.

Ratan makes a similar point in the context of the change of position defence. His focus is on the baseline against which a change in the defendant's position must be assessed.[89] According to him, the right question to ask is, 'how would the defendant have fared if the claimant had not been mistaken'?[90] This is justified by reference to the idea that the claimant must take the 'rough with the smooth'. The claimant enjoys the 'upside' of her defective decision-making, namely restitution from the defendant. Consequently, the claimant cannot deny its 'downside', namely the risk of the defendant's causally-related detriment.[91] Ratan's normative defence of the 'rough with the smooth' principle[92] mirrors the equality thesis. He says that this principle is justified by the need to prevent the claimant from relying on 'self-serving distinctions':[93]

> Why should the claimant be able to have the consequences of the defect in her decision making allocated to her by the law of unjust enrichment when it works to her advantage but not otherwise? … [T]he unjust enrichment claimant cannot justify distinguishing between the consequences of the defect in her decision making simply on the basis that this distinction furthers her own interests. Such self-serving distinctions are precisely what the 'rough with the smooth' principle rules out.

In Example 8, the claimant asserts the integrity of her pre-transaction entitlements to justify the restitution claim. The claimant cannot be permitted to draw a self-serving distinction between her entitlements and those of the defendant.

[87] James Edelman, 'Change of Position: A Defence of Unjust Disenrichment' (2012) 92 Boston University Law Review 1009.

[88] ibid 1021. See also, Elise Bant, 'Change of Position: Outstanding Issues' in Andrew Dyson, James Goudkamp and Frederick Wilmot-Smith (eds), *Defences in Unjust Enrichment* (Oxford, Hart, 2016) 144. For a similar argument in the context of restitution within subsisting contracts see, James Edelman, 'Liability in Unjust Enrichment where a Contract Fails to Materialize' in Andrew Burrows and Edwin Peel (eds), *Contract Formation and Parties* (Oxford, Oxford University Press, 2010) 171, 173.

[89] Ajay Ratan, 'The Unity of Pre-receipt and Post-receipt Detriment' in Andrew Dyson, James Goudkamp and Frederick Wilmot-Smith (eds), *Defences in Unjust Enrichment* (Oxford, Hart, 2016) 87.

[90] ibid 91.

[91] ibid 111–112.

[92] See, Tony Honoré, *Responsibility and Fault* (Oxford, Hart, 1999) 134 (stating that 'its moral force can hardly be denied').

[93] Ratan (n 89) 112.

It follows that she cannot assert a claim against the defendant that would deprive the defendant of the protection of his pre-existing entitlements.[94]

The equality thesis also derives support from Weinrib's work. In his exposition of the theoretical basis for claims based on unjust enrichment, he says:[95]

> Underlying the obligation-creating conditions is the idea that the parties each have an entitlement to what is one's own until one freely parts with it. As the owner of the value at the inception of the transfer, the plaintiff makes a claim that rests initially on not having freely parted with that value. However, the normative ground of this claim has equal validity for both parties. Accordingly, the plaintiff's entitlement to what is one's own until freely parted with has to co-exist with the similar entitlement of the defendant. The plaintiff's claim not to have freely parted with the transferred value cannot create an obligation that usurps a pre-existing entitlement of the defendant's with which the defendant also has not freely parted.

The underlined words in that passage have particular resonance in relation to the obligation rule.

The reasons outlined above focus, principally, on the inequity of the claimant's position. They suggest that the claimant cannot be permitted to assert an interest whilst denying a similar protection to the defendant. There are also good systemic reasons for the equality thesis, some of which have been explored in the literature on moral and political philosophy.[96] For example, in Roman law, 'justice' was understood as 'the willingness to render what is due as a matter of right, to *each*'.[97] As the opening passage of the *Institutes* states, '[j]ustice is the stable and lasting willingness to give *to each his right*'.[98] From a systemic point of view, therefore, it is 'unjust' to allow the claimant her due while denying the defendant her entitlements.

Finnis's exposition of the principle that 'like cases must be treated alike' supports this conclusion. One aspect of that principle, according to Finnis, is equality.[99] Finnis argues that all human beings who possess the capacity for moral personality are equal in some respects. According to Finnis, moral personality is about 'what is needed to be a person who respects other persons,

[94] See also, James Goudkamp and Charles Mitchell, 'Denials and Defences in the Law of Unjust Enrichment' in *The Restatement Third, Restitution and Unjust Enrichment: Critical and Comparative Essays* (Oxford, Hart, 2013) 147 ('If the distinction between actions and defences did not exist, so that the law of unjust enrichment consisted only in the elements of the actions, the claimant would be the only party placed under a burden ... This would be contrary to a fundamental tenet of procedural justice. It is a basic principle of law that litigants in the civil sphere must be treated as even-handedly in terms of procedural justice as is reasonably possible').

[95] Weinrib (n 21) 29 (emphasis added).

[96] I am grateful to Ajay Ratan for drawing my attention to this literature.

[97] John Finnis, 'Equality and Differences' (2011) 56 American Journal of Jurisprudence 17, 17 (emphasis in original).

[98] John Finnis, 'The Priority of Persons' in *Intention and Identity: Collected Essays* (Oxford, Oxford University Press, 2011) 22 (emphasis added).

[99] Finnis, 'Equality and Differences' (n 97) 17.

for their own sake, and who sees the need to give to *each* of them their due (*ius suum*: their right)'.[100] Protecting the claimant's interests alone would, on this account, be a denial of the defendant's moral personality. Dworkin has defended a similar view in the context of organisation of rights and responsibilities in a political community. In order to be morally defensible, he argues, the rights and responsibilities that flow from a political community's decisions must 'show not only concern but an *equal* concern for all members'.[101] This follows from the premise that 'each person is as worthy as the other, that each must be treated with equal concern'.[102]

In summary, the equality thesis offers an explanation for the obligation rule within the framework of the entitlement thesis. That explanation is based on the need for equal protection of the claimant's and defendant's interests. The claimant cannot be permitted to use the law of restitution to protect its entitlements while simultaneously denying similar protection to the defendant. The next chapter will consider an alternative account of the obligation rule. That explanation is based on the corrective justice theory of unjust enrichment.

[100] Finnis, 'Equality and Differences' (n 97) 19.

[101] Ronald Dworkin, *Law's Empire* (Cambridge, Massachussetts, Harvard University Press, 1986) 200.

[102] ibid 213.

7

The Obligation Rule and the Corrective Justice Theory

THE PREVIOUS CHAPTER offered an explanation for the obligation rule based on the entitlement thesis. This chapter will explain the obligation rule using the framework of the corrective justice theory, which has been widely approved in the theoretical literature,[1] by textbook writers[2] and by the courts.[3]

A preliminary point about terminology: as a normative explanation for unjust enrichment, the phrase 'corrective justice' is often used in two different senses.[4] In the first sense, the 'thin' version, corrective justice only explains the juridical structure of an unjust enrichment claim.[5] The injustice that underlies the claim is itself not a 'corrective injustice'.[6] According to the second 'thick' version, corrective justice not only explains the form of justice that a claim in unjust enrichment takes, but also accounts for the substantive injustice upon which the claim is based.[7] In the second sense, corrective justice functions as a 'substantive principle of liability and remedy'.[8] This chapter will use corrective justice in the second sense.

[1] Ernest Weinrib, *The Idea of Private Law* (rev edn, Oxford, Oxford University Press, 2012); Lionel Smith, 'Restitution: The Heart of Corrective Justice' (2001) 79 Texas Law Review 2115; Jules Coleman, *Corrective Justice and Property Rights* (Rodney Roberts ed, New York, Peter Lang, 2002). For criticisms of the corrective justice theory, see James Penner, 'Value, Property, and Unjust Enrichment: Trusts of Traceable Proceeds' in Robert Chambers, Charles Mitchell and James Penner (eds), *Philosophical Foundations of the Law of Unjust Enrichment* (Oxford, Oxford University Press, 2009) 309; Andrew Botterell, 'Book Review: Corrective Justice' [2014] Mind 1, 3; Peter Cane, 'Corrective Justice and Correlativity in Private Law' (1996) 16 Oxford Journal of Legal Studies 472.

[2] Andrew Burrows, *The Law of Restitution* (3rd edn, Oxford, Oxford University Press, 2011) 68–69; Graham Virgo, *The Principles of the Law of Restitution* (3rd edn, Oxford, Oxford University Press, 2015) 4–5, 104, 664.

[3] *Investment Trust Companies v Revenue and Customs Commissioners* [2017] UKSC 29; [2017] 2 WLR 1200 [43] (Lord Reed); *Benedetti v Sawiris* [2013] UKSC 50, [2014] AC 938 [96]–[99] (Lord Reed); *Kingstreet Investments Ltd v Province of New Brunswick* 2007 SCC 1; [2007] 1 SCR 3 [32].

[4] Robert Stevens, *The Laws of Restitution* (Oxford, Oxford University Press, 2023) 19–20.

[5] Dennis Klimchuk, 'On the Autonomy of Corrective Justice' (2003) 23 Oxford Journal of Legal Studies 49, 51.

[6] John Gardner, 'The Purity and Priority of Private Law' (1996) 46 The University of Toronto Law Journal 459, 470.

[7] Zoë Sinel, 'Through Thick and Thin: The Place of Corrective Justice in Unjust Enrichment' (2011) 31 Oxford Journal of Legal Studies 551.

[8] Klimchuk, 'On the Autonomy of Corrective Justice' (n 5) 51.

The most comprehensive account of an explanation for the law of unjust enrichment based on corrective justice is to be found in the writings of Weinrib. Weinrib's corrective justice theory is therefore the primary model that this chapter will draw upon. The chapter is in two parts. Section I will provide an outline of Weinrib's corrective justice theory and Section II will advance an explanation for the obligation rule using the corrective justice theory.

I. CORRECTIVE JUSTICE THEORY

Sub-section (A) below will examine the three overarching features of Weinrib's corrective justice theory. Sub-section (B) will then explain how these features crystallise into Weinrib's 'obligation creating conditions'.

A. The Overarching Features

Weinrib's account of corrective justice comprises three overarching features: correlativity, Aristotle's conception of the forms of justice and Kant's explanation of equality.

i. Correlativity

In private law, the liability of a defendant is always a liability towards the claimant.[9] According to Weinrib, this means that one party's legal position is only intelligible in the light of the other. The parties to a private law claim are, in his words, 'connected as doer and sufferer of the same injustice'.[10] This has important implications for the kind of reasons that can justify private law liability.[11] Such reasons for liability must be correlative. A justification satisfies correlativity if the reason for the claimant's right mirrors the reason for the defendant's liability.[12]

ii. Aristotle's Conception of the Forms of Justice

The second overarching feature of Weinrib's thesis is his reliance on Aristotle's account of the forms of justice. Weinrib borrows the justificatory structure of his theory from Aristotle's conception of corrective justice.

[9] Ernest Weinrib, 'Correlativity, Personality and the Emerging Consensus on Corrective Justice' (2001) 2 The University of Toronto Law Journal 107, 110.
[10] ibid.
[11] Ernest Weinrib, 'Corrective Justice in a Nutshell' (2002) 52 The University of Toronto Law Journal 349, 350.
[12] Ernest Weinrib, 'Restoring Restitution' (2005) 91 Virginia Law Review 861, 868.

According to Aristotle, corrective justice is to be contrasted from distributive justice. The former concerns the 'bipolar' justice between persons in their private transactions.[13] In their pre-transaction positions, the parties to an unjust enrichment claim are situated in a relationship of equality.[14] Corrective justice responds to a disruption of that equality. This usually consists of a gain to the defendant and a loss to the claimant. The purpose of the remedial act of restitution is to restore the equilibrium. The defendant is asked to give up the gain and the claimant is compensated for her loss.[15]

Not all forms of private law liability fit this conceptual structure neatly. For instance, if D's negligent driving injures C, it is not immediately apparent how D has acquired any gain. Weinrib's response to this problem is to recast gains and losses as being 'normative' rather than 'material'. He says, 'gains and losses refer to discrepancies between what the parties have and what they should have according to the norm governing their interaction'.[16] Therefore, given the norm against negligent driving, Weinrib says, D has more than what she ought to have. On this basis, D has acquired a normative gain.

iii. Kant's Explanation of Equality

Aristotle's conception of corrective justice presumes a state of 'equality' between the parties. But that raises the question: in what respect are they equal? Weinrib's response is based on Kant who asserts that the parties' equality lies in their status as 'self-determining agents'.[17] This aspect of Weinrib's thesis is explored in greater detail in a later section of this chapter.[18]

B. Weinrib's Obligation-Creating Conditions

In relation to claims based on unjust enrichment, the three overarching features identified above crystallise into three obligation-creating conditions.

i. Transfer of Value

According to Weinrib, value is 'quantitative' and 'relational'. It abstracts from particular uses of things.[19] Thus, it permits the quantitative comparison of

[13] Matthew Doyle, 'Corrective Justice and Unjust Enrichment' (2012) 1 The University of Toronto Law Journal 229, 234.

[14] Ernest Weinrib, 'The Gains and Losses of Corrective Justice' (1994) 44 Duke Law Journal 277, 292.

[15] Mitchell McInnes, 'Unjust Enrichment: A Reply to Professor Weinrib' [2001] Restitution Law Review 29, 34.

[16] Weinrib, 'The Gains and Losses of Corrective Justice' (n 14) 282–283.

[17] McInnes, 'Unjust Enrichment: A Reply to Professor Weinrib' (n 15) 36.

[18] See Chapter 7, Section II(B) below.

[19] Ernest Weinrib, 'Unjust Enrichment' in *Corrective Justice* (Oxford, Oxford University Press, 2012) 190, 191.

qualitatively different things.[20] On Weinrib's view, a 'transfer of value' from the claimant to the defendant is a necessary component of the normative justification for unjust enrichment claims.[21] However, in order for an unjust enrichment claim to arise, a transfer of value must be accompanied by two 'obligation-creating conditions': a claimant-oriented condition and a defendant-oriented condition.

ii. The Claimant-Oriented Condition

The claimant-oriented condition is that 'the benefit was non-donatively transferred'.[22] This comprises two requirements: the claimant did not intend to make a gift to the defendant and the claimant *did* intend to transfer value to the defendant. In Weinrib's words, this means that the claimant must have intended to give the defendant 'something for nothing'.[23] Whether the claimant did so is judged objectively.[24]

iii. The Defendant-Oriented Condition

The defendant-oriented condition is that the defendant must have 'accepted' the benefit as being 'non-donatively given'.[25] The defendant's acceptance is also judged objectively: '[w]hat matters is not the defendant's inner psychological state, but the judgments and assumptions that can reasonably be made against the background of the legal structure in which they operate'.[26]

II. CORRECTIVE JUSTICE AND THE OBLIGATION RULE

This section advances an explanation for the obligation rule using the framework of Weinrib's corrective justice theory. In summary, the explanation offered here argues that Weinrib's corrective justice thesis and the entitlement theory share a significant, albeit often-overlooked, feature: the normative relevance of the claimant's pre-transaction entitlements. The claimant's pre-transfer interests

[20] Ernest Weinrib, 'The Normative Structure of Unjust Enrichment' in Charles Rickett and Ross Grantham (eds), *Structure and Justification in Private Law: Essays for Peter Birks* (Oxford, Hart, 2008) 27.

[21] In relation to the idea of 'transfer of value', see also Chapter 2, Section (I)(B)(i)(c).

[22] Weinrib, 'Unjust Enrichment' (n 19) 205.

[23] Sinel (n 7) 557.

[24] Weinrib, 'Unjust Enrichment' (n 19) 208; Weinrib, 'The Normative Structure of Unjust Enrichment' (n 20) 43.

[25] Ernest Weinrib, 'Correctively Unjust Enrichment' in Robert Chambers, Charles Mitchell and James Penner (eds), *Philosophical Foundations of the Law of Unjust Enrichment* (Oxford, Oxford University Press, 2009) 43.

[26] Weinrib, 'Unjust Enrichment' (n 19) 208; Weinrib, 'The Normative Structure of Unjust Enrichment' (n 20) 43.

are a necessary component of Weinrib's account of claims based on unjust enrichment. This is also true of most other corrective justice accounts of the law of unjust enrichment. The primary task this section undertakes is to bring to light this aspect of the corrective justice theory. Once this is done, it can be seen that the equality thesis can explain the obligation rule under the corrective justice theory as well as the entitlement thesis.

A. Why Return to the Past?

Most corrective justice accounts rely on the normativity of re-establishing a prior state of affairs. Consider, for instance, this passage from Weinrib:[27]

> Corrective justice features the maintenance and restoration of the notional equality with which the parties enter the transaction … Injustice occurs when, relative to this baseline, one party realizes a gain and the other a corresponding loss. The law corrects this injustice when it re-establishes the initial equality by depriving one party of the gain and restoring it to the other party.

The 'correction' that Weinrib contemplates is the re-establishment of a pre-existing state. But why return to the past? The law of unjust enrichment makes no enquiry into the normative desirability of the pre-transaction state of affairs. Why, then, should the law insist on returning to it? Academic literature offers a number of potential responses.[28] For the present purposes, it will suffice to consider Weinrib's own response, which is based on the need to maintain 'equality' between the parties.

B. Equality, of What?

Aristotle's conception of corrective justice, upon which Weinrib builds his corrective justice theory, relies on the notion of 'transactional equality'.[29] On this account, the parties' pre-transfer positions are analogous to 'two equal lines'.[30] A defective transfer upsets that equality and, therefore, corrective justice calls for its reversal. There is an important gap in this analysis. As Weinrib says, Aristotle 'does not tell us what the equality is an equality *of*'.[31] It will be explained below that the 'equality' corrective justice presupposes is the parties'

[27] Ernest Weinrib, 'Correlativity and Personality' in *Corrective Justice* (Oxford, Oxford University Press, 2016) 16. See also, Weinrib, 'Corrective Justice in a Nutshell' (n 11) 349; Weinrib, 'The Gains and Losses of Corrective Justice' (n 14) 280; Doyle (n 13) 234.

[28] Coleman (n 1) 63.

[29] Weinrib, *The Idea of Private Law* (n 1) 57.

[30] Weinrib, 'Corrective Justice in a Nutshell' (n 11) 349. See also, Weinrib, 'The Gains and Losses of Corrective Justice' (n 14) 280 ('From the standpoint of corrective justice, the two parties are equals, and justice consists in vindicating their equality').

[31] Weinrib, *The Idea of Private Law* (n 1) 57 (emphasis added).

equal entitlement to their pre-transaction holdings. I draw support for that view from three sources.

i. Scholastics and Natural Lawyers

The application of Aristotle's corrective justice (or 'commutative justice',[32] as it was sometimes called) by the Scholastics provides useful insights. For example, Aquinas conceptualised restitution as 'nothing else but restoring someone to the possession or ownership of his goods'.[33] Although translations of Aquinas's work use the words 'his goods', Aquinas's original language referred not just to 'his' goods or 'his' belongings, but anything that was 'coming to him' or 'due to him' 'either because of the law or by reason of justice'.[34] When understood in this way, Aquinas's analysis comes very close to recognising that the claimant's pre-transaction entitlements are a necessary condition for restitution. Indeed, in some of his later work Aquinas explained that corrective justice was violated either by interfering with another's property (*acceptio rei*) or by having what belonged to another (*ipsa res accepta*).[35]

The claimant's pre-transaction entitlement was an important component of the Scholastics' conception of 'equality' and corrective justice more generally. As Hallebeek observes,[36]

> From the viewpoint of moral theology [of the Scholastics], what matters is that someone has been deprived of his belongings. This is the inequality which according to justice should be nullified.

Gordley's examination of the evolution of unjust enrichment through the age of the late Scholastics and the early natural lawyers reaches the same conclusion.[37] He demonstrates that the reasons for recognising claims based on unjust enrichment were inextricably connected with the recognition and preservation of private property and resources. While 'distributive justice gives each citizen a fair share of whatever resources the state has to divide', the role of commutative justice is to 'preserve the share of each citizen'.[38] On this view, a violation of commutative justice occurs when benefits are derived from 'another's resources'.[39] This is why Scholastics and natural lawyers premised their notion of unjust enrichment on the defendant's enrichment being derived from the claimant's 'resources'. As Gordley explains,[40]

[32] Ernest Weinrib, 'Corrective Justice' (1992) 77 Iowa Law Review 403, 414.
[33] Jan Hallebeek, *The Concept of Unjust Enrichment in Late Scholasticism* (Gerard Noodt Instituut, 1996) 47.
[34] ibid 48.
[35] James Gordley, *Foundations of Private Law: Property, Tort, Contract, Unjust Enrichment* (Oxford, Oxford University Press, 2006) 424.
[36] Hallebeek (n 33) 48.
[37] Gordley (n 35) 419.
[38] ibid 424.
[39] ibid.
[40] ibid 425.

> We should note the context in which they spoke of unjust enrichment. Resources, from which one party had the exclusive right to benefit, had been used to confer on someone else the very benefit to which the first party had the exclusive right. Commutative justice forbad the second party to keep the benefit. That is a quite different and much more defensible claim than to say that no one should benefit as the result of a loss or cost suffered or incurred by someone else.

In short, the 'equality' that Aristotle, the Scholastics and the natural lawyers had in mind when they spoke about corrective justice was 'an equality of entitlement to [the parties'] respective pre-interaction goods'.[41]

ii. The Modern Literature on Corrective Justice

There is overwhelming support for this conception of equality in the modern literature on corrective justice. Smith considers this issue in detail.[42] He adopts Aristotle's understanding of justice as a 'mean'. On this view, justice consists in not having too much or too little of something. But 'too much' or 'too little' with reference to what? In the context of distributive justice, the answer depends on the criteria for distribution. By contrast, corrective is concerned,[43]

> not with equality of proportions but equality of entitlement to pretransaction holdings ... Corrective justice requires that pretransaction holdings be respected, and it is achieved when they are. If D takes ten units from P, then corrective justice is violated and requires that the units be returned.

Consequently, Aristotle's idea of the 'mean' denotes 'nothing other than [the parties'] initial holding conceived and validated as an entitlement'.[44] In an article entitled 'The Protection of Entitlements via the Law of Restitution',[45] Friedmann develops this thesis further. He convincingly demonstrates that the law of restitution vindicates and protects the claimant's pre-existing entitlements. He says:[46]

> The causes of action and the rights of recovery in torts and restitution presuppose the existence of some initial entitlement which they are meant to protect against certain events. They operate to redress an injury or imbalance between the parties with regard to their initial entitlements.

[41] Richard Wright, 'Susbtantive Corrective Justice' (1992) 77 Iowa Law Review 625, 641–642.

[42] Smith (n 1).

[43] ibid 2118. See also, Hanoch Dagan, 'The Distributive Foundation of Corrective Justice' (1999) 98 Michigan Law Review 138, 140 ('Unjust Enrichment studies cases in which A holds a resource that B appropriates, to her own advantage and to A's harm').

[44] Peter Benson, 'The Basis of Corrective Justice and Its Relation to Distributive Justice' (1992) 77 Iowa Law Review 515, 541.

[45] Daniel Friedmann, 'The Protection of Entitlements via the Law of Restitution – Expectancies and Privacy' (2005) 121 Law Quarterly Review 400.

[46] ibid 401.

On this analysis, the equality that corrective justice seeks to preserve is the parties' equal entitlement to their pre-transaction holdings. The content of those entitlements is not determined by corrective justice or the law of unjust enrichment. As Friedmann explains, these entitlements are derived from other facilitative branches of the law.[47] In this sense, corrective justice is 'parasitic'[48] in nature. It follows that the equality that corrective justice demands is 'equal treatment with respect to [the parties'] independently definable just holdings'.[49] As Waluchow puts it,[50]

> [Corrective justice] presupposes an independently definable just status quo; a status quo of equality in which each party has, by law, his due – his entitlements – and which owing to the actions of the defendant, has been distributed.

The idea that corrective justice presupposes a pre-existing set of entitlements is also adopted by Coleman. He distinguishes between 'transactional rights' (ie rights generated by corrective justice) and 'underlying rights' (ie the parties' pre-transfer entitlements). Coleman recognises that transactional rights are conditional on the parties' underlying rights. Indeed, he considers that the underlying rights condition the nature of the transactional rights. Thus, it is impossible to 'disassociate the duty to make repair from the status of the underlying entitlements and treat the latter as if it had no bearing on the grounds or content of the former'.[51]

iii. Weinrib

Weinrib has also adopted the notion that the equality of corrective justice is the parties' equal entitlement to their pre-transaction entitlements:

> Corrective justice ... features the maintenance and restoration of the notional equality with which the parties enter the transaction. <u>The equality consists of persons having what lawfully belongs to them</u>. Injustice occurs when, relative to this baseline, one party realizes a gain and the other a corresponding loss.[52]
>
> Equality consists in persons' having what belongs to them. The parties do not have the same quantity of holdings, but they are <u>equal as the owners of whatever they do have</u>.[53]

[47] ibid 400. See also, Mark Gergen, 'What Renders Enrichment Unjust?' (2001) 79 Texas Law Review 1927, 1930 ('Consent by a person with power to allocate a resource will always bar a claim that the resource's allocation to D rather than to P was unjust').

[48] WJ Waluchow, 'Professor Weinrib on Corrective Justice' in Panagiotou S (ed), *Justice, Law and Method in Plato and Aristotle* (Edmonton, Academic Printing & Publishing, 1987) 156.

[49] ibid.

[50] ibid.

[51] Coleman (n 1) 63. See also, Steven Walt, 'Eliminating Corrective Justice' (2006) 92 Virginia Law Review 1311, 1321 ('the duty of repair arises upon the violation of legal entitlements, whether or not the entitlements are morally legitimate').

[52] Weinrib, 'Corrective Justice in a Nutshell' (n 11) 13 (emphasis added).

[53] Weinrib, *The Idea of Private Law* (n 1) 63 (emphasis added).

Cane examines this aspect of Weinrib's theory in detail. He concludes that Weinrib's corrective justice is 'more easily explained in terms of protection of an existing distribution of resources'.[54] Similarly, Barker considers it 'an immensely important insight' of Weinrib's work that 'corrective justice restores prior legal *entitlements*, not simply prior *factual positions*'.[55]

For present purposes, the key point is that a corrective justice theory of unjust enrichment is dependent on the pre-transfer entitlements of the claimant. As Weinrib says, 'of course corrective justice presupposes the existence of entitlements'.[56]

C. Entitlements, to What?

The proposition that the claimant's pre-transaction entitlements are a necessary component of the corrective justice account of unjust enrichment leads to a further question. What are these entitlements? The literature on corrective justice offers two broad approaches which I will outline briefly.

On one approach, pre-transfer entitlements that ground restitution claims are derived from other areas of the law.[57] Three non-exhaustive examples are commonly offered.[58] The first concerns proprietary entitlements.

> *Example 1*: C owes £100 to D1. C mistakenly pays the money to D2, D1's twin brother. D2 believes, in good faith, that he is entitled to the payment. C seeks restitution from D2.

[54] Peter Cane, 'Corrective Justice and Correlativity in Private Law' (1996) 16 Oxford Journal of Legal Studies 472, 476. See also, Martin Hevía, *Reasonableness and Responsibility: A Theory of Contract Law* (Dordrecht, Springer, 2013) 13 ('The purpose of corrective justice is the protection of entitlements: interferences with them are wrongful to entitlement holders, and justice requires the correction of the injustices that those interferences entail').

[55] Kit Barker, 'Understanding the Unjust Enrichment Principle in Private Law: A Study of the Concept and its Reasons' in Jason Neyers, Mitchell McInnes and Stephen Pitel (eds), *Understanding Unjust Enrichment* (Oxford, Hart, 2004) 100. See also, Kit Barker, 'Theorising Unjust Enrichment Law: Being Realist(ic)?' (2006) 26 Oxford Journal of Legal Studies 609, 618.

[56] Weinrib, *The Idea of Private Law* (n 1) 80. There is a substantial body of literature that examines whether corrective justice's reliance on pre-transaction entitlements breaks down the distinction between corrective justice and distributive justice. For that debate see, ibid 80 ('As an autonomous function of justice, corrective justice operates on entitlements without addressing the justice of the underlying distribution. Even if corrective justice works against a distributive background, it accepts the distribution as given and does not incorporate the justification of the distribution into its own structure. Therefore, the existence of a distribution in no way implies that the equality of corrective justice is identical to the equality embodied in the distribution'); Klimchuk, 'On the Autonomy of Corrective Justice' (n 5); Benson (n 44); Stephen Perry, 'On the Relationship between Corrective Justice and Distributive Justice' in Jeremy Horder (ed), *Oxford Essays in Jurisprudence* (Oxford, Oxford University Press, 2000) 237.

[57] Gordley (n 35) 425.

[58] For the view that restitution claims may also be justified by reference to other types of entitlements, see Friedmann (n 45); Daniel Friedmann, 'The Creation of Entitlements Through the Law of Restitution' in Peter Birks, CEF Rickett and Ross Grantham (eds), *Structure and Justification in Private Law* (Oxford, Hart, 2008) 189.

C's claim will succeed. On Weinrib's analysis, C's claim is based on the fact that the mistaken payment – a defective transfer of value – was made by C and received by D2 non-donatively. But a significant part of that normative justification is C's right to the £100 before it was transferred to D2. As Friedmann says, 'the source of the plaintiff's [restitutionary] right lies in his primary entitlement, namely his ownership of the £100 paid under mistake'.[59]

By analogy, restitution claims may also be justified by reference to entitlements that are not, strictly, property. Consider, for instance, a mistaken transfer from the claimant's bank account to the defendant's bank account. The claimant's entitlement here is 'a contractual right vis-à-vis the bank'.[60] The normative basis of C's restitution claim depends in part on this entitlement. Lord Goff's speech in *Lipkin Gorman*[61] illustrates this. In that case, the claimant firm of solicitors sought to recover a sum of money from the defendant club. This sum had been unauthorisedly withdrawn from the claimant's bank account by one of their partners and then used to place bets at the defendant club. In that context, Lord Goff recognised that,[62]

> there was of course no question of the solicitors having any legal property in any cash lying at the bank. The relationship of the bank with the solicitors was essentially that of debtor and creditor.

Having found that the claimants could not found their claim upon their property in the money, Lord Goff relied on a different entitlement:

> [S]ince the client account was at all material times in credit, the bank was the debtor and the solicitors were its creditors. Such a debt constitutes a chose in action, which is a species of property; and since the debt was enforceable at common law, the chose in action was legal property belonging to the solicitors at common law.[63]
>
> [T]he solicitors [were] owners of the chose in action constituted by the indebtedness of the bank to them in respect of the sums paid into the client account.[64]

An entitlement-based analysis may also be offered for cases where the defendant benefits from the claimant's mistaken provision of services. In these cases, the claimant's pre-transfer entitlement consists in her right to her own labour. As Friedmann puts it, '[t]hese services "belong" to the plaintiff who is ordinarily entitled to "sell" them'.[65]

[59] Friedmann, 'The Protection of Entitlements via the Law of Restitution – Expectancies and Privacy' (n 45) 403–404.

[60] ibid 406.

[61] *Lipkin Gorman v Karpnale Ltd* [1991] 2 AC 548 (HL).

[62] ibid 573–574.

[63] ibid 574.

[64] ibid.

[65] Friedmann, 'The Protection of Entitlements via the Law of Restitution – Expectancies and Privacy' (n 45) 409.

By contrast to the approach that was outlined above, Weinrib adopts a different method to answer the question: what are the claimant's pre-transaction entitlements? He relies on a monolithic conception of the claimant's pre-transfer rights. He conceptualises this as the claimant's entitlement to value.[66] As noted above, a defective 'transfer of value' is one of the three obligation-creating conditions that trigger restitution on Weinrib's account. The idea of a 'transfer of value' from the claimant, he says, presumes the claimant's initial entitlement to value:[67]

> [B]ecause one can transfer only that to which one has a right, the notion of a transfer of value recognizes that the transaction enriched the defendant with what was initially within the plaintiff's entitlement.

What is the basis of the claimant's entitlement to value at the beginning of the story? In response, Weinrib relies on the Hegelian notion that value is an incident of rights. 'As full owner of the thing', Hegel says, 'I am *eo ipso* owner of its value as well as of its use'.[68] Similarly, Weinrib argues, the claimants' pre-transfer right to value is an incident of her right to her own labour or property.[69] It will be apparent to the reader that this analysis is closely aligned with the first approach identified earlier. Weinrib simply characterises entitlements derived from other branches of the law in terms of the claimant's right to value. Ultimately, even on Weinrib's analysis, the claimant's entitlement to value is an incident of the claimant's rights to property, labour or other rights. What is significant, however, is Weinrib's recognition that the claimant's pre-transfer right to value is an indispensable component of a claim in unjust enrichment:[70]

> The plaintiff's right to the value at the inception of its transfer is the precondition of the claim that the value should be retransferred to the plaintiff once the transfer is shown to be defective.

If the claimant did not have a legitimate entitlement to value, Weinrib says, she 'would have no standing to have the value returned'.[71]

As explained above, one body of literature on corrective justice understands the claimant's entitlements as derived from other legal interests such as property, labour or contractual entitlements. Weinrib, by contrast, considers the claimant's 'right to value' as a common thread that runs across all unjust enrichment claims.[72] For present purposes, it is unnecessary to decide which approach is preferable. The key point is that, on either view, the claimants'

[66] For the broader role that the conception of 'value' plays in Weinrib's account, see Chapter 7, Section I(B)(i) above.
[67] Weinrib, 'Unjust Enrichment' (n 19) 199.
[68] GWF Hegel, *Outlines of the Philosophy of Right* (Oxford, Oxford University Press, 2008) 75.
[69] Weinrib, 'The Normative Structure of Unjust Enrichment' (n 20) 43.
[70] Weinrib, 'Unjust Enrichment' (n 19) 199.
[71] Weinrib, 'The Normative Structure of Unjust Enrichment' (n 20) 30–31.
[72] In relation to the idea of 'transfer of value', see also Chapter 2, Section (I)(B)(i)(c).

pre-transaction entitlements are an essential part of the corrective justice explanation for unjust enrichment.

D. Corrective Justice and the Equality Thesis

The previous section demonstrated that the claimant's pre-transfer entitlements are a necessary component of the corrective justice explanation for unjust enrichment. Once this is recognised, the equality thesis operates within the corrective justice framework just as it does within the entitlement theory. The claimant cannot use corrective justice to protect her entitlements while simultaneously denying similar protection to the defendant. This is what would happen if the claimant were granted the restitution of an enrichment which the defendant received in discharge of a valid legal obligation. Restitution must therefore be denied in such cases. This is the function the obligation rule performs. Indeed, the equality thesis stands on an even stronger footing in the corrective justice context than it does within the framework of the entitlement theory because the corrective justice explanation for unjust enrichment is itself based on a line of reasoning that mirrors the equality explanation.

Consider the defendant-centered enquiry: why must the defendant provide restitution? In the context of a simple mistaken payment, the defendant is not a wrongdoer. Nor is it at fault for the claimant's mistake. Why then is the defendant liable for restitution? Weinrib's answer is based on the equality of parties. Holding the defendant liable based solely on the claimant's unilateral mistake, he argues, would amount to treating the parties inconsistently:[73]

> The basis of the plaintiff's claim is that, in the absence of donative intent on her part, the transfer … has deprived her of value that belonged to her without her having freely parted with it. If the plaintiff's lack of donative intent were to suffice for liability, defendants in turn would be deprived of what belongs to them without their having freely parted with it. The principle of justice in transfer, that one is entitled to what one owns until one freely parts with it, would thereby be inconsistently asserted for the plaintiffs and denied for defendants.

Weinrib's reasoning in this passage is closely aligned with the equality thesis. Weinrib's concern is that, if a non-consensual transfer of value is considered objectionable from the claimant's perspective, why is it permissible to require the defendant to give up value non-consensually?

This reasoning has particular resonance in the context of the obligation rule. By asserting a restitution claim, the claimant says that the defendant's benefit was derived from its resources non-consensually. But when the enrichment is owed to the defendant under a valid legal obligation, granting restitution would

[73] Weinrib, 'Unjust Enrichment' (n 19) 203.

deprive the defendant of its legitimate entitlement. Permitting restitution would, therefore, amount to treating the parties inconsistently.

It was mentioned earlier that Weinrib analyses the defendant-sided enquiry as a concern about equality. Some corrective justice accounts rely on the equality thesis as an *answer* to that enquiry too. The crux of their analysis is the suggestion that the defendant cannot, without contradiction, deny the claimant's right to restitution. As McInnes explains,[74]

> By resisting liability, the defendant broadly asserts the right to retain his … enrichment until he freely chooses to part with it. Contrary to the Kantian imperative, however, he thereby claims for himself a right that he is unwilling to extend to others. Since the plaintiff's intention in conferring the benefit was vitiated by error, her payment was not truly an instance of self-determining agency. Consequently, if the defendant cannot be forced into an involuntary transaction, the plaintiff cannot be held to hers.

On this view, maintaining equality between the claimant and the defendant is a significant imperative of corrective justice. As Drassinower puts it,[75]

> [S]trictly formulated, the principle at the heart of the law of unjust enrichment is not the principle that a person is entitled to what is his until he freely parts with it. Rather, it is the bilateral principle that plaintiff and defendant are each equally entitled to what is theirs until they freely part with it. The import of this equality is that a denial of the one's entitlement must eo ipso amount to a denial of the other's.

The equality thesis states that in assessing whether the claimant is entitled to restitution based on the defendant's unjust enrichment the defendant's pre-existing entitlements must be taken into account. This proposition is entirely consistent with the corrective justice theory of unjust enrichment. As Weinrib explains:[76]

> 'One cleans another's shoes; what can the other do but put them on?' In this graphic example, the benefit has been so completely entangled in the recipient's property, that the cleaning of the shoes cannot be treated as an object of choice that is independent of his use of them.
>
> Nor can the mere wearing of the shoes count as acceptance, <u>for this would derogate from the pre-existing entitlement of the owner</u>, as having exclusive dominion over the shoes, to owe nothing to anyone else through their lawful use.

The same analysis applies when the enrichment is owed to the defendant under a valid legal obligation.

[74] Mitchell McInnes, 'The Measure of Restitution' (2002) 52 The University of Toronto Law Journal 163, 188. See also, McInnes, 'Unjust Enrichment: A Reply to Professor Weinrib' (n 15) 36.

[75] Abraham Drassinower, 'Unrequested Benefits in the Law of Unjust Enrichment' (1998) 48 The University of Toronto Law Journal 459, 468.

[76] Weinrib, 'Unjust Enrichment' (n 19) 204, 205 (emphasis added).

In summary, a large part of this chapter was devoted to explaining an often-overlooked aspect of Weinrib's corrective justice theory: the significance of the claimant's pre-transfer entitlements. Once this aspect is brought to light, it is easy to understand why the obligation rule defeats the reason(s) for restitution within the scheme of corrective justice. The equality thesis states that the claimant should not be permitted to use the law of restitution to protect its entitlements while simultaneously denying the same protection to the defendant. By denying restitution in these cases, the obligation rule ensures that the parties to an unjust enrichment claim are treated equally.

8

The Equality Thesis in Practice

CHAPTERS 6 AND 7 advanced the equality thesis. These chapters explained that the obligation rule is best explained on the basis of the need to maintain equality between the claimant and the defendant. This chapter will examine the practical consequences of the equality thesis. It will show that they are largely in line with the prevalent judicial and academic thinking on the operation of the obligation rule.

The remainder of this chapter is in three parts. Section I will explain that the obligation rule is not a defence but a denial of primary liability. Section II will examine the operation of the obligation rule in the context of different unjust factors. Section III will consider the application of the obligation rule to different countervailing obligations.

I. QUALIFICATION ON PRIMARY LIABILITY

The equality thesis helps locate where the obligation rule fits within the doctrinal scheme of unjust enrichment. It suggests that the normative reasons for an unjust enrichment claim are not satisfied if the defendant can assert a valid legal entitlement to the enrichment. It follows that the obligation rule denies the defendant's primary liability based on unjust enrichment.[1] This analysis is consistent with most academic and judicial authorities.

Most academic commentators say that a defendant's enrichment is not 'unjust' if the defendant has a valid legal entitlement to the enrichment.[2] This analysis has also been adopted by the courts. For example, in *Kleinwort*

[1] In the taxonomy proposed by Goudkamp and Mitchell, the obligation rule is a 'denial', not a 'defence': James Goudkamp and Charles Mitchell, 'Denials and Defences in the Law of Unjust Enrichment' in *The Restatement Third, Restitution and Unjust Enrichment: Critical and Comparative Essays* (Oxford, Hart, 2013) 133.

[2] Andrew Burrows, 'Is There a Defence of Good Consideration?' in *The Restatement Third, Restitution and Unjust Enrichment: Critical and Comparative Essays* (Oxford, Hart, 2013) 167; Graham Virgo, *The Principles of the Law of Restitution* (3rd edn, Oxford, Oxford University Press, 2015) 133; Sonja Meier, 'Unjust Factors and Legal Grounds' in David Johnston and Reinhard Zimmerman (eds), *Unjustified Enrichment: Key Issues in Comparative Perspective* (Cambridge, Cambridge University Press, 2002) 53.

Benson,[3] Lord Hope said that 'the payee cannot be said to have been unjustly enriched if he was entitled to receive the sum paid to him'.[4] Similarly, in *DD Growth Premium 2X Fund*, Lord Sumption said,[5]

> It is fundamental that a payment cannot amount to enrichment if it was made for full consideration; and that it cannot be unjust to receive or retain it if it was made in satisfaction of a legal right.

The same view was adopted by the High Court of Australia in *David Securities*, where Brennan J said:[6]

> [T]o say that a defendant has been unjustly enriched by the receipt of a payment is to say that the defendant has no right to receive it … If a defendant has a right to receive a payment, whether under a statute, in discharge of a liability owing to him or pursuant to a contract, a mistake by the plaintiff in making the payment does not convert the receipt into an unjust enrichment.

Understanding the obligation rule as a restriction on primary liability in unjust enrichment has several practical implications. The most important of these relates to burden of proof.[7] The burden of establishing that the defendant's enrichment is 'unjust' falls on the claimant. Therefore, the burden of proving that the enrichment was not owed to the defendant must also fall on the claimant.[8] As Lord Millet said in *Tribe v Tribe*,[9] 'the burden lies on the plaintiff to prove that the money was not paid by way of gift or pursuant to an enforceable contract'.

If the defendant received nothing more than what it was entitled to, it is only fair that the burden of disproving that fact must fall on the claimant. As Burrows says:[10]

> D is merely receiving what it was, on the face of it, entitled to receive from C … Why should D be put to the burden of proving that the obligation was valid rather than putting the burden on C, who after all is bringing the claim, to prove that the prior obligation is not as it seems?

However, it would be virtually impossible for the claimant to disprove that the enrichment was not owed to the defendant pursuant to any conceivable obligation.

[3] *Kleinwort Benson Ltd v Lincoln City Council* [1998] UKHL 38, [1999] 2 AC 349.

[4] ibid 408 (Lord Hope). See also, *Deutsche Morgan Grenfell Group Plc v Inland Revenue Commissioners* [2006] UKHL 49, [2007] 1 AC 558 [85] (Lord Scott) ('*DMG*').

[5] *DD Growth Premium 2X Fund v RMF Market Neutral Strategies* [2017] UKPC 36, [2018] Bus LR 1595 [62].

[6] *David Securities v Commonwealth Bank of Australia* [1992] HCA 48, (1992) 175 CLR 353, 392 (Brennan J).

[7] See, James Goudkamp, *Tort Law Defences* (Oxford, Hart, 2016) 138–139.

[8] Burrows, 'Is There a Defence of Good Consideration?' (n 2) 182–183; Duncan Sheehan, *The Scope and Structure of Unjust Enrichment* (Oxford, Hart, 2024) 39, 81, 133, 181.

[9] *Tribe v Tribe* [1995] Ch 107 (CA) 125. See also, *National Mutual Life Association v Walsh* (1987) 8 NSWLR 585 (NSWSC).

[10] Burrows, 'Is There a Defence of Good Consideration?' (n 2) 183. See also, Andrew Burrows, *A Restatement of the English Law of Unjust Enrichment* (Oxford, Oxford University Press, 2012) 31. For a contrary view, see, Virgo, *The Principles of the Law of Restitution* (n 2) 173.

Therefore, the preferable approach is to impose the burden of proof on the claimant once the defendant has pleaded an entitlement to the enrichment.[11] In other words, there should be an initial evidential burden on the defendant. Once the defendant has discharged the evidential burden, the legal burden is on the claimant. Scott proposes the following useful scheme:[12]

> (a) the claimant begins by pleading (and proving) that he made the payment by mistake;
> (b) the defendant pleads that the payment was in fact due under a valid contractual, statutory or other obligation;
> (c) it then falls to the claimant to prove that no such valid contract or other obligation exists.

This scheme is consistent with the equality thesis, and has the merit of clarity and convenience.

II. UNJUST FACTORS

The equality thesis suggests that the obligation rule will apply regardless of the unjust factor upon which the unjust enrichment claim is based. The application of the obligation rule is not restricted to claims based on mistake.

For example, the obligation rule has been applied to claims based on duress. In *Flower v Sadler*,[13] the employee sought to set aside some bills of exchange drawn in favour of the defendant. The claimant alleged that the bills were procured as a consequence of the defendant's threat to prosecute him. Even if that were true, it was held, the payment would be irrecoverable because,[14]

> [A] debt was actually due from [the claimant], and there is nothing illegal in a creditor endeavouring to obtain payment of his debt … if a debt really exists, the right to sue for it must be upheld even although there may have been a threat by the creditor of criminal proceedings.

In *Ward v Lloyd*,[15] a claim for restitution based on duress was dismissed on the basis that the claimant did nothing more than demand what was legitimately owed to him. *Astley v Reynolds*[16] offers another illustration. The claimant had pawned his plate with the defendant for £20. The defendant threatened not

[11] Virgo, *The Principles of the Law of Restitution* (n 2) 133.

[12] Helen Scott, 'Defence, Denial or Cause of Action? 'Enrichment Owed' and the Absence of a Legal Ground' in Andrew Dyson, James Goudkamp and Frederick Wilmot-Smith (eds), *Defences in Unjust Enrichment* (Oxford, Hart, 2016) 65.

[13] *Flower v Sadler* (1882) 10 QBD 572 (CA). For the contrary view, see, *Clark v Woods* (1848) 2 Ex 395, 154 ER 545.

[14] *Flower* (n 13) 575.

[15] *Ward v Lloyd* (1843) 6 Man & G 785, 134 ER 1109.

[16] *Astley v Reynolds* (1731) 2 Str 915, 93 ER 939.

to return the plate unless an additional amount of £10 was paid. Though the claim based on duress succeeded, the claimant was only allowed to recover the surplus of £10. One explanation for this result is that the sum of £20 was owed to the defendant.[17]

Australian courts have also adopted the view that the application of the obligation rule is not restricted to mistake claims. For example, three judges of the Supreme Court of Western Australia held that a claim based on duress will not succeed if the relevant payment was owed to the defendant.[18] Giles J adopted a similar approach in *Equiticorp Financial Services*.[19] In that case, a claim based on duress failed because the defendant was owed a greater sum than the amount he received.[20]

On principle, there is no reason why the obligation rule should be inapplicable to claims based on the policy-motivated unjust factors. Consider, for example, the decision of the New Zealand Supreme Court in *Stiassny*.[21] In that case, the claimant partnership firm brought a claim against the Revenue seeking to recover mistakenly paid Goods and Services Tax (GST). The claim was based on the *Woolwich* principle. The claim failed. Although the Court applied the good consideration rule rather than the obligation rule, either principle would have led to the same result. The key point is that the amount of GST that the claimant sought restitution of was owed to the Crown pursuant to a valid legal obligation.[22]

III. COUNTERVAILING LEGAL OBLIGATIONS

This section will examine the operation of the obligation rule in the context of different countervailing legal obligations such as contracts, statutes, judgments and other legal entitlements. Natural obligations and gifts are also considered briefly.

A. Contracts

The existence of a contractual regime may impact an unjust enrichment claim in a number of different ways. Parties may contractually exclude a

[17] Graham Virgo, 'Demolishing the Pyramid: the Presence of Basis and Risk-Taking in the Law of Unjust Enrichment' in Andrew Robertson and Hang Wu Tang (eds), *The Goals of Private Law* (Oxford, Hart Publishing, 2009) 495.

[18] *Scolio Pty Ltd v Cote* (1992) 6 WAR 475 (SCWA) 482 (Ipp J & Seaman J), 484 (Rowland J).

[19] *Equiticorp Financial Services Ltd v Equiticorp Financial Services Ltd* (1992) 29 NSWLR 260 (NSWSC).

[20] ibid 300–301. See also, James Edelman and Elise Bant, *Unjust Enrichment* (2nd edn, Oxford, Hart, 2016) 346.

[21] *Stiassny v Commissioner of Inland Revenue* [2012] NZSC 106.

[22] ibid [65].

restitution claim, expressly or impliedly.[23] The contractually agreed price may influence the valuation of a restitution claim.[24] The existence of a contractual regime between one of the parties to the restitution claim and a third party may also influence the unjust enrichment analysis.[25] This section will not attempt to examine all these contractual consequences. The focus here is only on cases where the enrichment was owed to the defendant pursuant to a valid contractual obligation.

i. Valid Contracts

In the context of valid contracts, the key question is: did the defendant have a valid contractual entitlement to the enrichment in respect of which the claimant seeks restitution? If the answer is yes, restitution will be denied.

Steam Saw Mills v Baring Bros Co Ltd[26] illustrates this. This decision was examined in Chapter 1. In summary, the claimant held a licence from the Russian government to import timber. As a condition of the licence, the claimant was required to deposit the purchase price with the defendant in advance. The dispute concerned payments made by the claimant on 9 November 1917. By then, the Russian government had been overthrown by revolution. The claimant argued that, had it been aware of this fact, it would not have made the advance payment. Lord Sterndale rejected the claim for restitution:[27]

> [I]f a man pays money under a mistake of fact, there being a liability to pay it, if the fact of which he was ignorant does not discharge him from that liability, he cannot recover it back.

Despite the claimant's mistake, the defendant had a valid contractual entitlement to the 9 November payment, which is why restitution was unavailable.

Bell v Lever Bros[28] is another example. The defendants were employed by the claimant companies. As the result of a corporate restructuring exercise, their employment was terminated prematurely. The claimant entered into two separate compensation agreements with the defendants offering them compensation for the early termination of their services. Subsequently,

[23] See Charles Mitchell, Paul Mitchell and Stephen Watterson, *Goff & Jones: The Law of Unjust Enrichment* (10th edn, London, Sweet & Maxwell, 2022) [3-28]; Virgo, *The Principles of the Law of Restitution* (n 2) 141.

[24] Andrew Burrows, *The Law of Restitution* (3rd edn, Oxford, Oxford University Press, 2011) 348–350.

[25] See *Pan Ocean Shipping Co Ltd v Creditcorp Ltd (The Trident Beauty)* [1994] 1 WLR 161 (HL); *MacDonald Dickens & Macklin v Costello* [2011] EWCA Civ 930, [2012] QB 244. See also, Mitchell, Mitchell and Watterson (n 23) [3-62]–[3-66]; Virgo, *The Principles of the Law of Restitution* (n 2) 142.

[26] *Steam Saw Mills Company Ltd v Baring Brothers* [1922] 1 Ch 244 (CA).

[27] ibid 250. See also, *DMG* (n 4) [85] (Lord Scott); *Re Magarey Farlam Lawyers Trust Accounts (No 3)* [2007] SASC 9, 96 SASR 337 [177]; Virgo, *The Principles of the Law of Restitution* (n 2) 134.

[28] *Bell v Lever Bros* [1932] AC 161 (HL).

the claimant discovered that the employees had entered into certain unauthorised transactions on behalf of the company. This was a breach of the terms of their service agreement and would have entitled the employer to terminate their services without paying compensation. Upon realising their mistake, the employers sought restitution of the benefits paid out under the compensation agreements.

The claim failed. The employees had a valid contractual entitlement to the benefits they received under the compensation agreement. Consequently, no restitution claim could be brought in respect of those benefits. Lord Atkin said:[29]

> A buys B's horse; he thinks the horse is sound and he pays the price of a sound horse; he would certainly not have bought the horse if he had known as the fact is that the horse is unsound. If B has made no representation as to soundness and has not contracted that the horse is sound, A is bound and cannot recover back the price.

Steam Saw Mills and *Bell* are straightforward cases. The defendant had a valid contractual entitlement to the enrichment in both cases and, therefore, the restitution claims failed. In some other cases, the nature of the defendant's entitlement is less straightforward. For example, the defendant's entitlement may be conditional on a prior event. If that condition is not satisfied, the entitlement will be rendered inoperative. In effect, this leaves the defendant in the same position as if it had no entitlement to the enrichment. There is then no reason why a restitution claim should not succeed.

In some cases, the condition attached to the defendant's contractual entitlement is the claimant's counter-performance. *Deglman v Guaranty Trust Co* illustrates this.[30] This decision was considered in detail in Chapter 4, Section III. In summary, there was an oral contract between the plaintiff and his aunt. Pursuant to that contract, the plaintiff performed certain services for the aunt. In return she promised him that she would make provision for him in her will. The contract was found to be valid but unenforceable under the Statute of Frauds. The plaintiff subsequently sought restitution of the value of services he rendered. The Supreme Court of Canada granted the claim. As explained in Chapter 4, Section III the aunt's contractual right to the plaintiff's services was conditional on her counter-performance. She failed to fulfil her promise to make provision for the plaintiff in her will. As a consequence, a necessary pre-condition for her contractual entitlement was not satisfied. This is why the obligation rule did not preclude restitution in this case.

In some cases, the defendant's entitlement is conditional on matters other than counter-performance by the defendant. *Barnes v Eastenders Cash & Carry plc*[31]

[29] ibid 224. See also, *Kwei Tek Chao v British Traders and Shippers* [1954] 2 QB 459 (QB); *RJ Brady Contracting Pty Ltd v Kellyville Christmas Tree Farm Pty Ltd* [2005] NSWCA 22.

[30] *Deglman v Guaranty Trust Co of Canada* [1954] SCR 725 (Supreme Court of Canada).

[31] *Barnes v Eastenders Cash & Carry plc* [2014] UKSC 26; [2015] AC 1.

illustrates this. In that case, the claimant was appointed the receiver for a group of companies upon an application made by the Crown Prosecution Service (CPS). The claimant rendered his services on the basis that he would be remunerated out of the companies' assets. This was also agreed between the claimant and the CPS.[32] Subsequently, the order appointing the claimant was quashed. This meant that the claimant could no longer make a claim over the companies' assets. The claimant sought restitution of the value of his services from the CPS. His claim was based on failure of consideration. He argued that the basis upon which he rendered services was that he would be remunerated from the companies' assets. The claim succeeded despite the agreement between the claimant and the CPS. The best explanation for this result is that the claimant's obligation to provide his services was conditional. The condition was not counter-performance but the existence of a state of affairs. As Lord Toulson put it,[33]

> [T]he receiver agreed to accept the burden of management of the companies on the basis that he would be entitled to take his remuneration and expenses from the companies' assets, and that state of affairs which was fundamental to the agreement has failed to sustain itself.

In other words, the claimant's obligation to provide services and the defendant's entitlement to receive them were both conditional on the claimant's right to remunerate himself from the companies' assets. When that condition failed, the defendant's entitlement to the claimant's services was rendered inoperative. As a result, the defendant had no contractual entitlement to the claimant's services.[34]

Whether the defendant has earned an unconditional entitlement to the enrichment is a question of contractual construction. The fact that the contract provides that a sum has fallen 'due' does not necessarily mean that it has been unconditionally earned. This is illustrated by *Shell-Mex Ltd v Elton Cop Dyeing Co Ltd*.[35] The claimant sellers were contractually entitled to invoice the defendant buyers for quantities of oil that were not taken up by the buyer. Clause 15 of the contract provided that:

> Sellers have the right at any time to invoice to buyers the due quantities of oil not taken up, and to demand payment of the invoice amounts, and such quantities (or a proportionate quantity of the bulk) shall be at the buyer's risk and expense, or the sellers may, at their option, instead of invoicing, cancel such undelivered balance.

[32] ibid [98].

[33] ibid [114].

[34] For another example where the defendant's entitlement was conditional on the existence of a state of affairs, see *Roxborough v Rothmans of Pall Mall Australia Ltd* [2001] HCA 68, (2001) 208 CLR 516. For a detailed examination of that decision see Chapter 4, Section I above. See also, *Clifton v Coffey* [1924] HCA 35, (1924) 34 CLR 434.

[35] *Shell-Mex Ltd v Elton Cop Dyeing Co Ltd* (1928) 34 Com Cas 39.

Payment for the quantities not taken up by the buyers was 'due' upon the receipt of the seller's invoice. However, the seller's right to the payment was conditional on actual delivery. Wright J said:[36]

> What is invoiced under clause 15 is still the price payable under the contract, which includes the sellers' services in actually delivering the goods to the buyers' works. The sellers have never earned the price as such, and can only claim damages because they have been prevented from fulfilling their contract.

By contrast, in some cases, the proper construction of the contract will be that the defendant's entitlement is unconditional despite the defendant not rendering proper, or any, counter-performance. In these cases, the obligation rule will preclude any claim for restitution. This is exemplified by *Wuhan Guoyu Logistics v Emporiki Bank*.[37] That was a dispute between the buyer and seller in a shipbuilding transaction and the defendant bank. The bank had provided an 'on-demand performance guarantee' on behalf of the buyer. On 11 May 2009, the seller demanded payment of the second instalment. The buyer refused to pay, contending that the instalment was not yet due. In June 2011, the seller made a demand against the bank relying upon the guarantee. The bank complied. Subsequently, the dispute between the buyer and the seller was referred to arbitration. The tribunal found that the second instalment was in fact not due. The bank sought restitution of the instalment payment. The claim failed.

This was because the bank's obligation and the seller's corresponding contractual entitlement were unconditional in nature. As Tomlinson LJ said:[38]

> [O]n making its demand of the bank … the Seller acquired a complete and immediately enforceable cause of action against the Bank. The Bank was obliged to pay immediately, as paragraph 4 of the Payment Guarantee spells out in terms. Thereafter the Seller's right to payment from the Bank was indefeasible, and it is of no relevance that the Seller subsequently discovers that his demand, although made in good faith, was in fact made upon an incorrect premise.

On a proper construction of the contract, the bank's obligation under the guarantee was *not* conditional on the buyer's obligation.[39] Consequently, regardless of the fact that there was no liability as between the buyer and seller, the bank remained contractually obliged to honour the guarantee. For the same reason, the seller was contractually entitled to the bank's payment.

Howes Percival LLP v Nicolas Page[40] is another example. The claimants were a firm of solicitors and the defendants were the owners of a family company.

[36] ibid 45 (emphasis added).

[37] *Wuhan Guoyu Logistics Group Co v Emporiki Bank of Greece SA* [2013] EWCA Civ 1679, [2014] 1 All ER (Comm) 870.

[38] ibid [20].

[39] See also, *Ministry of Sound (Ireland) Limited v World Online Limited* [2003] EWHC 2178 (Ch), [2003] 2 All ER (Comm) 823 [33].

[40] *Howes Percival LLP v Nicolas Page* [2013] EWHC 4104 (Ch).

The claimants had provided legal services to the defendants on the basis of a 'Conditional Fee Agreement' (CFA). Subsequently, disputes arose between the parties regarding their compliance with the CFA and the agreement was terminated. After termination, the claimants sought restitution of the value of their services from the defendants. This claim was dismissed.

This result is seemingly inconsistent with the decisions in *Deglman* and *Barnes*. Like in both those cases, in *Howes*, the claimants' services were rendered on the basis that they would be remunerated. However, there is a key difference. In *Howes*, the claimants' right to remuneration was itself conditional. Behrens J emphasised this point:[41]

> The cases cited by [counsel for the claimant] are distinguishable because none of them involved a conditional right to payment. Suppose for example it had become clear that [the defendants] were going to lose. In that event [the claimant] would be entitled to no fee.

Thus, in *Howes* (unlike in *Deglman* or *Barnes*), the claimants' services were not conditional on remuneration. The claimants' contractual right to remuneration was contingent on something else, namely the defendants' success in the litigation. Therefore, the claimants' services had been unconditionally earned under the contract. Therefore, the obligation rule applied.

Howes also illustrates that contractual termination is not a sufficient reason for a restitution claim to succeed. The legal services agreement in *Howes* had been terminated before the restitution claim was brought. Yet, the restitution claim failed. This is consistent with the principle that termination does not wipe away accrued contractual entitlements.[42] If the defendant's entitlement has unconditionally accrued before contractual termination, the restitution claim will fail.[43] Termination is neither necessary nor sufficient.

Bank of Boston v European Grain[44] illustrates this further. In that case, the dispute between the charterers and the ship owners was about the construction of the following contractual provision:

> Clause 16: Freight shall be prepaid within five days of signing and surrender of final bills of lading, full freight deemed to be earned on signing bills of lading, discountless and non-returnable, vessel and/or cargo lost or not lost and to be paid to [a named bank in the Piraeus].

[41] ibid [310].

[42] *Odfjell Seachem A/S v Continentale des Petroles et d'Investissements* [2004] EWHC 2929 (Comm).

[43] Robert Stevens, 'Is There a Law of Unjust Enrichment?' in Simone Degeling and James Edelman (eds), *Unjust Enrichment in Commercial Law* (Sydney, Thomson Reuters, 2008) 24–30; Stephen Waddams, 'Contract and Unjust Enrichment: Competing Categories, or Complementary Concepts?' in Peter Birks, Charles Rickett and Ross Grantham (eds), *Structure and Justification in Private Law: Essays for Peter Birks* (Oxford, Hart, 2008) 172. See also, Edelman and Bant (n 20) 167 ('restitution will be permitted notwithstanding the existence of a juristic reason to *receive* the benefit if considerations of coherence of the law have the effect that the juristic reason is not one which continues to permit the *retention* of the benefit') (emphasis added).

[44] *Bank of Boston v European Grain and Shipping Ltd* [1989] AC 1056 (HL).

The charterers argued that they had lawfully terminated the agreement by accepting the owner's repudiation. Consequently, it was argued that no payment was due under Clause 16. Relying on the words 'full freight deemed to be earned on signing bills of lading' in Clause 16, Lord Brandon rejected this contention. Bills of lading had been signed before termination. This was held to be a sufficient condition for freight to fall unconditionally due under the agreement.[45] The restitution claim, therefore, failed despite contractual termination.

ii. Voidable Contracts

A voidable contract creates valid contractual rights and obligations until it is rescinded. Until rescission, the defendant may rely on a voidable contract in support of its right to the enrichment in respect of which restitution is sought.[46] Before rescission, the obligation rule operates in the same way as it does in the context of a valid contract. Upon rescission, the contractual obligations under a voidable contract are wiped away retrospectively. Unlike in the context of a terminated contract, therefore, the defendant cannot rely on accrued rights under a voidable contract.[47] There are no such rights. Therefore, after rescission, there is no scope for the obligation rule to apply.

There is considerable support for this view in the authorities. The proposition that a voidable contract must first be rescinded before restitution can be sought was adopted in the eighteenth century decisions in *Towers v Barrett*[48] and *Weston v Downes*,[49] which were followed in *Load v Green*.[50] In *Load*, the defendant had obtained goods from the claimant through fraudulent misrepresentation. The claimant sought to recover the goods. It was held that rescission was a necessary pre-condition for the claim to succeed.

In cases where rescission is unavailable, the defendant's contractual entitlements remain in place. As a consequence, restitution is precluded by the obligation rule. This is illustrated by *Clarke v Dickson*.[51] The claimant was induced by fraudulent misrepresentations to subscribe to shares in a company. The company was subsequently wound up. During the winding up proceedings, the claimant discovered that representations were false. He sought restitution of the deposits that he had paid to subscribe to the shares. It was held that rescission was not available to the claimant. This was because *restitutio in integrum* was impossible as the shares had changed their nature following the claimant's subscription. Therefore, the claimant's restitution claim failed.

[45] ibid 1098. See also, *Stocznia Gdanska SA v Latvian Shipping Co* [1998] 1 WLR 574 (HL).

[46] Edelman and Bant (n 20) 146.

[47] Andrew Tettenborn, *The Law of Restitution in England and Ireland* (3rd edn, London, Cavendish, 2002) 154.

[48] *Towers v Barrett* (1786) 1 Term Reports 133; 99 ER 1014.

[49] *Weston v Downes* (1778) 1 Douglas 23; 99 ER 19.

[50] *Load v Green* (1846) 15 M&W 216; 153 ER 828.

[51] *Thomas Clarke v Samuel Dickson* (1858) EB & E 148; 120 ER 463.

It is doubtful whether a modern court would come to the same conclusion on whether rescission is available in these circumstances.[52] Nevertheless, *Clarke v Dickson* illustrates the point that rescission is a necessary pre-condition for seeking restitution of the benefits conferred under a voidable contract.

iii. Void Contracts

The obligation rule has no application in the context of void contracts for the obvious reason that such contracts do not create any contractual obligations.[53] But this does not mean that restitution necessarily follows. It was explained in Chapter 1, Section II(A) that the good consideration rule may deny restitution in some cases where benefits were conferred pursuant to a void contract.

The availability of restitution in such cases also depends on whether the other elements of unjust enrichment are satisfied. For example, in the Privy Council's decision in *Linz v Electric Wire Co*,[54] the claimant had applied for preference shares in the defendant company. After the shares were allotted, the claimant sold them off. It later turned out that the initial allotment was void. Upon discovering this, the claimant sought restitution from the company. The claim was based on failure of consideration. Although the contract between the claimant and the company was void, the claim failed. Lord Simonds explained that,[55]

> having been duly registered as a shareholder and having parted for value with her shares by a sale which the company recognized by issue of a share certificate to, and registration of, her transferee, she got exactly that which she bargained to get.

In other words, although the contract was void, there was no failure of consideration. The claimant had received what she had bargained for.[56]

Linz illustrates that the invalidity of a contract does not always mean that there has been a failure of consideration. Whether there has been a failure of consideration depends on what the parties bargained for. In *Linz*, the parties had not bargained for an enforceable promise. But there are cases in which that is the nature of the bargain. On one view, this is the best explanation for swaps cases such as *Guinness Mahon*.[57] In that case, the Court granted restitution to reverse a fully performed swap.[58] Why was the claim not dismissed on the basis

[52] *Erlanger v New Sombrero Phosphate Co* (1878) 3 App Cas 1218.

[53] Edelman and Bant (n 20) 142. See also, Anne Sanders, 'Absence of Basis: A German Perspective' in Steven Elliot, Birke Häcker and Charles Mitchell (eds), *Restitution of Overpaid Tax* (Oxford, Hart, 2014) 229.

[54] *Linz v Electric Wire Company of Palestine* [1948] AC 371 (PC).

[55] ibid 377.

[56] See also, *Sharma v Simposh Ltd* [2011] EWCA Civ 1383, [2013] Ch 23.

[57] *Guinness Mahon & Co Ltd v Kensington and Chelsea Royal London Borough Council* [1999] QB 215 (CA).

[58] ibid 230 (Morrit LJ).

that the parties got what they bargained for? Stevens and McFarlane argue that this is because:[59]

> whatever happened, the local authority could always recover money it paid out on the ground of its lack of capacity. It was never on risk and could never lose under the bet. The other party bargained for the opportunity to win under the bet and it never could. Receiving counter-performance is of little comfort if the local authority is always entitled to get it back.

In other words, the parties bargained for a legally enforceable promise. They did not get it. There was, therefore, a failure of consideration despite the fact that the transaction had run its full course.

B. Statutes

The operation of the obligation rule in the context of statutory entitlements is relatively straightforward. If the defendant has a valid entitlement to the relevant enrichment under a statute, restitution will be precluded by the obligation rule.[60]

The decision of the Court of Appeal in *FII Test Claimants*[61] illustrates this. In that case, certain aspects of the United Kingdom's corporation tax regime were successfully challenged on the basis that they contravened European Union law. As a result, some of the tax that had been collected from the claimants in 'Year 1' was found to have been collected unlawfully. The claimants had used up some of their available tax relief to offset this unlawful levy. The claimants argued that, had they not used their tax relief to offset the unlawful exaction of tax in Year 1, those reliefs would have been available to reduce their tax liability in 'Year 2'. By depriving the claimants of their opportunity to reduce their tax liability in Year 2, they argued, the Revenue had been enriched. Arden LJ rejected this submission:[62]

> The short answer to the claim is that the tax paid in year 2 or subsequent years was lawfully due and so cannot be the subject of recovery under *Woolwich* or as a payment under a mistake: see *Kleinwort Benson v Lincoln City Council* [1998] UKHL 38, [1999] 2 AC 349 at 408B (Lord Hope).

Arden LJ's reasoning is an application of the obligation rule. The Revenue, whose enrichment was the receipt of tax in Year 2, had a valid entitlement

[59] Robert Stevens and Ben McFarlane, 'In Defence of Sumpter v. Hedges' (2002) 118 Law Quarterly Review 569, 577. See also, Frederick Wilmot-Smith, 'Reconsidering "Total" Failure' (2013) 72 Cambridge Law Journal 414, 434.

[60] Mitchell, Mitchell and Watterson (n 23) [2-08]; Virgo, *The Principles of the Law of Restitution* (n 2) 146.

[61] *Test Claimants in the FII Group Litigation v Revenue & Customs Commissioners* [2010] EWCA Civ 103, [2010] STC 1251.

[62] ibid [181].

to that tax. No restitution claim is available in these circumstances. It is irrelevant that the claimants *could have* reduced their tax liability. What is relevant is that they did not, in fact, do so. Consider an analogous example:[63]

> *Example 1*: C's liability for inheritance tax is in dispute. Had C made an election in a deed of variation, C's inheritance tax liability could have been avoided. C made a mistake of law in failing to exercise the election. C seeks restitution from the Revenue of tax already paid.

C's claim will fail. Just as in *FII Test Claimants*, the Revenue has a valid entitlement in respect of C's inheritance tax liability. Despite C's mistake, therefore, there is no valid claim for restitution on these facts.[64]

Lord Scott's dissent in *DMG*[65] is another example of the application of the obligation rule in a statutory context.[66] As explained in Chapter 4, Section II, the Advance Corporation Tax (ACT) in respect of which the claimant sought restitution in that case was owed to the Revenue when it was paid. Despite the claimant's mistake, Lord Scott would have denied restitution:[67]

> [I]f the legal obligation under which the money was paid cannot be, or has not been, invalidated, then, in my opinion, whether or not it can be shown that 'but for' the mistake in question the money would not have been paid, a restitutionary remedy for the recovery of the money would not be available.

The majority of the House of Lords reached the opposite result. It was explained in Chapter 4, Section II that the result reached by the majority judges is explicable on the basis of the principle of 'EU estoppel'.[68]

In relation to the application of the obligation rule to statutory entitlements, two further points fall to be made.

First, the claimant may contest the validity of the defendant's statutory entitlement.[69] If such a challenge succeeds, the obligation rule will not apply. *Woolwich Equitable Building Society v Inland Revenue Commissioners*[70] was such a case. The question before the House of Lords in that case was whether the claimant could recover tax paid to the Revenue on the basis that it was an ultra vires exaction. In prior proceedings, the claimant had challenged the validity of

[63] See *The Test Claimants in the FII Group Litigation v The Commissioners for Her Majesty's Revenue & Customs* [2008] EWHC 2893 (Ch) [257]. See also, Burrows, *The Law of Restitution* (n 24) 89–90.

[64] Mitchell, Mitchell and Watterson (n 23) [2–58]. It was explained in Chapter 4, Section II(B)(ii) that these examples are materially different from the facts of *DMG*.

[65] *DMG* (n 4).

[66] For a detailed analysis of this decision, see Chapter 4, Section II above.

[67] *DMG* (n 4) [85].

[68] For the view that the majority is wrong on this point, see Robert Stevens, *The Laws of Restitution* (Oxford, Oxford University Press, 2023) 86–87; Stevens, 'Is There a Law of Unjust Enrichment?' (n 43) 17–20.

[69] Charles Mitchell and Monica Chowdry, 'Tax Legislation as a Justifying Factor' [2005] Restitution Law Review 1, 10–18.

[70] *Woolwich Equitable Building Society v Inland Revenue Commissioners* [1993] AC 70 (HL).

the statutory regulation that authorised the Revenue's collection of tax from the claimant.[71] The claimant was a building society. As a consequence of the Income Tax (Building Societies) Regulations 1986, building societies had been asked to comply with a new taxing regime. The Regulations were challenged on the basis that they were ultra vires section 343(1A) of the Income and Corporation Taxes Act 1970. The House of Lords upheld the challenge. Thus, even before the House of Lords heard the restitution claim, the statutory regulation that entitled the Revenue to exact the impugned tax had been declared invalid. This is why the Revenue did not have a statutory entitlement to the enrichment in that case.[72]

Second, the obligation rule is not the only basis upon which a statutory regime may defeat restitution claims. There are a number of other ways in which a statute may preclude an unjust enrichment claim.[73] For example, statutes may expressly or impliedly exclude an unjust enrichment claim. Section 7(3) of the Civil Liability (Contribution) Act 1978 is an example of the former. It provides that the statutory regime,

> supersedes any right, other than an express contractual right, to recover contribution (as distinct from indemnity) otherwise than under this Act in corresponding circumstances.

Monro v HMRC[74] exemplifies implied statutory exclusion. In that case, the Court of Appeal held that the statutory recovery regime provided in section 33 of the Taxes Management Act 1970 impliedly suggested that the Parliament intended to exclude the common right of recovery based on unjust enrichment.

Furthermore, restitution claims may also be denied on the basis that, if permitted, they would stultify statutory policy.[75] For example, in *R Leslie Ltd v Sheill*,[76] a restitution claim was denied on the basis that permitting recovery would be contrary to the Parliamentary policy which was reflected in the Infants Relief Act 1874. This is not an application of the obligation rule but a distinct restriction on unjust enrichment claims.

C. Judgments

A restitution claim will fail if the enrichment was owed to the defendant pursuant to a court judgment. The equality thesis suggests that denying restitution

[71] *Woolwich Equitable Building Society v Inland Revenue Commissioners* [1991] 4 All ER 92.

[72] For an example of a similar challenge, see *British Sky Broadcasting Group Plc v C & E Commissioners* [2000] BVC 2067.

[73] Mitchell, Mitchell and Watterson (n 23) [2-07].

[74] *Monro v Revenue and Customs Commissioners* [2008] EWCA Civ 206, [2009] Ch 69. See also, *Sevastopoulos v Spanos* [1991] 2 VR 194 (Supreme Court of Victoria).

[75] Edelman and Bant (n 20) 160; Mitchell, Mitchell and Watterson (n 23) [2-21].

[76] *R Leslie Ltd v Sheill* [1914] 3 KB 607 (CA). See also, *Equuscorp Pty Ltd v Haxton* [2012] HCA 7, (2012) 246 CLR 498.

in these circumstances is necessary to protect the defendant's entitlement to the enrichment which is based on the judgment.

There is unanimity among academic commentators that there can be no restitution of benefits conferred in furtherance of judgments.[77] *Huffer v Allen*[78] is an illustration of this principle. The claimant owed £28 to the defendant. The defendant had commenced proceedings to recover this sum. Before judgment was entered, the claimant paid the defendant £10 in partial discharge of the debt. Notwithstanding this, the defendant sought and obtained judgment for £28. The judgment was enforced against the claimant who was compelled to pay £28. The claimant sought restitution on the basis that, as at the date of the judgment the claimant only owed the defendant £18. The claim failed. It was held that the claimant's argument was precluded by the judgment under which the defendant was entitled to £28 from the claimant. Kelly CB said,[79]

> But he cannot make this averment, and therefore cannot maintain this action, whilst the judgment, against which no averment can be admitted, stands as evidence that when judgment was signed the debt which the then defendant owed was 28l., and not 18l.

On similar facts, the same approach was adopted in *Sophia de Medina v Grove*.[80] There, again, the claimant sought restitution of a sum that had been paid to the defendant in execution of a valid judgment. Dismissing the claim, Lord Denman said,[81]

> If there was any fraud in the case, that might be a ground for the interference of the Court to set aside the judgment or the execution: but, whilst both remain unreversed, it would be contrary to principle to reverse them in effect by an action to recover back the amount levied.

It is apparent from this reasoning that the position would have been different if the judgment had been set aside.[82] In that scenario, the obligation rule no longer applies.[83]

Moses v Macferlan,[84] a formative decision on the law of unjust enrichment in England, was a case in which the enrichment was owed to the defendant under a judgment. Moses indorsed four promissory notes to Macferlan. This was subject to an agreement between the parties that Moses would not be held liable on these notes. In breach of the agreement, Macferlan sued Moses in the Court of Conscience. The Court refused to receive evidence of the collateral

[77] Peter Birks, *Unjust Enrichment* (2nd edn, Oxford, Oxford University Press, 2005) 139–140; Edelman and Bant (n 20) 165; Stevens, 'Is There a Law of Unjust Enrichment?' (n 43) 17; Virgo, *The Principles of the Law of Restitution* (n 2) 147.

[78] *Huffer v Allen* (1866–67) LR 2 Ex 15.

[79] ibid 18.

[80] *Sophia de Medina v Grove* (1846) 10 QBR 152; 116 ER 59.

[81] ibid 67.

[82] *Huffer* (n 78) 18–19; *Sophia de Medina* (n 80) 67.

[83] Edelman and Bant (n 20) 165; Virgo, *The Principles of the Law of Restitution* (n 2) 147.

[84] *Moses v Macferlan* (1760) 2 Burr 1005, 97 ER 676.

agreement. Therefore, Moses was held liable on his indorsement. Subsequently, Moses brought an action for money had and received. Through this claim, Moses was effectively seeking to reverse the payment made to Macferlan under the earlier judgment. Since the judgment against Moses had not been set aside, Macferlan had a valid entitlement to that sum. On principle, therefore, Moses's claim ought to have failed. But Lord Mansfield reached the opposite conclusion.

Rejecting the submission that granting Moses's claim would contradict the earlier judgment, Lord Mansfield said:[85]

> The ground of this action is not, 'that the judgment was wrong:' but, 'that, (for a reason which the now plaintiff could not avail himself of against that judgment,) the defendant ought not in justice to keep the money.'

With respect, this aspect of Lord Mansfield's reasoning is incorrect. Macferlan had a valid entitlement to receive the sum in respect of which Moses was seeking restitution. Restitution ought not to have been awarded.

Lord Mansfield's decision to sidestep the subsisting judgment has attracted unanimous criticism from commentators.[86] The authoritative value of *Moses* on this point has also been doubted. In *Marriot v Hampton*,[87] Lord Kenyon said of *Moses*:[88]

> I am afraid of such a precedent. If this action could be maintained I know not what cause of action could ever be at rest. After a recovery by process of law there must be an end of litigation, otherwise there would be no security for any person.

In the same case, Grose J went so far as to say that he would have no difficulty 'in disregarding the whole authority of [*Moses*]'.[89] In *Phillips v Hunter*,[90] Lord Eyre said that he could not 'subscribe to the authority of [*Moses*]'[91] as it seemed to 'unsettle foundations'.[92] In short, *Moses v Macferlan* is wrongly decided, and should not be followed, on this point.[93]

D. Other Entitlements

It was explained above that the obligation rule applies whether the defendant's entitlement is based on contracts, statutes or court judgments. On principle, the

[85] ibid 679.

[86] Mitchell, Mitchell and Watterson (n 23) [2-33]–[2-35]; Stevens (n 43) 17; Daniel Friedmann, 'Unjust Enrichment, Pursuance of Self-Interest and the Limits of Free Riding' (2003) 36 Loyola of Los Angeles Law Review 831, 833–834; Ernest Weinrib, 'Unjust Enrichment' in *Corrective Justice* (Oxford, Oxford University Press, 2012) 202.

[87] *Marriot v Hampton* (1797) 7 Term Reports 269, 101 ER 969.

[88] ibid.

[89] ibid.

[90] *Phillips v Hunter* [1795] 2 Hy Bl 402.

[91] ibid 414.

[92] ibid 416. See also, *Brisbane v Dacres* 5 Taunt 160, 128 ER 641.

[93] The result in *Moses* may be justified by interpreting the claim as one for breach of contract. For that view, see Stevens (n 43) 17; *Phillips* (n 90) 625.

same must be true of obligations owed to the defendant that arise out of civil wrongs. The decision of the South Australian Supreme Court in *Re Magarey Farlam*[94] confirms this. That decision was considered in Chapter 5, Section II(A).

What about customary obligations? *Brisbane v Dacres*[95] has sometimes been relied on to support the view that a defendant may rely on customary obligations to defeat restitution claims.[96] In fact, *Brisbane v Dacres* does not support that proposition. The dispute in that case arose from a practice in the navy pursuant to which captains of government ships conveying public money would pay one-third of their freight to the Admiral. Pursuant to this custom, the claimant paid £2500 to Admiral Dacres. The claimant later discovered that the Admiral had no legally enforceable right to this payment. A claim for restitution was brought. The claim was dismissed by Gibbs J, Heath J and Mansfield CJ (Chambre J dissented). None of the judges relied on the defendant's customary entitlement.

Gibbs J said that restitution was not available for mistakes of law. He relied on *Bilbie v Lumley*[97] for this proposition. He said:[98]

> I think that where a man demands money of another as a matter of right, and that other, with a full knowledge of the facts upon which the demand is made has paid a sum, he never can recover back the sum he has so voluntarily paid. It may be, that upon a further view he may form a difference opinion of the law, and it may be, his subsequent opinion may be the correct one. If we were to hold otherwise, I think many inconveniences may arise; there are many doubtful questions of law.

Chambre J's dissenting judgment also did not rely on the defendant's customary entitlement. Instead, he rejected the mistake of law bar:[99]

> [I]t seems to be a most dangerous doctrine, that a man getting possession of money, to any extent, in consequence of another party's ignorance of the law, cannot be called on to repay it.

Heath J agreed with Gibbs J that the claim should be dismissed. However, he did not rely on any notion of customary entitlement. Instead, his reasoning was that there was no relevant mistake upon which a claim could be brought:[100]

> [I]t is very difficult to say that there is any evidence of ignorance of the law here; an officer is sent on a profitable service, the admirals are in the habit of receiving a proportion of the officer's recompense, and it is very likely the officer should acquiesce in the demand. He might not like to contest the point with his superior officer.

[94] *Re Magarey Farlam Lawyers Trust Accounts (No 3)* [2007] SASC 9, 96 SASR 337.
[95] *Brisbane* (n 92).
[96] Ben Kremer, 'The Action for Money Had and Received' (2001) 17 Journal of Contract Law 93, 112.
[97] *Bilbie v Lumley* (1802) 2 East 469; 102 ER 448.
[98] *Brisbane* (n 92) 645 (Gibbs J).
[99] ibid 647 (Chambre J).
[100] ibid 648 (Heath J).

Now consider Mansfield CJ's judgment. His reasoning was as follows:[101]

> The admiral and captain each thinking that their rights continue as before, the admiral, that he has his contractual right, the captain, that it is his duty to pay the accustomed share, the one pays, and the other receives it. This then being so, the admiral doing no more than all admirals do, is it against his conscience for him to retain it? … So far from its being contrary to æquum et bonum, I think it would be most contrary to æquum et bonus, if he were obliged to repay it back. For see how it is! If the sum be large, it probably alters the habits of his life, he increases his expenses, he has spent it over and over again; perhaps he cannot repay it at all, or not without great distress: is he then, five years and eleven months after, to be called on to repay it?

Mansfield CJ's reasoning in this passage mirrors the modern change of position defence. No part of his reasoning relies on the customary status of the practice. Indeed, it would have been surprising if Mansfield CJ relied on this custom at all. This is because, two years before *Brisbane v Dacres* was decided, in *Montagu v Janverin*,[102] he had denied that this practice had the status of a custom. In *Montagu*, he said:

> It is very difficult to conceive how there can be a custom to divide money given by way of bounty. For this money, paid to the captain as a gratuity for carrying bullion, is a gratuity which they have no right to demand.[103]
>
> It seems to me quite impossible that such a custom should exist in law, or that the practice should be known to the lords of the admiralty.[104]

Therefore, *Brisbane v Dacres* is not authority for the proposition that a customary obligation which does not give rise to legal rights and liabilities may form the basis for denying a restitution claim.

E. Discharge

In relation to each of the legal obligations considered above, namely, contractual entitlements, statutes, judgments and other obligations, the operation of the obligation rule is contingent on the 'discharge' of the defendant's entitlement. In other words, it is not the existence of a countervailing legal obligation but its discharge upon the receipt of a benefit by the defendant that attracts the application of the obligation rule.[105] This requirement was emphasised by Lord Sumption in *Fairfield Sentry v Migani*[106] where he said that 'to the extent

[101] ibid 648–649 (Mansfield CJ).

[102] *Montagu v Janverin* (1811) 3 Taunt 442.

[103] ibid 453 (Mansfield CJ).

[104] ibid 454 (Mansfield CJ).

[105] Graham Virgo, 'Demolishing the Pyramid – the Presence of Basis and Risk-Taking in the Law of Unjust Enrichment' in Andrew Robertson and Tang Wu (eds), *The Goals of Private Law* (Oxford, Hart, 2009) 493–497.

[106] *Fairfield Sentry Ltd (In Liquidation) v Migani* [2014] UKPC 9, [2014] 1 CLC 611.

that a payment made under a mistake discharges a contractual debt of the payee, it cannot be recovered'.[107]

What about premature payments?

> *Example 2*: C owes D £100 due on 1 April. C does not intend to discharge the debt, but mistakenly pays D £100 on 25 March. On 1 April, D notifies C that her payment is accepted in discharge of the debt. On 5 April, C brings a claim to recover £100 from D on the basis that it was a mistaken payment.

Assuming, for the present purposes, that the debt was discharged on 1 April, the obligation rule operates from that date. Therefore, on principle, C could have brought a claim against D for the time value of money between 25 March and 1 April. This is confirmed by the decision of the New South Wales Court of Appeal in *Equiticorp Financial Services*.[108] Giles J said,[109]

> It could be argued that any enrichment of Bank of New Zealand lay not in receipt of the $44,460,976.85 in the liquidity reserve, since undoubtedly it was owed a sum greater than that, but in receipt of that amount some two months before the Uruz Pty Ltd debt was strictly repayable.

However, in the light of the Supreme Court's decision in *Prudential Assurance Company Ltd v Commissioners for Her Majesty's Revenue and Customs*,[110] C no longer has an unjust enrichment claim for the time value of money between 25 March and 1 April. However, since the decision in *Prudential* was not based on the obligation rule, it is not considered further here.

F. Natural Obligations

It was explained above that countervailing legal obligations preclude restitution through the operation of the obligation rule. Do 'natural obligations' have a similar effect? Commentators are divided on this issue.[111] This section will consider whether the equality thesis offers any insights as to this question.

As a starting point, it is necessary to ask: what are natural obligations? A precise answer is difficult, not least because of divergences amongst the legal systems that employ this doctrine. But there is agreement as to some of its common features. Natural obligations are not fully recognised and enforceable legal obligations.[112] Thus, they cannot form the basis of a positive claim. However, they impose moral duties. In this context, it is often said that natural

[107] ibid [18].
[108] *Equiticorp Financial Services* (n 19).
[109] ibid 322.
[110] *Prudential Assurance Company Ltd v Commissioners for Her Majesty's Revenue and Customs* [2018] UKSC 39, [2018] STI 1499.
[111] See, Duncan Sheehan, 'Natural Obligations in English Law' [2004] Lloyd's Maritime and Commercial Law Quarterly 172; Sheehan (n 8) 131; Birks, *Unjust Enrichment* (n 77) 257–258; Burrows, *A Restatement of the English Law of Unjust Enrichment* (n 10) 35; Virgo, *The Principles of the Law of Restitution* (n 2) 147.
[112] Pedro F Entenza-Escobar, 'Natural and Moral Obligations' (2016) 8 The Catholic Lawyer 308, 311.

obligations 'bind the obligor's conscience'.[113] Natural obligations have some legal consequences. On one view, one of these consequences is that they can form the basis for a valid performance. On that view, money paid or performance rendered in furtherance of a natural obligation cannot be recovered through restitution.[114]

This section will examine natural obligations as reasons for denying restitution through three historical phases. The first phase comprises decisions from the late eighteenth century. This period marks the highpoint of the natural obligation doctrine.[115] Second, by the beginning of the nineteenth century the trend had changed. By then, *Bilbie v Lumley*[116] had adopted the 'mistake of law' bar. Most cases that invoked the natural obligation bar thus far had been claims based on mistakes of law. *Bilbie*, therefore, had the consequence of rendering the natural obligation doctrine largely redundant. Third, the mistake of law bar was abolished in the late twentieth century.[117] In theory, this makes the natural obligation bar relevant again. However, modern judicial reasoning offers sparse support for this doctrine.

This section will make two claims. First, the eighteenth century jurisprudence on the natural obligation bar is consistent with the equality thesis. Second, the modern law of unjust enrichment should not recognise a defence based on natural obligations.

i. Natural Obligations in the Eighteenth Century

Some decisions from the late eighteenth century offer emphatic support for the natural obligation bar. The first among them is *Moses v Macferlan*.[118] Although it was strictly unnecessary for the resolution of the case, Lord Mansfield said:[119]

> This kind of equitable action, to recover back money, which ought not in justice to be kept … lies only for money which, ex æquo ot bono, the defendant ought to refund: it does not lie for money paid by the plaintiff, which is claimed of him as payable in point of honor and honesty, although it could not have been recovered from him by any course of law; as in payment of a debt barred by the Statute of Limitations, or contracted during his infancy, or to the extent of principal and legal interest upon an usurious contract, or, for money fairly lost at play: because in all these cases, the defendant may retain it with a safe conscience, though by positive law he was barred from recovering.

[113] Mitchell McInnes, 'Natural Obligations and Unjust Enrichment' in Elise Bant and Matthew Harding (eds), *Exploring Private Law* (Cambridge, Cambridge University Press, 2010) 176; Peter Birks, 'Mistakes of Law' (2000) 53 Current Legal Problems 205, 215.

[114] RW Leage and AM Prichard, *Leage's Roman Private Law: Founded on the Institutes of Gaius and Justinian* (3rd edn, London, Macmillan, 1961) 432.

[115] Sheehan (n 111) 178.

[116] *Bilbie* (n 97).

[117] *Kleinwort Benson* (n 3).

[118] *Moses* (n 84).

[119] ibid 680–681.

Lord Mansfield's reasoning in this passage effectively transplanted the Roman-civilian doctrine of natural obligations into English law.[120] His reliance on Vinnius's edition of Justinian's Institutes reveals the origins of this doctrine.[121] Two decades later *Bize v Dickason*[122] was decided. There, again, the natural obligation doctrine did not influence the final decision. However, Lord Mansfield reiterated his support for this doctrine in almost identical language.[123]

In the meantime, *Farmer v Arundel*[124] had been decided. In *Farmer*, unlike in *Moses* and *Bize*, the Court may have reached a different result had it not been for the natural obligation doctrine. The decision in *Farmer* arose from a dispute between two parishes. The defendant parish had maintained a pauper for several years. In fact, it was the claimant's obligation to do so. The defendant sought reimbursement of their expenses from the claimant. Unaware that the claimant was not under a legal obligation to pay, the claimant obliged. The claimant later sought restitution. The Court proceeded on the basis that there was no countervailing legal obligation: '[t]his money could not have been demanded by the defendant'.[125] Yet, the claim failed. De Grey CJ held that the claimant did nothing more than discharge an 'honest debt'.[126] Adopting Lord Mansfield's language, he said:[127]

> Money due in point of honour or conscience, though a man is not compellable to pay it, yet if paid, shall not be recovered back.

This view was affirmed in *Munt v Stokes*.[128] In that case, the defendant had borrowed money from the claimant under a transaction that was prohibited by law. Unaware of this, the claimant repaid the loan. Upon discovering the true position, the claimant sought restitution. Can a natural obligation be founded on a contract prohibited by law? The Court held that it could. It was held that the loan was 'not malum in se, but malum prohibitum'.[129] Having found that the contract was not inherently unobjectionable despite the legal prohibition, Lord Kenyon denied restitution:[130]

> There was nothing contrary to conscience in the defendants receiving the money which they had advanced; the plaintiffs therefore are not intitled either in law or in equity to recover it back again.

[120] Peter Birks, 'English and Roman Learning in Moses v Macferlan' (1984) 37 Current Legal Problems 1, 15.
[121] Sheehan (n 111) 176.
[122] *Bize v Dickason* (1786) 1 Term Rep 285, 99 ER 1097.
[123] ibid 286–287.
[124] *Farmer v Arundel* (1772) Blackstone W 824; 96 ER 485.
[125] ibid 826.
[126] ibid.
[127] ibid 825–826 (De Grey CJ).
[128] *Munt v Stokes* (1792) 3 Term Reports 561; 100 ER 1176.
[129] ibid 564.
[130] ibid (Kenyon CJ).

Thus, at the turn of the eighteenth century, there was considerable judicial support for the natural obligation doctrine as a bar on restitution claims.

The reasoning of the courts during that period is consistent with the equality thesis. This is because, although it was recognised that natural obligations could not form the basis of a positive claim, they were conceptualised as reasons why the defendant had a valid right to retain the enrichment.[131]

That is how natural obligations were understood in Roman law. Consider, for instance, the nature of the action in *condictio indebiti*. '*Indebiti*' connotes something that is not due. *Condictio indebiti* reverses payments or performances rendered under the belief that they are due under valid obligations whereas the obligation was in fact non-existent.[132] The Roman law explanation for the natural obligation doctrine was that the payment is not *indebitum*.[133] As Hume explains,[134]

> To make way for the *condictio indebiti* it seems to be necessary that the payment have been absolutely and utterly *indebitum*, not due to that party, by any even natural bond of obligation.

For these purposes, Roman law equated a 'natural' obligation to a legal obligation.[135] Thus, Evans explains that:[136]

> [W]hat is due according to natural justice is considered as being really due; and, although the payment of it could not be enforced, yet if it is actually paid, though by a person who supposes himself to be liable in point of law, it cannot be reclaimed.

In the eighteenth century, restitution was often conceptualised as an equitable action. On that basis, commentators such as Erskine argued that, since the claim was based on equity, the defendant's 'equitable' right was sufficient to defeat it.[137] Kremer offers a similar analysis. He focuses on the fact that restitution claims were pleaded as actions for 'money had and received'. This was a procedurally liberal action, which meant that:[138]

> any circumstance the defendant could point to which showed some valid legal, equitable or moral claim to be entitled to the money and hence to retain it would repel the plaintiff's claim.

131 Sheehan (n 8) 39, 181.

132 JAC Thomas, *Textbook of Roman Law* (Philip McDonald, 2013) 327.

133 Leage and Prichard (n 114) 385.

134 David Hume, *Baron David Hume's Lectures*, vol 3 (George Paton ed, Edinburgh, Stair Society, 1939) 172.

135 Vinnius's Commentary on the Institutes of Justinian, 3.27.6 cited in Birks, 'English and Roman Learning in Moses v Macferlan' (n 120) 17–18.

136 William Evans, 'An Essay on the Action of Money Had and Received' in *Essays: On the Action for Money Had and Received, on the Law of Insurances, and on the Law of Bills of Exchange and Promissory Notes* (1802) (reprinted in [1998] Restitution Law Review 1) 5.

137 Erskine Institute III cited in Scottish Law Commission, *Recovery of Benefits Conferred Under Error of Law* (Discussion Paper Number 95, Vol 2, 1993) [2.70]. For a similar justification in the context of civilian jurisdictions, see Meier (n 2) 37.

138 Kremer, 'The Action for Money Had and Received' (n 96) 109.

On the Roman law understanding of the natural obligation bar, therefore, it appears to have been the defendant's natural *right* to the enrichment that precluded restitution.

The eighteenth century case law often resorted to the language of 'unconscionability' to explain the natural obligation bar. But when one examines what 'unconscionability' in fact meant in this context, it is apparent that the key question was whether the defendant had a valid right to retain the enrichment. In *Moses*, Lord Mansfield relied on the 'iniquity of [the defendant] *keeping* that money'[139] 'which ought not in justice to be *kept*'.[140] In *Clarke v Shee*,[141] similarly, restitution was granted because it was found that the defendant 'cannot in conscience retain the enrichment'.[142] *Dale v Sollet*[143] makes the point clearer. In that case, in response to a claim for money had and received, the defendant asserted a set-off in respect of certain sums that were due to him. The defendant's argument was upheld. The plaintiff's right to restitution, it was held,[144]

> can be no more than what remains after deducting all just allowances which the defendant has a right to retain out of the very sum demanded.

Kremer's comprehensive study of the 'money had and received' cases from this era confirms this view:[145]

> [T]he notion of 'conscience' did not operate at large … the rule to which it gave rise to was that the plaintiff had to show that the defendant had no 'right to retain' that which he received. The rule meant that any valid reason the defendant could adduce in evidence – 'any equity' to keep it –would 'rebut the action'.

The natural obligation doctrine, when rationalised on the basis of the defendant's right to retain the enrichment, is consistent with the equality thesis. The equality explanation suggests that the claimant cannot rely on the law of restitution to protect her pre-transaction interests while depriving the defendant of his legal entitlement to the enrichment. The claimant's pre-transfer interests, although legally recognised, are not necessarily enforceable legal claims. More often than not, they are protected legal interests, not claim rights. By parity, the defendant's interests that the obligation rule accords protection to may similarly be legally recognised interests, albeit not enforceable legal rights. This appears to have been the basis upon which eighteenth century courts denied restitution based on the natural obligation bar.

[139] *Moses* (n 118) 679.
[140] ibid 680.
[141] *Clarke v Shee and Johnson* (1774) 1 Cowper 197; 98 ER 1041.
[142] ibid 1042.
[143] *Dale v Sollet* (1767) 3 Burrow 2133; 98 ER 112.
[144] ibid 113.
[145] Kremer, 'The Action for Money Had and Received' (n 96) 22. See also, Ben Kremer, 'Restitution and Unconscientiousness: Another View' (2003) 119 Law Quarterly Review 188, 190.

ii. A Modern Natural Obligation Bar?

The previous section explained that the eighteenth century natural obligation doctrine is consistent with the equality thesis. Does the modern law of unjust enrichment recognise a natural obligation bar? Should it? This section will argue that the answer to both questions is 'no'. There are four main reasons that may be offered in support of that view.

a. Judicial Support

By the turn of the eighteenth century, the tide had turned against the recognition of natural obligations as reasons for denying restitution claims.[146] There is almost no support in modern judicial reasoning for a doctrine of natural obligations.

Two decisions are often relied on in support of the natural obligation qualification:[147] *Tootal Clothing v Guinea Properties*[148] and *Re Magarey Farlam*.[149] On analysis, neither case supports the natural obligation doctrine.

Tootal Clothing was a dispute between Guinea (the landlord) and Tootal (the tenant). Under a lease agreement, Guinea had agreed to lease a commercial property to Tootal. Tootal was to carry out shop-fitting works on the premises. In return, the first three months of Tootal's tenancy were to be rent-free. By a supplemental agreement, Guinea had also agreed to pay Tootal a sum of £30,000. Tootal carried out the works and demanded payment. Guinea refused to pay, arguing that the supplemental agreement did not comply with the formality requirements under section 2 of the Law of Property (Miscellaneous Provisions) Act 1989 and was, therefore, void. This argument was rejected. Scott LJ said:[150]

> [S]ection 2 is of relevance only to executory contracts. It has no relevance to contracts which have been completed. If parties choose to complete an oral land contract or a land contract that does not in some respect or other comply with section 2, they are at liberty to do so. Once they have done so, it becomes irrelevant that the contract they have completed may not have been in accordance with section 2.

This reasoning is relied upon to support the view that money paid under a contract which is void for reason of informality cannot be recovered. That in turn, it is argued, supports the natural obligation bar. With respect, *Tootal Clothing* does not support either proposition. In *Tootal*, the claimant was seeking to enforce Guinea's promise to pay £30,000. A natural obligation could

[146] Sze Ping-fat, '*Obligatio Naturalis*: A Concept or a Fallacy' (2007) 28 Business Law Review 209, 209–210.

[147] Sheehan (n 111) 189; Robert Goff and Gareth Jones, *The Law of Restitution* (6th edn, London, Sweet & Maxwell, 2002).

[148] *Tootal Clothing Ltd v Guinea Properties Ltd* (1992) 64 P & CR 452 (CA).

[149] *Re Magarey Farlam Lawyers* (n 27).

[150] ibid 455.

not have formed the basis of such a positive claim. At best, it could have justified Tootal's retention of £30,000, once that amount had been paid. But that was not the nature of the claim in *Tootal*. Furthermore, the Court in *Tootal* found that Guinea's supplemental promise to pay £30,000 was enforceable as a separate contract despite the statutory formality requirement. Scott LJ said,[151]

> If parties choose to hive off part of the terms of their composite bargain into a separate contract distinct from the written land contract that incorporates the rest of the terms, I can see nothing in section 2 that provides an answer to an action for enforcement of the land contract, on the one hand, or of the separate contract on the other hand. Each has become, by the contractual choice of the parties, a separate contract.

Thus, the supplemental agreement was a valid and subsisting contract. Even if Guinea had mistakenly paid £30,000 to Tootal, that sum would have been irrecoverable. It is unnecessary to rely on any natural obligation to reach that conclusion. The obligation rule suffices.

As for the decision in *Re Magarey Farlam*,[152] this case was considered in Chapter 5, Section II. The claimants were partners in a solicitors' firm. One of the firm's employees had misappropriated funds from the firm's trust account. When the partners learnt of the defalcations they paid $93,000 into the account. This was intended to replenish funds belonging to eight clients of the firm who were thought to be victims of the misappropriation. Subsequently, it turned out that the claimants had underestimated both the quantum of misappropriation as well as the number of its victims. Upon discovering this, they sought restitution of the amount that they had paid into the trust account. It was argued that the payment was caused by a mistake as to the extent of the fraud. The claim failed. Debelle J's reasons for reaching that conclusion are not entirely easy to discern. On the one hand, relying on *Farmer v Arundel*,[153] he said:[154]

> The claim by the partners of Magarey Farlam concerns money due in point of honour and conscience. It was money paid when there was no compulsion to do so.

This passage appears to support the natural obligation bar. In a later passage, however, Debelle J relied on the defendants' *legal* right to the enrichment:[155]

> There is no criterion by which it can be said that the eight clients were not entitled to be reimbursed for the loss each had suffered. The payment was not unjust.

The claimants had been found vicariously liable for the employee's wrongdoing. This meant that they were liable to reimburse the defendants for their loss. Based on this finding, Debelle J said, 'a payment cannot be recovered if, in fact, the

[151] ibid 456.
[152] *Re Magarey Farlam Lawyers* (n 27).
[153] *Farmer* (n 124).
[154] *Re Magarey Farlam Lawyers* (n 27) [166] (Debelle J).
[155] ibid [168] (Debelle J).

payer is liable to the payee'.[156] This analysis suggests that he was merely applying the obligation rule. In any case, having found that the defendant was entitled to the enrichment under a valid legal obligation, the natural obligation bar was unnecessary to dispose of the case. Thus, *Re Magarey Farlam* offers limited support for the natural obligation bar.

b. Lord Mansfield's Categories

In *Moses*, Lord Mansfield identified four instances of the application of the natural obligation doctrine: time-barred debts, payments due under a usurious contract, debts contracted during minority and gambling debts.[157] Subsequent legal developments have rendered the operation of the natural obligation bar redundant in all four contexts.

As far as time-barred debts are concerned, expiry of the limitation period does not render a legal obligation void.[158] Despite their unenforceability, time-barred debts create valid legal obligations. As explained earlier, a mistaken payment that discharges an unenforceable obligation is irrecoverable.[159] This is an application of the obligation rule. The natural obligation bar has no useful function to perform in this context.[160]

The same may be said about Lord Mansfield's second category. At the time when *Moses* was decided usurious contracts were subject to a special regulatory regime. In response to the lender's demand for repayment, it was open to the borrower to plead usury. Such a plea, if successful, would have rendered the contract void.[161] However, contracts in this category are no longer subject to special regulation.[162] Their legal status is determined in the same way as other contracts.

The third category in *Moses* – namely debts contracted during minority – is less straightforward. Within this category, contracts to supply necessary goods or services to minors are relatively unproblematic. Such contracts are valid.[163] Restitution is therefore precluded by the obligation rule. In other cases, the contract is either void or voidable at the instance of the minor. In either case, the natural obligation doctrine offers no assistance. This is because, as Sheehan says,[164]

> The fact that the contract is void for lack of capacity often means that there can be no natural obligation. The reason we render the contract void for lack of capacity is to protect the party which lacks capacity.

[156] ibid [177].
[157] *Moses* (n 84) 680–681.
[158] Tang Hang Wu, 'Natural Obligations and the Common Law of Unjust Enrichment' (2015) 6 Oxford University Commonwealth Law Journal 133, 141.
[159] See Chapter 4, Section III.
[160] Virgo, *The Principles of the Law of Restitution* (n 2) 147.
[161] Warren Swain, *The Law of Contract 1670–1870* (Cambridge, Cambridge University Press, 2015) 162.
[162] Virgo, *The Principles of the Law of Restitution* (n 2) 148.
[163] *Ryder v Wombwell* (1868) LR 4 Ex 32; Edwin Peel, *Treitel on the Law of Contract* (15th edn, London, Sweet & Maxwell, 2020) [12-003].
[164] Sheehan (n 111) 191.

Another category of contracts upon which proponents of the natural obligation bar rely are contracts entered into with a minor which are affirmed by the minor after attaining the age of majority.[165] In these cases, restitution is not available after affirmation. But here, again, the denial of restitution is explicable without reference to natural obligations. Once ratified upon attaining majority, the contract becomes enforceable.[166] No fresh consideration is necessary for this purpose.[167] Thus, affirmation creates a valid subsisting contract entitling the defendant to retain the enrichment. This result is explicable based on the obligation rule.

The final category is gambling debts. Ever since 1845, gambling debts have been governed by legislation. The Gaming Act 1845 provided that gaming and wagering contracts are void. However, the recovery of sums paid in furtherance of gaming or wagering was prohibited.[168] In 2005, a new Gaming Act came into force. This statute provided that gaming contracts were enforceable. They may therefore create a valid legal right to retain the enrichment[169] and, therefore, attract the application of the obligation rule.

c. The Doctrine of Moral Consideration

The late eighteenth century also witnessed the development of the doctrine of moral consideration, namely the idea that moral obligations could constitute 'consideration' that would render a bare promise enforceable as a contract.[170] As with the natural obligation bar, the doctrine of moral consideration was also pioneered in England by Lord Mansfield. In *Hawkes v Saunders* he said,[171]

> Where a man is under a moral obligation, which no Court of Law or Equity can inforce [sic], and promises, the honesty and rectitude of the thing is a consideration.

This proposition had garnered some judicial support in the late eighteenth century.[172] By the first half of the nineteenth century, however, it suffered the same fate as the natural obligation bar. In *Eastwood v Kenyon*, the moral consideration doctrine was decisively rejected. It was held that, if accepted, it would:[173]

> annihilate the necessity for any consideration at all, inasmuch as the mere fact of giving a promise creates a moral obligation to perform it.

[165] ibid.

[166] *Williams v Moor* (1843) 11 M & W 256; 152 ER 798.

[167] Peel (n 163) [12-029].

[168] Gaming Act 1845, s 18 ('no Suit shall be brought or maintained in any Court of Law or Equity for recovering any Sum of Money or valuable Thing alleged to be won upon any Wager').

[169] Virgo, *The Principles of the Law of Restitution* (n 2).

[170] Sheehan (n 111) 178–180.

[171] *Hawkes v Saunders* (1782) 1 Cowper 289; 98 ER 1091.

[172] See *Atkins v Hill* (1775) 1 Cowper 284; 98 ER 1088; *Trueman v Fenton* (1777) 2 Cowper 544; 98 ER 1232.

[173] *Eastwood v Kenyon* (1840) 11 A&E 438; 113 ER 482, 486.

There have been no significant attempts to revive the doctrine of moral consideration thereafter. Present day contract textbooks unequivocally reject the proposition that an antecedent moral or natural obligation can constitute good consideration for a promise.[174]

The rejection of the moral consideration doctrine is a powerful reason why a natural obligation bar should not be recognised in the modern law of unjust enrichment. This is because the natural obligation bar and the moral consideration doctrine are logical corollaries. This is evident from Lord Mansfield's reasoning in *Hawkes* in which case the moral consideration doctrine was first affirmed. Referring to the restitution claim, which was then conceptualised as being quasi-contractual in nature, he said:[175]

> Where a man is under a legal or equitable obligation to pay, the law implies a promise, though none was ever actually made.

This proposition served as the basis for the recognition of the moral consideration doctrine. In the next sentence of his speech, Lord Mansfield said:[176]

> '[a] fortiori, a legal or equitable duty is a sufficient consideration for an actual promise'.

The proposition that the moral consideration doctrine and the natural obligation bar are logical corollaries is strongly supported by the academic literature. Atiyah describes these rules are 'mutually complementary'.[177] Baloch argues that 'theoretical consistency' demands the recognition of both or neither.[178] In his examination of Lord Mansfield's contract law decisions from the eighteenth century, Oldham confirms this view:[179]

> [Lord Mansfield's] belief that courts should honor promises prompted by legal or equitable duty was only half the formula. The other half was what came to be known as quasi-contract, in which 'the honesty and rectitude of the thing' generated an equitable obligation to pay, customarily described as a promise implied by law.

This also appears to have been the accepted understanding in Roman law. Pothier, for instance, says:[180]

> If, upon the result of a fair inquiry it should appear that money paid under a mere mistaken idea of legal obligation, without any purpose of gratuitous donation or

[174] See eg HG Beale, *Chitty on Contracts* (35th edn, London, Sweet & Maxwell, 2023) [6-036].

[175] *Hawkes* (n 171) 1091.

[176] ibid.

[177] PS Atiyah, *The Rise and Fall of Freedom of Contract* (Oxford, Clarendon Press, 1985) 181.

[178] Tariq A Baloch, 'The Unjust Enrichment Pyramid' (2007) 123 Law Quarterly Review 636, 641–642.

[179] James Oldham, 'Reinterpretations of 18th-Century English Contract Theory: The View from Lord Mansfield's Trial Notes' (1988) 76 Georgetown Law Journal 1949, 1962–1963; See also, James Oldham, *The Mansfield Manuscripts and the Growth of English Law in the Eighteenth Century* (Chapel Hill, North Carolina, University of North Carolina Press, 1992) 225.

[180] Joseph Pothier, *A Treatise on the Law of Obligations, Or Contracts* (William Evans tr, London, Joseph Butterworth, 1806) 379.

> liberality, and for the payment of which there was no moral duty, is subject to repetition, it seems to follow, as a necessary consequence, that a promise of payment founded merely upon such mistake cannot be obligatory.

Similarly, Sheehan – a modern proponent of the natural obligation bar – says:[181]

> '[i]t is after all logically necessary, as Lord Mansfield saw, that, if the obligation provides consideration for a future promise, fulfilment of the obligation is irreversible'.

The rejection of the moral consideration doctrine is therefore yet another reason why the modern law of unjust enrichment should not recognise a natural obligation bar.

d. Natural Obligations and Bilateral Transactions

One of the key difficulties with the doctrine of natural obligations is its vagueness.[182] In response to this problem, Sheehan has proposed a modern version of the natural obligations doctrine. He appears to offer a broad version and a narrow version of the doctrine. The broad version is formulated in these terms:[183]

> The defence should arise where the claimant has undertaken to do an act, but the contract, under which he undertook the duty, is void. Nonetheless, we see the undertaking of the duty as worthy of some recognition. However, the reason why the contract, or agreement is void ought not indicate a disapproval of the act itself, or a need to protect the claimant.

This analysis suggests that there is a moral obligation behind every promise, a view Sheehan ascribes to Fried.[184] However, Sheehan ultimately resiles from this proposition, partly because it was rejected by Lord Mansfield in *Lee v Muggeridge*.[185] Sheehan then proposes a narrower version of the natural obligation bar, which is formulated as follows:[186]

> The reason why we deny recovery in the void contract cases is exactly the same as the reason we deny recovery where there is an enforceable contract; we cannot destroy bargains … even if Fried's arguments are unsatisfactory on some level, there must be something that justifies our giving effect to the promises that make up a contract.

On this analysis, it is not the normative weight of a promise that justifies the natural obligation bar; it is the need to protect bargains. Notably, on Sheehan's account, this is the only category of case where a natural obligation bar to

[181] Sheehan (n 111) 179.
[182] Burrows, *A Restatement of the English Law of Unjust Enrichment* (n 111) 35; Virgo, *The Principles of the Law of Restitution* (n 2) 148; Ping-fat (n 146) 215.
[183] Sheehan (n 111) 185.
[184] Charles Fried, *Contract as Promise: A Theory of Contractual Obligation* (Cambridge, Massachusetts, Harvard University Press, 1981) ch 2.
[185] *Lee v Muggeridge* (1813) 5 Taunton 36; 128 ER 599.
[186] Sheehan (n 111) 185.

restitution claims ought to be recognised. Thus, restitution in respect of performance rendered under a contract that is subsequently found to be void for informality is the 'central case'[187] for the application of the natural obligation bar.

> *Example 3*: C wanted to buy a black car. She entered into a contract with D for this purpose. The purchase price, £10,000, was paid upfront. When the car was delivered, C realised that it was a red car. The contract contained no term as to the colour of the car. Therefore, C continued to be bound by the contract. Later, C realised that the contract was void for non-compliance with a formality requirement. C seeks restitution from D. She relies on her mistake.[188]

Will C's claim succeed? Had C's claim been for failure of consideration, the answer may have been easier. One could have said, as Toulson LJ did in *Sharma v Simposh*, that C 'got what she paid for'.[189] Consequently, there is no failure of consideration. But C's claim is based on mistake. On one view, C's claim should nevertheless fail.[190] Sheehan agrees with that result, and says that the denial of restitution is best explained by reference to the natural obligation bar.

Why is there a natural obligation in Example 3? Sheehan's answer is based on the 'bargain' between C and D. But if the reason for denying restitution in that example is the need to protect the integrity of the bargain between C and D, it is preferable to rely directly on that reason. As Edelman says:[191]

> [W]here the claimant labours under a unilateral mistake when entering into a bilateral contract with the defendant ... recovery is not generally possible ... this principle is based on the need for respect for mutual autonomy in bilateral arrangements. In bilateral exchanges, a claim for unjust enrichment (whether expressed as mistake or as failure of consideration) is only possible where the objective condition of the claimant's transfer to the defendant has failed. The conditionality means that the autonomy of both parties to the bilateral arrangement is protected. This is true even if the bilateral arrangement is a void contract.

Thus, if restitution is to be denied in Example 3, it is possible, and preferable, to do so without importing the amorphous notion of natural obligations into English law.

In summary, the eighteenth century case law offers some support for a natural obligation bar to restitution claims. These cases are consistent with the equality thesis. As to whether the modern English law of unjust enrichment should recognise a doctrine of natural obligation, the preferable answer is that it should not.

[187] ibid 188.
[188] Loosely based on *Sharma v Simposh* [2011] EWCA Civ 1383, [2013] Ch 23.
[189] ibid [26] (Toulson LJ).
[190] See, James Edelman, 'Liability in Unjust Enrichment where a Contract Fails to Materialize' in Andrew Burrows and Edwin Peel (eds), *Contract Formation and Parties* (Oxford, Oxford University Press, 2010) 171.
[191] James Edelman, 'Change of Position: A Defence of Unjust Disenrichment' (2012) 92 Boston University Law Review 1009, 1024–1025.

G. Gifts

'Causative mistake' was first adopted as the standard for the restitution of mistaken payments in 1979.[192] This standard, applied on the basis of 'but for' causation, has received consistent judicial approval since then.[193] In 2013, seven Justices of the Supreme Court held that a different, higher, standard applied to restitution in the context of mistaken gifts.[194]

The claim in *Pitt v Holt* arose from a road traffic accident that Mr Derek Pitt suffered in 1990 which left Mr Pitt mentally incapacitated. Mrs Pitt was appointed as his receiver. Subsequently, Mr Pitt's damages claim was compromised and the proceeds were invested in a discretionary trust. Mrs Pitt's decision to create the trust was based on advice from her solicitors and financial advisers. She only found out later that the settlement would attract significant inheritance tax liability. The inheritance tax could have been avoided had the trust been structured differently, but Mrs Pitt had not been advised of the inheritance tax consequences. She commenced proceedings seeking to set aside the 'Derek Pitt Trust' based on her mistake.

Lord Walker delivered the unanimous judgment of the Supreme Court which held in favour of Mrs Pitt. Although setting aside the Derek Pitt Trust was not strictly the same as seeking restitution of a mistaken gift,[195] he proceeded on the basis that the standards applicable were identical:[196]

> I would provisionally conclude that the true requirement is simply for there to be a causative mistake of sufficient gravity; and, as additional guidance to judges in finding and evaluating the facts of any particular case, that the test will normally be satisfied only when there is a mistake either as to the legal character or nature of a transaction, or as to some matter of fact or law which is basic to the transaction.

Lord Walker also said that the Court would conduct an evaluation of the 'injustice (or unfairness or unconscionableness) of leaving a mistaken disposition uncorrected', with 'an intense focus on the facts'.[197]

The circularity of the words 'causative mistake of sufficient gravity'[198] and the indeterminacy of the 'unconscionableness' criterion[199] have been

[192] *Barclays Bank Ltd v WJ Simms Son & Cooke (Southern) Ltd* [1980] QB 677 (QB).

[193] *Nurdin & Peacock Plc v DB Ramsden* [1999] 1 WLR 1249 (Ch D); *Kleinwort Benson* (n 117).

[194] *Pitt v Holt* [2013] UKSC 26; [2013] 2 AC 108. Whether the higher standard applies to all mistaken gifts, or to some sub-specie thereof, remains unclear. As to that debate, see sub-sections (i) and (ii) below.

[195] Andrew Burrows, 'Inner Temple Lecture on Unjust Enrichment' (February 17, 2014) wwwinnertempleorguk/downloads/members/lectures_2014/lecture_burrows_2014pdf accessed 5 January 2024.

[196] *Pitt* (n 194) [122].

[197] ibid [126].

[198] Frederick Wilmot-Smith, 'Taxing Questions' (2015) 131 Law Quarterly Review 531, 534 (in the context of the 'at the expense of' requirement).

[199] Graham Virgo and Paul Davies, 'Relieving Trustees' Mistakes' [2013] Restitution Law Review 74, 82; Burrows, 'Inner Temple Lecture on Unjust Enrichment' (n 195) 7 ('[The Court] suggests that

criticised elsewhere. What is relevant for the present purposes is that the Court adopted a standard higher than the simple causative mistake test. Can the equality thesis offer any useful insights as to the rationale for this distinction? The remainder of this section considers that question.

The true scope of the decision in *Pitt v Holt* is not easy to discern. As Burrows has pointed out, part of the difficulty arises from the Court's failure to place the issues in their legal context.[200] As a consequence, there are at least two interpretations of the reasoning in *Pitt v Holt*. On the narrow reading, the higher 'serious mistake' standard only applies to 'formal gifts' such as a structured formal settlement or a gift made under a deed. On a broader reading, on the other hand, the higher standard in *Pitt v Holt* applies to all mistaken gifts regardless of their formality.[201] Both possibilities will now be examined.

i. Pitt v Holt*: The Narrow Reading*

On one view, the serious mistake standard in *Pitt v Holt* was based on the formality of the transaction. Consequently, that higher standard only applies to the restitution of formal gifts such as those made under a deed. Virgo and Davies adopt this view:[202]

> [I]f a claimant transfers property to a defendant by mistake, whether or not the claimant can recover the value of his property will depend upon precisely how that property was transferred: if by contract, a fundamental mistake will be required; if by deed, a serious mistake will be necessary to rescind it in Equity; if by gratuitous transfer without a deed, a mere 'but for' mistake appears to suffice.

The idea that, for the purposes of restitution, there is a hierarchy among gifts depending on the formality of the transaction, has also been approved by other commentators. For example, Krebs has suggested that the restrictions in *Pitt v Holt* 'may well be explained on the basis [of] the formality of the transaction'.[203] Edelman and Bant similarly note that 'a deed of gift constitutes a juristic reason to retain the enrichment'.[204]

Through the lens of the equality thesis, the application of a higher standard to the restitution of gifts made under deed is readily explicable. Deeds have

something more serious than a mere 'but for' test is required to rescind gifts and voluntary dispositions but it does not explain what that more serious test is other than by a resort to the justice of the case on the facts').

[200] Burrows, 'Inner Temple Lecture on Unjust Enrichment' (n 195) 7.

[201] A third reading of *Pitt v Holt* based on the proprietary consequences of Mrs Pitt's claim for rescission has also been proposed: see Terence Etherton, 'The Role of Equity in Mistaken Transactions' (2013) 27 Trust Law International 159. For a contrary view see, Mitchell, Mitchell and Watterson (n 23) [9-151].

[202] Virgo and Davies (n 199) 83.

[203] Thomas Krebs, *Restitution at the Crossroads: A Comparative Study* (London, Cavendish, 2001) 80.

[204] Edelman and Bant (n 20) 151 (emphasis added). See also, Stephen Watterson, 'Reversing Mistaken Voluntary Dispositions' (2013) 72 Cambridge Law Journal 501, 503–504.

an obligatory effect;[205] even when they are unsupported by consideration, gifts made under deed bind the donor.[206] They also create valid entitlements in favour of the donee. For instance, the donee may bring a claim for damages for the breach of a covenant contained in a gift deed.[207] It is unsurprising, therefore, that the deed must be set aside before the restitution of a gift made under it can follow. As long as the deed subsists, the donee has a valid entitlement to the gift.

This analysis is consistent with the equality thesis. Granting the donor's restitution claim while the deed subsists would deprive the donee of her right to the gift, while affirming the donor's pre-transaction entitlements. As Häcker puts it, therefore, 'a mistake-based claim to recover the gift or its value cannot succeed before the deed of promise has been avoided'.[208] When a gift is made by deed, setting aside the deed is a necessary pre-condition for restitution.[209] On this view, the higher, serious mistake standard in *Pitt v Holt* is the threshold for setting aside the formal deed at equity.

ii. Pitt v Holt*: The Broad Reading*

On the broad reading, the serious mistake standard in *Pitt v Holt* applies to mistaken gifts in general regardless of formality.[210] This appears to have been the view adopted by Mackie J in *Pagel v Farman*.[211] That was a dispute between the partners of a hedge fund. Following the hedge fund's collapse, the claimant gifted a sum of money to the defendant. This was meant to help the defendant tide over his financial difficulties. Subsequently, the claimant realised that the defendant's declarations of financial trouble were exaggerated. He sought restitution of the gift. The gift was not made under a deed. Yet, the Court held that the applicable standard was the serious mistake threshold.[212]

The broad reading of *Pitt v Holt* is seemingly inconsistent with the equality thesis. Informal gifts, such as the one in *Pagel*, do not impose legal obligations on the donor. Nor do they create entitlements in favour of the donee. A gift, even an informal one, conveys title to the defendant,[213] but so does a mistaken payment. The defendant cannot rely on the title transferred through a mistaken transaction to defeat the claimant's unjust enrichment claim. The same must be true of a mistaken gift.

[205] Birke Häcker, 'Mistaken Gifts after *Pitt v Holt*' (2014) 67 Current Legal Problems 333, 370.
[206] *Hall v Palmer* (1844) 3 Hare 532; 67 ER 491. See also, Peel (n 163) [3-170].
[207] *Cannon v Hartley* [1949] Ch 213 (Ch D).
[208] Häcker (n 205) 371. See also, Keith Mason, John Carter and Gregory Tolhurst, *Mason & Carter's Restitution Law in Australia* (2nd edn, Melbourne, LexisNexis Butterworths, 2008) 153.
[209] Dominic O'Sullivan KC, Steven Elliott KC and Rafal Zakrzewski, *The Law of Rescission* (3rd edn, Oxford, Oxford University Press, 2023) [29.25].
[210] ibid [29.30].
[211] *Scott Pagel v Ivor Farman* [2013] EWHC 2210 (Comm).
[212] ibid [40].
[213] Ben McFarlane, *The Structure of Property Law* (Oxford, Hart, 2008) 311.

Is there a good justification for adopting a higher threshold in respect of mistaken gifts in general? The academic literature offers two different answers. On one view, there is no reason why the reversal of mistaken gifts ought to be held to a higher standard. The causative mistake approach tempered by the change of position defence offers sufficient protection for the donee.[214] Etherton adopts that view:[215]

> [I]t is not easy to see why, in principle, there should be any different policy as regards personal restitution claims in respect of mistaken gifts and other mistaken non-contractual transactions.
>
> [T]he true principal distinction is between, on the one hand, upsetting contracts, which should be very difficult … and upsetting other non-contractual transactions, whatever their character or subject matter.

Krebs adopts a similar position. Applying the serious mistake standard to mistaken gifts in general, he argues, 'would be raising the status of gifts onto a higher plane which would be almost contractual'.[216] According to him, the key question is whether there has been an allocation of risks. As gifts and other voluntary dispositions do not allocate risks, they do not merit special protection.[217]

By contrast, it has also been suggested that the higher threshold ought to apply to gifts in general, regardless of their formality. For instance, Virgo has argued that gifts are legal transactions that should not be undermined by restitution.[218] Other commentators have gone one step further to justify the protection of gifts as a separate legal category. Stoljar was a pioneer in this respect. He argued that English law recognises a promissory theory that protects reliance upon promises, even when they are rendered gratuitously.[219]

The broader reading of *Pitt v Holt*, and the general application of a higher standard to mistaken gifts, is also supported by the law on setting aside testamentary gifts. It is well established that a threshold higher than the standard usually required by the law of unjust enrichment needs to be met before a testamentary disposition can be successfully challenged.[220] A common example of the application of this rule may be found in cases that consider challenges to wills on the basis of undue influence.[221] In these cases, the probate doctrine of undue influence displaces the equitable doctrine.[222] The former imposes a

[214] Etherton (n 201) 171.
[215] ibid 167.
[216] Krebs (n 203) 79.
[217] ibid.
[218] Virgo, *The Principles of the Law of Restitution* (n 2) 148. See also, Meier (n 2) 52.
[219] Samuel Stoljar, 'Enforcing Benevolent Promises' (1989) 12 Sydney Law Review 39. See also, SJ Stoljar, 'A Rationale of Gifts and Favours' (1956) 19 Modern Law Review 237.
[220] John McGhee KC and Steven Elliott KC, *Snell's Equity* (34th edn, London, Sweet & Maxwell, 2019) [8-012]–[8-013].
[221] See Law Commission, *Making A Will* (Consultation Paper 231 2017) [7.50]–[7.56].
[222] Pauline Ridge, 'Equitable Undue Influence and Wills' (2004) 120 Law Quarterly Review 617, 622.

higher threshold as compared to the latter. First, 'presumed' undue influence is inapplicable in the testamentary context; the claimant must prove actual undue influence.[223] Second, the authorities suggest that challenges to testamentary dispositions ought to be judged on the basis of a higher version of the civil standard of proof.[224] Third, the nature of undue influence that can successfully impugn a testamentary gift is also limited. Usually, evidence of 'coercion' or 'fraud' is required.[225] 'Influences' falling below this standard will usually be considered insufficient to set aside a will.

In my view, the disagreement as to whether a higher standard applies to the reversal of gifts, testamentary or otherwise, is best understood as a debate about whether English law recognises gifts as a protected legal category. In particular, does English law recognise the donee's interest in the retention of a gift? Wu argues that it does.[226] In order to substantiate that claim, he relies on the social functions that gifts perform:[227]

> [J]ust as it is important to protect the market economy from being subverted by the law of restitution by recognising the sanctity of contracts, it is equally essential to protect the moral economy by defending the completed gift from an overzealous application of the law of restitution. The gift is an important social practice meant to generate trust so as to form the basis of future action.

Harding and Hickey have similarly justified protecting gifts on the basis of the values of obligation, reciprocity and altruism.[228] However, they admit – rightly in my view – that 'donative values never ground conclusive reasons for action'.[229] They are weighed against, and often overridden by, other considerations.

This section does not aim to express a conclusive view on the extent to which gifts are protected as a legal category. As Harding's and Hickey's exploratory study demonstrates, English law's treatment of gifts is characterised by remarkable plurality.[230] However, it should be apparent from what was said above that the right questions to ask are: to what extent does English law treat gifts as a protected legal category? In particular, does the donee of a completed gift have an interest protected by law? If the answers to these questions are 'yes', then there may be a good reason for requiring that the restitution of mistaken gifts should be held to a higher standard.

[223] *Edwards v Edwards* [2007] EWHC 1119, [2007] WTLR 1387 (Ch) [47](i); *Boyse v Rossborough* (1857) VI House of Lords Cases (Clark's) 2, 10 ER 1192, 1212.

[224] *Edwards* (n 223) [47](iii).

[225] ibid [47](iv).

[226] Tang Wu, 'Restitution for Mistaken Gifts' (2004) 20 Journal of Contract Law 1.

[227] ibid 24.

[228] Matthew Harding and Robin Hickey, 'Equity and the Value of Gifts' (2014) 8 Journal of Equity 1, 2–3.

[229] ibid 25.

[230] ibid 24.

Conclusion

THIS BOOK EXAMINED the relationship between unjust enrichment claims and countervailing legal obligations owed to the defendant. It did so by considering cases in which restitution is denied on the basis that the enrichment was owed to the defendant under a valid legal obligation.

The book began in Chapter 1 by explaining that, from a doctrinal standpoint, there are two different rules that operate in this area: the good consideration rule and the obligation rule.

Part I of the book considered the good consideration rule. Chapters 2 and 3 argued that the good consideration rule is best understood as a principle that relates to the defendant's enrichment. The rationale for the good consideration rule is that the 'consideration' provided by the defendant offsets the enrichment it received. Overall, this leaves the defendant in an enrichment-neutral position. Therefore, no restitution claim is available.

Part II examined the obligation rule. Chapter 4 explained that the obligation rule is a bright-line rule. It does not require courts to weigh against each other the relative weight of the unjust factor and the defendant's right to the enrichment in individual cases. The commonly offered explanations for the obligation rule were then considered in Chapter 5. It was suggested that most academic accounts of the rule presume the subsidiarity of unjust enrichment without justifying that assumption.

Chapters 6 and 7 set out the positive case. It was explained in those chapters that, in order to account for the obligation rule, one must ask two key questions. First, what are the normative reasons that justify an unjust enrichment claim? Second, does the presence of a countervailing legal obligation owed to the defendant defeat any of these reasons?

Chapters 6 and 7 used two prominent normative accounts of the law of unjust enrichment – the entitlement thesis and the corrective justice theory – to explain the obligation rule. On both accounts, the normative justification for an unjust enrichment claim relies on the claimant's pre-transaction entitlements. That being so, the best justification for the obligation rule is based on the need to maintain equality between the claimant and the defendant. The claimant cannot use the law of restitution to protect its entitlements while denying similar protection to the defendant. That would be the consequence if the claimant were awarded restitution of an enrichment to which the defendant has a valid legal right. The obligation rule prevents that outcome. Chapter 8 set out the practical consequences of this explanation, which is referred to in this book as the 'equality thesis'.

Two issues remain to be considered: (a) in view of the equality-based explanation for the obligation rule, what should be the relationship between the good consideration rule and the obligation rule? and (b) how does the absence of basis model deal with the relationship between unjust enrichment claims and the defendant's countervailing legal entitlements? These questions are considered in Sections I and II below.

I. THE GOOD CONSIDERATION RULE AND THE OBLIGATION RULE: A RE-EVALUATION

Chapter 1 explained the distinction between the good consideration rule and the obligation rule. It was explained that, in one sense, the scope of the good consideration rule is broader than that of the obligation rule. The obligation rule requires the presence of a legal obligation whereas the good consideration rule does not. The defendant may give 'good consideration' in a way that does not entail the discharge of any legal obligation owed to it. In other respects, the good consideration rule is narrower. It requires that the claimant must have intended to confer the enrichment on the defendant and that the defendant received the enrichment in good faith. The obligation rule is not subject to either of these requirements.

A key question regarding the relationship between the good consideration rule and the obligation rule remains to be asked: does the obligation rule operate even if the countervailing entitlement was owed to the defendant by a third party other than the claimant? The equality thesis suggests that it does.

The equality thesis states that the claimant cannot use the law of unjust enrichment to protect its pre-transaction entitlements while denying equivalent protection to the defendant. The law of unjust enrichment does not require that, in order for there to be a restitution claim, the claimant's pre-transaction entitlements must have been owed to it *by the defendant*. By parity of reasoning, the obligation rule should apply whether the defendant's entitlements were owed by the claimant, or by a third party whose obligation the claimant discharges. In short, the obligation rule may apply in both two-party and three-party cases.

It follows from this proposition that there is inevitably a large degree of overlap between the good consideration rule and the obligation rule. As to when each of these two rules should apply, the preferable analysis is as follows:

(a) In any case where the defendant received the enrichment in discharge of a valid legal obligation – whether owed by the claimant or by a third party – restitution is denied by the obligation rule. It is unnecessary, and unhelpful, to invoke the good consideration rule in such cases.

(b) This does not mean that the good consideration rule should be abandoned altogether. There remains a category of case in which the good consideration rule continues to serve a useful purpose. These are cases in which the defendant provides 'good consideration' without discharging any legal obligation owed to it, either by the claimant or a third party. This may happen, for example, if the claimant and the defendant exchanged mutual benefits pursuant to a common basis, only to discover later that the contract under which they purported to do so was void. The denial of restitution in such cases is not explicable by reference to the obligation rule. As explained in Section I of Chapter 1, the decisions in *Ovidio Carrideo*,[1] *Adrenaline Pty Ltd*[2] and *Redland City Council*[3] are examples of this category.

II. ABSENCE OF BASIS

It has sometimes been suggested that the absence of basis framework offers easy and elegant solutions to the issues addressed in this book. The defendant's right to the enrichment constitutes a valid legal basis or 'a good reason' that justifies the enrichment. This is why, it is said, there can be no restitution.[4] In reality, the position is more complex. I will use the German law of unjustified enrichment, which is based on the absence of basis model, to illustrate this.

In Germany, the general unjustified enrichment action is codified in §812(I)(1) of the BGB. That provision reads:[5]

> A person who obtains something by performance [*Leistung*] by another person or in another way at the expense of this person without legal ground is bound to give it up to him.

Two aspects of this formulation have proved particularly controversial in German law: first, the distinction between enrichment through 'performance' and 'in another way' and, second, the meaning of the phrase 'without legal ground'. For the present purposes, it suffices to focus on the latter question.

The basis of an unjustified enrichment action in Germany is the defendant's receipt of an enrichment from or performance by the claimant 'without legal

[1] *Ovidio Carrideo Nominees Pty Ltd v The Dog Depot Pty Ltd* [2006] VSCA 6, 1 BFRA 612.

[2] *Adrenaline Pty Ltd v Bathurst Regional Council* [2015] NSWCA 123.

[3] *Redland City Council v Kozik* [2024] HCA 7.

[4] Robert Stevens, 'Is There a Law of Unjust Enrichment?' in Simone Degeling and James Edelman (eds), *Unjust Enrichment in Commercial Law* (Sydney, Thomson Reuters, 2008); Robert Stevens, *The Laws of Restitution* (Oxford, Oxford University Press, 2023) 85.

[5] Translated in Helen Scott, 'Restitution of Extra-contractual Transfers: Limits of the Absence of Legal Ground Analysis' [2006] Restitution Law Review 93, 95.

ground'. But what is a 'legal ground'? Ever since Grotius and Savigny,[6] German law has offered two potential answers to this question.[7] On one view, legal ground is an objective idea.[8] It may be understood as consisting of a valid legal obligation,[9] or as 'a relationship of indebtedness'.[10] On this view, the conception of a legal ground is detached from the intentions and purposes of the parties. The more dominant view, however, is that legal ground depends on the subjective purpose that underlies a transaction.[11] If that purpose is achieved, there is a valid legal basis, otherwise there is not.

> *Example 1*: C transfers his house to D, his estranged wife. The transfer is made on the shared basis that D would return to C. D does so. C's claim for restitution from D will fail.[12]

On the subjective view, the basis here is the parties' shared purpose. On this conception, the legal basis performs a function similar to the unjust factor of failure of basis.[13]

> *Example 2*: C owes £100 each to D and X. C intended to pay X but mistakenly paid D. C's claim for restitution from D will fail.[14]

Is there a valid basis for D's receipt of the £100? The difficulty here is that the subjective and objective conceptions of basis pull apart. On the objective view, there is a valid basis. The basis is the debt owed by C to D. But the subjective notion of 'basis' gives a different answer. The purpose of C's transfer was to discharge C's debt to X, but the transfer failed to achieve that purpose. The fact that C succeeded in discharging a different debt owed to D should be irrelevant as this was not the purpose C intended to achieve.

Then how does the absence of basis model explain Example 2? The answer is that it can only do so by prioritising the objective conception of legal basis over its subjective version. In other words, in order to provide a defensible explanation for the denial of restitution in Example 2, the absence of basis model must explain why the objective meaning of basis overrides the subjective notion when

[6] For an account of the historical evolution of this concept, see Anne Sanders, 'Absence of Basis: A German Perspective' in Steven Elliott, Birke Häcker and Charles Mitchell (eds), *Restitution of Overpaid Tax* (Oxford, Hart, 2014) 218.

[7] Jacques Du Plessis, 'Towards a Rational Structure of Liability for Unjustified Enrichment: Thoughts from Two Mixed Jurisdictions' (2005) 122 South African Law Journal 142, 150.

[8] Sanders (n 6) 224.

[9] Gerhard Dannemann, *The German Law of Unjustified Enrichment and Restitution: A Comparative Introduction* (Oxford, Oxford University Press, 2009) 41.

[10] Du Plessis (n 7) 173; Scott (n 5) 98.

[11] Sanders (n 6) 224; Thomas Krebs, *Restitution at the Crossroads: A Comparative Study* (London, Cavendish, 2001) 218.

[12] Scott (n 5) 99.

[13] Sanders (n 6) 219.

[14] Based on dicta in *Platt v Bromage* (1854) 24 LJ Ex 63, 65. See also, Andrew Burrows, *A Restatement of the English Law of Unjust Enrichment* (Oxford, Oxford University Press 2012) 32–33.

they come into conflict. No convincing reasons have been offered for adopting such a rule of hierarchy. This is particularly so since the subjective notion of basis represents the dominant view in Germany.[15]

Most attempts to justify a hierarchical relationship between the two conceptions of legal basis are unconvincing. Consider Krebs's reasoning for example:[16]

> [I]n German law, it is first of all the contract which governs the relationship between the parties. If the failure of purpose relied on for the restitutionary claim is not due to a circumstance which vitiates the contract rendering it void or voidable, it is thus of no restitutionary relevance and cannot lead to restitution. Thus it is always the outer, as opposed to the inner purpose of a *Leistung* whose failure has restitutionary consequences. It is only in situations where no outer purpose (such as the discharge of a liability or a creation of an underlying contract) exists, that such purposes as referred to above come to the fore, that is, in the cases of the *datio ob rem*.

With respect, this analysis is conclusory. What is needed is an account of why there appears to be a rule of priority between what Krebs calls the 'outer' and 'inner' purposes of a transaction. Krebs offers no justification for any such hierarchy.

Dannemann identifies this problem in the context of the German law action for *condictio causa data causa non secuta*.[17] This action arises from the second part of the second sentence in §812(1) of the BGB, which provides for restitution:[18]

> if the result does not occur which the performance had been aimed at to produce according to the content of the legal transaction.

In this context, the legal ground analysis depends on 'the result ... which the performance had been aimed to produce'. This is a subjective idea. As Dannemann explains, this provision usually applies in cases where the claimant renders performance for a particular purpose and 'both parties have agreed that this purpose was the reason for the performance'.[19] But what happens if the subjective purpose fails, yet the performance is justifiable by reference to an objective legal ground such as a valid legal obligation owed to the defendant?

This question came up before the Bundesgerichtshof in 2008.[20] In that case, an unmarried couple had pooled their resources to build a family home. The property was registered in one of their names. The couple fell out and

[15] Sanders (n 6) 224.
[16] Krebs (n 11).
[17] Dannemann (n 9).
[18] Translated in ibid 45.
[19] ibid 45.
[20] BGH 9.7.2008, NJW 2008, 3277 (non-marital property) translated in ibid 290.

the disappointed partner sought restitution. His case was that he had invested €83,806.25 and 1,000 hours of work into building the family home. The Bundesgerichtshof remitted the case to the lower court with two directions. The first was to examine whether there was a shared purpose between the parties. The Court said:[21]

> A claim in unjustified enrichment for failure of this expectation requires that the recipient has consented to this expectation; one-sided expectations are not sufficient. However, a tacit agreement in this sense can be assumed if one party intends its performance to achieve a particular result, and if the other party recognises this and accepts this performance without objection.

The Bundesgerichtshof also instructed the lower court to consider the possibility of a claim under §313 of the BGB. Such a claim is based on the premise that the basis of a contract has significantly changed since it was entered into (a scenario akin to frustration in English law). But what if the lower court were to find that the parties' subjective purpose had failed but the contract remained open? What should happen if the parties' intended purpose failed but the performance was owed to the defendant under the contract? The Bundesgerichtshof did not grapple with this difficult question.

As Dannemann observes, in these circumstances, allowing an action based on *condictio causa data causa non secuta* would cause difficulties even within the German law of unjustified enrichment. As he explains, if allowed, a claim of this nature would 'distort the harmony between contract and unjustified enrichment by allowing a person to claim back what was performed under a valid obligation'.[22] Therefore, Dannemann says:[23]

> As a minimum, the *causa data causa non secuta* should no longer be allowed for a claim in unjustified enrichment where the enrichment is supported by a valid legal ground.

But he offers no convincing reasons for this assertion. In particular, he does not explain why there should be a hierarchy between the two conceptions of legal basis. For that reason, his proposed solution is no better than the academic accounts that were considered in Chapter 5. As explained in that chapter, they simply assume that unjust enrichment claims are subsidiary to other legal obligations. The difficult question is: *why* is unjust enrichment subsidiary to other legal entitlements?

Does Birks's absence of basis model offer a more satisfactory solution? Birks divides enrichments into two classes: participatory and non-participatory. Participatory enrichments are further divided into 'obligatory'[24] and 'voluntary'[25]

[21] ibid 293.
[22] ibid 49.
[23] ibid.
[24] Peter Birks, *Unjust Enrichment* (2nd edn, Oxford, Oxford University Press 2005) 130.
[25] ibid 142.

enrichments. In this way, Birks adopts a 'mixed' approach to understanding legal grounds.[26] For obligatory enrichments, legal basis is understood as an objective notion[27] whereas, for voluntary enrichments, basis is a subjective notion.[28] This scheme offers an easy answer to Example 2. In that example, C owed £100 to D. C's payment to D was obligatory. Therefore, what matters is the existence of an objective basis, ie a valid legal obligation.

The difficulty is in justifying Birks's scheme. Although Birks does not say so in terms, his model assumes that, in every case that involves a valid objective basis, subjective failure of basis is irrelevant. This raises the same difficult question which was identified earlier: why does the presence of an objective basis exclude claims based on a subjective failure of basis? Birks's model seeks to sidestep this difficulty by simply asserting that subjective basis is irrelevant if an enrichment is obligatory. But this is no better than Krebs's assertion that when there is an 'outer purpose' (such as a contractual obligation), 'inner purpose' (subjective failure of basis) is irrelevant. What the absence of basis model must offer is an account of why such a rule of priority must be adopted. On that difficult question, the absence of basis framework does no better than the unjust factors model.

[26] Tariq A Baloch, 'The Unjust Enrichment Pyramid' (2007) 123 Law Quarterly Review 636, 641.
[27] Birks (n 24) 130.
[28] ibid 142.

Index

www.ingramcontent.com/pod-product-compliance
Ingram Content Group UK Ltd.
Pitfield, Milton Keynes, MK11 3LW, UK
UKHW020819290926
15470UKWH00003B/1244

9 781509 966394